WAR AND DEMOCRACY

WAR AND DEMOCRACY

Labor and the Politics of Peace

Elizabeth Kier

CORNELL UNIVERSITY PRESS   ITHACA AND LONDON

First published 2021 by Cornell University Press

Library of Congress Cataloging-in-Publication Data

Names: Kier, Elizabeth, 1958– author.
Title: War and democracy : labor and the politics of peace / Elizabeth Kier.
Description: Ithaca [New York] : Cornell University Press, 2021. |
    Includes bibliographical references and index.
Identifiers: LCCN 2020043173 (print) | LCCN 2020043174 (ebook) |
    ISBN 9781501756405 (hardcover) | ISBN 9781501756412 (ebook) |
    ISBN 9781501756429 (pdf)
Subjects: LCSH: Politics and war. | Democracy. | World War, 1914–1918
    —Influence. | World War, 1914–1918—Social aspects—Great Britain. |
    World War, 1914–1918—Social aspects—Italy. | Labor movement—Political
    aspects—Great Britain. | Labor movement—Political aspects—Italy.
Classification: LCC D639.D45 K54 2021 (print) | LCC D639.D45 (ebook) |
    DDC 940.3/1—dc23
LC record available at https://lccn.loc.gov/2020043173
LC ebook record available at https://lccn.loc.gov/2020043174

To Jon

Contents

Acknowledgments

This book combines my interest in war with my commitment to rights. I hoped to find a sliver of light in war's destruction. I knew that a deepening of democracy could not justify the bloodletting of the Great War, but perhaps there was evidence of democracy's advance in the otherwise senseless ruin. Those hopes were dashed. British labor gave so much for so little in return, and Italy's turn to Fascism is directly linked to its wartime mobilization. But I found my sliver of light. Justice is more powerful than I imagined, and this book reasserts the power and influence of contentious politics, for good and ill. It also dispels false hopes about war as a democratizer while offering practical advice for democratic governance.

My good fortune in colleagues, friends, and family made writing this book a pleasure. Sid Tarrow assisted this project before he (or I) knew it existed, and his enthusiasm and advice have been invaluable. Sid is as remarkable a colleague as he was a seminar instructor, which is a high bar indeed. Ron Kreb's irrepressible energy helped to get this project off the ground, and his incisive comments set it off in a better direction. I learned a lot from Ron about democracy and war while working with him on our edited volume, *In War's Wake: International Conflict and the Fate of Liberal Democracy*. I am grateful to the participants at our Austin and Seattle workshops for *In War's Wake*, and especially to Nancy Bermeo, Miguel Centeno, Mark Wilson, and Jay Winter for their comments and critiques. John Owen's review of the nearly completed manuscript was fabulous. His sophisticated critiques and detailed comments sharpened my argument and improved every chapter. I cannot thank him enough.

My colleagues at the University of Washington always impress me with their insight and generosity. I owe a special thanks to George Lovell for his intellectual engagement, his careful read of initial drafts, and his unflagging encouragement. Jim Caporaso was also especially generous with his feedback and his support, and Aseem Prakash provided just the right measure of encouragement at a crucial point. Thanks also to the many graduate students and undergraduates who enrich my academic life.

I am grateful to Jens Meierhenrich for the opportunity to be a visiting fellow at the Centre for International Studies at the London School of Economics (LSE). The depth of resources at LSE—both intellectual and practical—made it an ideal environment to complete this book.

I also benefited enormously from presenting various stages of this project at LSE; the Department of Political Science, University College, London; the John Sloan Dickey Center for International Understanding, Dartmouth College; the Institute for Security and Conflict Studies, Elliott School of International Affairs, George Washington University; the Norwegian Institute of International Affairs, Oslo; the Peace Studies Program, Cornell University; the Swedish National Defense College and the Department of Political Science, Stockholm University; and the Watson Institute for International Studies, Brown University. I thank Fiona Adamson, Jan Joel Andersson, Steve Biddle, Neta Crawford, Jan Hallenberg, Charlie Glaser, John Kent, Jonathan Kirshner, Jenny Lind, Iver Neumann, Judith Reppy, Ole Jacob Sending, Sid Tarrow, Leslie Vinjamuri, and Bill Wohlforth for making these visits possible. I am also grateful to the many faculty and students who attended these talks. This project has taken so many twists and turns that they might not recognize it, but that is partly due to their excellent feedback.

Roger Haydon is a wonderful editor. He always provided thoughtful criticism and excellent counsel with a dry humor that made him a joy to work with. I also thank him for identifying reviewers who provided astonishingly careful and constructive reviews. Ellen Labbate and the production team at Cornell University Press, and Kristen Bettcher at Westchester Publishing made this an easy and pleasurable process. I am also grateful to Amron Gravett of Wild Clover Book Services for her indexing skills and Bill Nelson for his excellent maps. I thank Cambridge University Press for permission to publish some of the ideas presented in my chapter, "War and Reform: Gaining Labor's Compliance on the Homefront," from *In War's Wake*.

My parents, Mary and Porter, have been unstinting in their enthusiasm, support, and affection. I thank Kathleen and Bill, as well as Elspeth and Ben, for their love, conversation, and cat videos. Renée de Nevers and Brian Taylor brought their creativity to the book's completion. For sustaining me with her friendship and martinis, I thank Virginia Sly. Thanks also to Pina and Issy for their unbounded joy and dogged determination to chase after an idea, or anything else. I owe the most to Jon, to whom this book is dedicated.

WAR AND DEMOCRACY

MOBILIZING LABOR FOR WAR AND ITS IMPLICATIONS FOR DEMOCRACY

From the death and destruction of the Great War arose the conviction that the Armistice would usher in a new world. The link between war and democracy seemed obvious. The Italian workforce expected to be rewarded with worker management and "land to the peasants." Even Antonio Salandra, the conservative politician who took Italy into war, acknowledged the demands for a radical reordering of society: "Yes, the war is a revolution; a great, a very great revolution. . . . Let no one think that a peaceful return to the past will be possible after this storm" (quoted in Tasca 1938, 10). Such convictions were common across Europe. British labor believed that its wartime sacrifices would be repaid with democratic reform. There would be "homes for the heroes" and the extension of social rights. German and French trade unionists also emerged from the war with blueprints for reform. Activists often shared these expectations. They believed that World War I would advance political, civil, and social rights. Persuaded that the war would help win the battle against discrimination at home, W. E. B. Du Bois supported US entry in 1917: "Out of this war will rise, too, an American Negro, with a right to vote and a right to work and a right to live without insult" (quoted in Ellis 1992, 100). American progressives shared Du Bois's optimism that war could transform the country. One newspaper noted that "the sufferings of war are the birth pains of a worldwide social rebirth. . . . An age of freedom lurks around the corner of our tragedy" (quoted in S. Shapiro 1971, 325).

Scholars disagree about this purported link between war and democracy. Max Weber ([1923] 1983, 142) claimed that military service "meant the triumph of democracy." Many contemporary scholars concur. They suggest that the broadening of the franchise after World War I, and the promotion of social rights after World War II, is not coincidental. One historian entitled her book *War Is Good for Babies and Other Young Children* (Dwork 1987). Others are skeptical.[1] For every Weber who links fighting wars to emerging rights, there is an Alexis de Tocqueville ([1835] 1945, 268) who fears that "protracted war [will] endanger the freedom of a democratic country." Indeed, some scholars argue that it is peace—not war— that leads to democracy (Wright 1942, 841).[2] Skeptics argue that, at best, war influences the timing of democratic reforms, accelerating or postponing a change that would occur regardless (Snyder and Mansfield 2010). Whatever the causal claim, skeptics dismiss wartime promises as fool's gold, designed to elicit support but revealed as hollow once the emergency has passed.

This book takes a new approach to this timeless question. Instead of directly examining whether war builds democracy—an approach that generates important insights but little consensus—it takes an indirect route that begins with a simple observation: what happens to a democracy after a war depends in part on what happens to organized labor during the war. This connection is especially strong during total wars.[3] States must field huge forces with incessant demands for materiel. They must mobilize home-front factories to maximize productivity and minimize social unrest. States must ask of their societies—and especially of labor—much more than they ask in peacetime. But states use different strategies to mobilize labor, and with different results. Some states develop procedurally unjust strategies to gain labor's compliance with the war effort. Other states gain labor's consent through increased wages and benefits. Still others appeal to labor's sense of what is "just," reaching out to labor and including it in decision-making forums. Wartime mobilization profoundly (and predictably) affects the development of labor's interests, identity, and attitudes about the state. Some mobilization strategies encourage labor to adopt reformist goals. Others radicalize labor and generate working-class solidarity. Mobilization for war also shapes labor's allegiance to, and trust in, the state. By the time the war ends, the labor movement can differ radically from its prewar organization, and such transformations help explain the fate of postwar democratic reform.

I do not posit a relationship between the type of mobilization strategy and the nature of a postwar regime. The links from war to democracy are too complex to expect a direct relationship between the two. However, since organized labor is often vital to the strength and success of democracy, the search for sources of democracy should return us to the outbreak of war and the mobilization strategies that follow. The experience of war can transform the labor movement in ways that are central to postwar political settlements.

Not all paths to democracy include labor, but a rich tradition in sociology and political science concurs that labor activism and contentious politics can push liberalization forward.[4] Organized pressure from below creates openings for re-gime change and ensures the transition continues. A parallel literature on civil-ian resistance suggests that nonviolent protest—often led and organized by the labor movement—enhances the prospects for democratization.[5] Labor activism can also be central to the durability and strengthening of democracy.[6] Labor's par-ticipation in government increases the likelihood of redistributive policies that promote social rights. Many scholars argue that strong reformist labor unions and parties explain the advent and growth of the welfare state, and conversely that the decline in working-class power contributes to welfare retraction and socioeco-nomic inequality.[7]

It is by leveraging this wide-ranging literature on organized labor's role in democratization that I link war to democracy. I deduce hypotheses from research on social justice to explain how the strategies states use to mobilize their econo-mies transform labor's interests, identity, and attitudes about the state. I then draw on democratic theorists to assess the implications of these wartime changes for postwar politics. After the war ends, organized labor can play a central role in helping to sustain and build democracy or sometimes to undermine it. As the fol-lowing chapters detail, the strategies that Britain and Italy used to mobilize labor for the Great War transformed their labor movements. These wartime develop-ments explain labor's activism in postwar Britain and Italy and so the likelihood of democratic reform. War-induced changes help explain why so few democratic advances occurred in Britain and why democracy collapsed in Italy.

In analyzing how the wartime mobilization of labor shapes the prospects for democracy, this book makes several contributions. The first is to place the debate about war's effect on democracy within the larger scholarship about the sources of democracy. Historians and political scientists have posited causal claims about how war advances democracy, but this research works in isolation from the vast literature in sociology and political science that explains transitions to, and the strengthening of, democracy. This isolation reflects the tendency to see war as a phe-nomenon apart from normal politics, a tendency reinforced by the challenge in cre-ating parsimonious models about war's effect on politics. Bridging the gap between these two literatures—especially given the quality of the scholarship on democracy—enriches our understanding of the links between war and democracy.

Second, this book's interdisciplinary approach uncovers the crucial role that justice plays in the politics of war and peace. Many social scientists collapse con-cerns about justice into concerns about material rewards: a fair process helps to ensure a favorable outcome. But decades of social psychological research show that concerns about justice are not only pervasive, they are also motivated by more than narrow self-interest. How people assess the justice or injustice of their experi-ences influences their beliefs and behavior. I draw on this research in organizational justice to explain how and why identity and interests change. I explore how labor's assessments of the "justness" of the state's mobilization strategy systematically reshapes what labor wants, who it imagines it is, and what it thinks of the state. This transformation can become a watershed in labor's development, in turn influencing the nature of postwar politics and the extent of democracy.

Third, this book provides a new explanation for the origins of Italian Fascism. The collapse of Italy's fledgling democracy was not an inevitable consequence of the war or of structural features of the state and the economy. It was not the fact of war but the *type of mobilization* that was key. Italian officials chose policies that (unintentionally) transformed the rural and urban workforce. The experience of war turned labor relations with pockets of radical demands into a revolutionary situation. After the war, popular unrest intensified, challenging the economic status quo and provoking a countermobilization that Fascists road to power and the destruction of the liberal regime.

Fourth, this book corrects a tendency to treat war as a temporary interruption of routine politics. Studies examine either war or peace, but with the exception of the state-building literature, scholars rarely examine how wartime politics bleeds into the postwar environment. Yet we cannot understand how war affects politics if we focus exclusively on how war changes the state. Policies designed to prosecute wars also restructure society and alter its links to the state. Wartime mobilization can generate new ideas about what is necessary and possible, and what should be done to achieve it. These societal aspirations influence postwar politics and the success of democratic reform. Just as we search for the origins of war in the preceding years of peace, we should search for the origins of the domestic order in the preceding years of war.

This book's final contribution is a warning against undue optimism about war as a democratizer. Even in easy cases for conventional accounts, war rarely advances democracy. The British and Italian working class had every reason to expect compensation for their wartime service: there should have been a new social order in Britain and a reordering of Italian politics. There was not, which speaks to the limits of war as a democratic reformer. Some actors—and most likely veterans—can leverage wartime service to further their rights. But no one should look to war to advance democratic agendas, nor should scholars regret the decline of mass mobilization because of its apparently positive effects. But the implication is not that scholars should ignore the domestic consequences of war—the intuition that war affects democratic reform is correct. The link, however, is not what we often imagine. The experience of war shapes societal actors in ways that can determine democracy's fate.

War and Democracy: Conventional Accounts

Many social scientists believe that large-scale wars build democracy. They see war as contributing to important political advances, ranging from the abolition of serf-dom and the creation of representative institutions to the expansion of suffrage and the adoption of progressive taxation. Most of this scholarship emerged after World War II in response to the creation of European welfare states. Scholars have recently returned to this topic, again finding evidence of war's role in democracy's advance. They propose three pathways from war to democratic reform: through changes in societal values, increases in state capacity, and bargaining between state and societal actors. These arguments capture facets of war's creative impulse, but they remain unpersuasive.

War Creates Social Solidarity

The first set of arguments explores war's effect on values and beliefs. Scholars argue that war cuts across societal divides, brings the nation together, and engenders support for the creation of a just and inclusive society. Richard Titmuss first popularized this argument in his volume on Britain's official history of World War II. The war years generated "different conceptions of the meaning of social duty" and led to a "revision of ideas and a rearrangement of values" across society. Months of destruction and deprivation changed "the mood of the people, and in sympathetic response, values changed as well." No longer must the poor fend for themselves. More and more people, including those from privileged classes, now believed that "if dangers were to be shared then resources should also be shared" (Titmuss 1950, 516–17, 508). This increase in social solidarity encouraged the development of egalitarian policies. It was only fair that those who shouldered so much of the war's hardship should be brought into the collective fold.

Claims about the generation of solidarity initially examined British commitment to a mixed economy, Keynesianism, and a generous welfare state. World War II's equalization of risk dissolved distinctions between soldiers and civilians, rich and poor. German bombing did not discriminate between Georgian townhomes and slum dwellings. "I'm glad we've been bombed," the Queen remarked after Buckingham Palace was hit. "It makes me feel I can look the East Ender in the face." Out of this rubble, the notion of "fair shares" became irresistible. "I feel quite exhausted after seeing and hearing so much sadness, sorrow, heroism and magnificent spirit," the Queen wrote. "The destruction is so awful, and the people so wonderful—they deserve a better world" (quoted in Calder 1995, 58). This newfound belief that "we're all in the same boat" reoriented British politics. The experience shattered the Conservative Party's resistance to assisting the so-called undeserving poor, and it led civil servants and Tories to support the Labour Party's call for fundamental reform. From 1940, "egalitarianism and community feeling became to a great extent the pervasive ideals of social life," claimed Paul Addison, the historian who wrote the foremost account of the British experience. "The national unity of the war years gave rise to a new consensus at the top which dominated Britain long after the last bomb had fallen," he explained. "All three parties went to the polls in 1945 committed to principles of social and economic reconstruction" (1975, 18, 13–14).

Many scholars concur that a common enemy and common hardships enhance solidarity and encourage egalitarian norms. "War may be one of the larger class of national crises that inspire a collective willingness to move fast in the development of the welfare state," Harold Wilensky claims. Large-scale wars are "oddly egalitarian" because "the thirst for equality" inspires redistributive policies (1975, 72, 71). Gregory Kasza argues that this process contributed to the development of the Japanese welfare state. The drive for healthy and loyal soldiers and civilians partly explains this revolution in social rights (2002, 417–18). But Kasza stresses that the collective effort involved in fighting the Pacific War caused elites to rethink cultural norms about the provision of social services. The official wartime slogan of "All people are soldiers" soon morphed into "All people should have pensions" and "All people should have insurance" (Kasza 2002, 428).

Kenneth Scheve and David Stasavage generalized this argument in a sweeping account of the rise and fall of progressive taxation in Europe and the United States during the twentieth century. Mass mobilization transformed beliefs about tax fairness. Just as Wilensky noted decades earlier that large-scale wars raise questions about why "some profiteer and others die" (1975, 71), Scheve and Stasavage argue that mass casualty lists decisively shift tax debates from equal treatment and the ability to pay to a "compensatory" principle that underpins support for progressive taxation. This demand for comparative sacrifice dominated British, French, Canadian, and American legislative debates during and after World War I. "Across the political spectrum, politicians, bureaucrats, and other elites argued for higher taxes on the rich in order to compensate for these new inequalities" (Scheve and Stasavage 2016, 169). "Soaking the rich" who profited from war resonated while thousands of young and poor men were paying with their lives.

Activists and scholars believe that women also benefit from the goodwill that wartime service creates. Female labor helps to win wars and so reshapes popular and elite assumptions about women's place in the democratic polity. "Woman can never be accounted a negligible factor in the community again," an American suffragist declared during World War I. "Her economic value has been substantiated" (quoted in Wynn 1986, 148). Having resisted female suffrage for years,

President Woodrow Wilson reversed course in 1918: "We have made partners of the women in this war. Shall we admit them only to a partnership of suffering and sacrifice and toil but not to a partnership of privilege and right?" (quoted in J. Adams 2014, 238). Some scholars suggest that Wilson's change of heart was common. Noting the number of states that extended voting rights to women during or shortly after World War I, Robert Saldin (2010, 97) concludes that "their service on the homefront made women full partners in the war and, as a result, created a consensus that they deserved full citizenship rights." A study of twentieth-century voting rights also attributes the robust association between war and female suffrage to a new "domestic zeitgeist" (D. Hicks 2013, 72). Women's pivotal wartime roles generate support for equal rights.

Many scholars argue that World War II caused a similar transformation in white America. The war years were a turning point in white attitudes.[8] Knowledge of the vital contributions African Americans made to defeating Fascism led many whites "to question racial discrimination and to redefine American national identity in broad, inclusive terms that encompassed long-ostracized minorities" (Mershon and Schlossman 1998, 94). The contrast between the country's avowed war aims and the reality of Jim Crow was central to this shift. It became increasingly difficult for white America to square racism at home with the fight for freedom abroad. It became especially difficult to deny rights to African Americans when confronted with the real-life effects of Nazi theories of Aryan supremacy. The need to draw a bright line between Deutschland and Dixieland contributed to progress in civil rights (Klinkner and Smith 1999, 139). A legal scholar explains the Supreme Court's 1944 decision to abolish the white primary: "Justices cannot have failed to observe the tensions between a purportedly democratic war fought against the Nazis . . . and the pervasive disenfranchisement of Southern blacks" (quoted in Steven White 2019, 161).

Arguments about wartime solidarity usually stress that the vast collective efforts of total war foster support for an inclusive nation. Saldin (2010, 10) agrees that major wars are more likely to have this effect, noting that war against Fascism created a "new moral and intellectual environment" that furthered civil rights in the United States. But he also finds that small wars enhance democracy. The Korean War led to the racial integration of the military, and the Vietnam War was central to eighteen-to-twenty-year-olds gaining the vote. The wartime service of young and African American men "created new and compelling moral reasons to extend full citizenship rights to these groups." Wars act as "focusing events" that change elite and mass values and lead to fundamental changes in the provision of rights (Saldin 2010, 9, 12, 15).

It is true, as these scholars argue, that total wars sometimes generate a sense of community, but such sentiments often last no longer than a victory parade—or do not occur at all. American industrialists spoke eloquently during World War I of a more just future. John D. Rockefeller Jr. described "Labor and Capital as partners." The head of Bethlehem Steel referred to "a new age" and "a world for the workers." Yet routine politics had reemerged with a vengeance by 1919, when the National Association of Manufacturers declared its goal of "liquidating labor's wartime achievements" (quoted in Wynn 1986, 203). A generation later, another postwar period exposed the reality of America's home-front solidarity. Steven White (2019) shows that fighting Nazi Germany did not—as the conventional argument assumes—lead whites to revise racist beliefs. There was some decline in racial prejudice, but when it came to policies to redress racial injustice, the experience of war did not reform white America. To the contrary, support for federal antilynching laws *declined* during World War II. President Franklin Roosevelt had declared that the "four freedoms" must triumph "everywhere in the world," but Norman Rockwell's visual depiction of an all-white America in his *Freedom from Fear* portrays the more exclusive truth (Engel 2015, 26).

Even in World War II Britain—the quintessential example of the rise of egalitarian norms—later historians question the account. The British were joined in their commitment to defeating Nazi Germany, but there was no consensus on domestic reform. Most Conservatives opposed Labour's agenda for national insurance, medical reform, and employment, housing, and education policies. Tories "had not really budged from their prewar positions" (Jefferys 1987, 132).[9] Despite a party platform supporting reconstruction, the 1945 electoral campaign "put into sharp relief the distinctions between the reforming vision of Labour and the fundamentally unreconstructed nature of Conservativism under Churchill" (Cronin 1986, 10). In his first speech during the campaign (and following revelations of the horrors at German concentration camps), Winston Churchill declared that if Labour were elected, it "would have to fall back on some form of Gestapo" to implement its policies. The "spirit of Dunkirk" had only papered over deep-seated differences about welfare reform. "Winston jumped straight off his pedestal as world statesman to deliver a fantastical exaggerated onslaught on socialism," a member of his government declared (both quoted in Toye 2010, 656). Tories might support welfare reform, but only within the existing (prewar) structure.

To accept parliamentary debates and electoral campaigning as evidence of wartime solidarity confuses rhetoric with reality. Politicians are attuned to the popular aspirations that wars raise. Soldiers and civilians across Europe and North America believed they were fighting for a better world. Members of Britain's Conservative Party understood that World War II had been a "People's War." They often spoke of their support for the Beveridge Report, which outlined Britain's comprehensive welfare state. They knew they had to appear committed to its various provisions. But away from the public eye, they "whittled it away by detailed criticism" (Jefferys 1987, 131). A prominent Tory conceded as much. There was within the party "a feeling that Beveridge is a sinister old man, who wishes to give away a great deal of other people's money" (quoted in Jefferys 1987, 131).

Arguments about the rise of wartime solidarity tend to conflate national unity with support for an inclusive nation. Americans were united in their war against Fascism, but racial violence and discrimination persisted. The "arsenal of democracy" was a *divided arsenal*, as the title of Daniel Kryder's (2000) history of US race relations during the war suggests. Britain's evacuation of children to the countryside before the Blitz was said to have encouraged genuine concern among middle-class families about the horrific conditions in urban slums. But housing evacuees often generated disgust among their rural hosts and confirmed their prejudices about the urban poor (McKibbin 1990, 287). Suffering the same fate under German bombing often did more to reinforce class divides than bridge them. An air raid warden disparaged those in working-class shelters, acknowledging that "she had acquired a good deal of contempt for the ordinary person. . . . They made no attempt to amuse their children, for instance, nor to take responsibility for themselves" (quoted in Mitchison 1985, 146). The much-heralded solidarity on the British home front "is a mirage, an illusion which rapidly fades the closer one gets to it" (Pimlott 1985, 366).

War Strengthens the State

The second set of arguments linking war to democracy focuses on state capacity. Scholars recognize that wars strengthen executive authority and threaten representative institutions. But they also stress that wartime state building can clear the path to democracy. Not only do dysfunctional states provide a weak foundation for democratic polities (Tilly 2006, 23–24), but mobilization for war creates legacies that ease the adoption of progressive reform. The expanded scope of wartime governments gives postwar reformers the administrative capacity, fiscal strength, and knowledge to expand social citizenship (Obinger, Petersen, and Starke 2018). Many Progressives supported US entry into World War I for precisely this reason. They hoped that mobilization would build the strong "positive" state essential to realizing their goals (Porter 1994, 275). Wars also furnish governments with new fiscal powers and introduce a ratchet effect. States increase taxes and spending in wartime, but like a ratchet that permits tightening in only one direction, taxation and state spending never return to their prewar levels. "It is harder to get the saddle on the horse than to keep it there," a study of the growth in public expenditures concludes (Peacock and Wiseman 1961, xxxiv). The public accepts tax rates in wartime it would otherwise find intolerable, and it soon normalizes to this increase. Nancy Bermeo (2007) suggests that Portugal's fiscal capacity eased its democratization following the end of its costly colonial wars in 1975.

Bruce Porter argues that the bureaucratic, regulatory, and tax structure built during World War I made possible the expansion of the US welfare state (1994, 281–82). Maurizio Ferrera makes a similar claim about the influence of both world wars on the Italian welfare state: increased state capacity made possible "the elaboration of very ambitious and comprehensive reform plans" (2018, 99). Jytte Klausen argues that this pattern occurred across Europe and the United States after World War II. The need to manage wartime economies led to an unprecedented growth in state capacity that made possible the creation of welfare states (2001). Historians concur. James Cronin and Peter Weiler (1991) note that the wartime transformation of the British state meant that upon victory in 1945, the Labour government could turn immediately to the implementation of its ambitious program for reconstruction.

The experience of war also enlightens state actors about the need for reform. Wars have an "inspection effect" (Peacock and Wiseman 1961). International conflict "often casts a spotlight on deficiencies that might otherwise be ignored," a scholar of American political development explains (Saldin 2010, 236). The exposure of chronic social problems prompts government action. German bombing during World War II exposed the desperate conditions in British slums, and the 1899 Boer War revealed the wretched health of the working class. The knowledge that thousands of men were unfit for military service prompted London's quest for "national efficiency" and policies to improve the nation's health (Bourne 1989, 201). Managing a wartime economy also gives political elites the expertise to tackle chronic problems. Total wars join public and private actors, and administrators gain detailed knowledge about the economy. Alan Milward ([1977] 1987) found in his classic study of the economics of World War II that mobilization stimulated the collection of economic data and encouraged officials to rethink their view of the economy, the extent of their economic power, and their responsibility to use this power to better society. This new expertise can be crucial. The viability of policy initiatives often rests on the presence of coherent bureaucracies staffed by well-trained and experienced officials.

Wars do build states, and these increases in state capacity can become vehicles for democratic reform. But these newly empowered agencies can also vanish in postwar calls to return to the status quo. Woodrow Wilson's wartime administration expanded the scope and size of the federal government, and Progressives hoped to use a version of this wartime state to revitalize the democratic promise. Yet few of these agencies survived the Armistice. Traditional fears of big government resurfaced. Republicans sought to end wartime regulatory powers and to curb taxes and spending. The War Industries Board was shut down so quickly that its director had to personally pay for some of his employees' trips home (Rockoff 2005, 336). The government slashed the number of federal employees and by 1921 had dismantled most of the wartime state. Only public transportation continued to be regulated. The wartime state seemed to go "to pieces in a night," an observer remarked (quoted in Wynn 1986, 199). Even the benefits of the ratchet effect failed to materialize. Government spending was higher after 1918, but war costs—not a growth in social expenditures—absorbed that increase (Rockoff 1998, 47–48). This rapid dismantling of the wartime state is most evident in economically liberal states when officials call for a "return to normalcy," as Warren Harding promised during his 1920 presidential campaign. But even when the empowered state survives demobilization, officials can use the state's enhanced capacity to crush social unrest, not to address its root causes.

A fundamental problem with arguments about increases in state capacity and social solidarity is that they are apolitical. There is a *granting* of reforms: from the rich to the poor, from the state to society. The privileged recognize the plight of the poor and commit to address it; the state reflexively uses its larger capacity and newfound expertise to address social ills. In these accounts, even learning is an apolitical process where officials apply the appropriate lessons. Addison (1975, 13) depicts a conflict-free process leading to the British welfare state: "When Labour swept to victory in 1945 the new consensus fell, like a branch of ripe plums, into the lap of Mr. Attlee." Alan Peacock and Jack Wiseman (1961) assume that the newly enlightened state channels its larger budget into social needs. This neglect of political contention is equally true of recent accounts. Scheve and Stasavage (2016, 117) argue that mass mobilization created the political will across income levels to impose progressive taxes. Left and right parties "felt compelled" to respond to fairness demands even after the war ended.

These accounts depict, at best, an enlightened self-interest where the state acts on its own initiative to ensure the ready supply of healthy soldiers and loyal workers, as London did in the wake of the Boer War and Tokyo did during the Pacific War. Either way, those who benefit from reform barely figure in the accounts. Elites "reward" the disenfranchised who have "earned" or "deserve" full citizenship rights (and not fought long and hard to attain them). It is as if war suspends organized political contention. The absence of political conflict is all the more notable given the stakes involved in redistributive policies and the extension of civil and political rights.

War Allows Society to Extract Paybacks from the State

A third set of arguments stresses the contestation inherent in any expansion of democratic citizenship. Payback arguments see the state as striking a bargain with civilians: cooperate with the war effort and you will be repaid with democratic reform. Stanislav Andreski first popularized this argument, positing a "military participation ratio," whereby the greater the proportion of the population mobilized for war, the greater the leveling of social inequalities after the war. "An effort must be made to win them over, to convince them that they are fighting for themselves" (1954, 27). Charles Tilly argues that wars force rulers into bargaining situations—however imbalanced—where societal actors extract concessions in exchange for their support (1992a, 83–103). New social contracts must be negotiated as the cost of warfare escalates. "The most general effect of the war is to make the common people more important," the author of the report that laid the foundation for the British welfare state noted about World War II (quoted in Stevenson 1990, 196). Michael Mann's pithy comment that "the people sacrificed but not for nothing" captures the payback logic (1988, 158).

Scholars claim the flip side as well. Regimes that do not depend on domestic extraction, either because they have access to other resources or because they do not fight costly wars, are not forced to concede rights (Tilly 2006, 23). Robert Bates suggests that leaders of states that rely on foreign aid can ignore popular demands for democratization (2001, 82). John Ferejohn and Frances McCall Rosenbluth claim that African Americans did not benefit from the Spanish-American War or World War I because manpower needs were comparatively slight (2017, 262).

Scholars draw on every corner of history to illustrate this argument, but they focus on three turning points when the evolution of warfare forced rulers to extract ever-greater resources from their societies, and to provide ever more rights in return. The first transition came in the 1600s with the Revolution in Military Affairs. The widespread adoption of firepower, the construction of complex fortifications, and the creation of large standing armies dramatically increased the cost of war. Fighting these larger, longer, and more expensive wars forced rulers to offer political rights to various groups in return for their collaboration. Douglass North and Barry Weingast (1989) argue that the British Crown recognized parliamentary sovereignty in the late seventeenth century in order to attain support for its wars. Bates (2001, 78) agrees: this era's representative institutions were a "byproduct of the effort to transform private wealth into public revenues."

The French Revolution's introduction of the nation in arms was the second transition in warfare. "The implicit strategy of rulers was to grant national rights to the minimum set of persons that would guarantee the delivery of militarily essential resources to the state" (Tilly 1992b, 17). Mass conscript armies exploded those demands and fundamentally changed the relationship between states and their subjects. Swedish working-class men demanded the vote under the slogan "One man, one gun, one vote" (Gunitsky 2017, 83). Whether it was Napoleonic France, the United States in 1812, or Austria and France in the 1870s, reliance on conscript forces required expanded rights (Porter 1994; Vagts 1959, 207–8). Two comprehensive analyses of the expansion of voting rights concur on the "martial origins of democracy." Ferejohn and Rosenbluth (2017, 1) argue that the desperate need for military manpower led to some of the most significant franchise reform in history. Tony Ingesson et al.'s study (2018) of male suffrage since the Napoleonic Wars finds that the "quid pro quo mechanism" is significant when the risk of death is high.

Modern warfare "made any state vulnerable to popular resistance and answerable to popular demands" (Tilly 1992a, 83). These demands include social rights, especially for veterans demanding payback for their wartime service (Mann 1993, 499–502). The US welfare state began as pensions for Civil War veterans (Skocpol 1992), and the GI Bill further developed it (Mettler 2005). Activists also see military service as a route to citizenship rights. In the midst of the Civil War, Frederick Douglass asserted, "Once let the black man get upon his person the brass letters, U.S. . . . there is no power on earth . . . which can deny that he has earned the right to citizenship in the United States" (quoted in Wickenden 1990, 108). This link is not automatic—autocratic Prussia mastered the use of conscripts. Nevertheless, scholars agree that "conscription and citizenship were two sides of the same coin" (Centeno 2002, 242).

The advent of total war marked the third transition in warfare. Previously only soldiers could cash a "patriotic check," but as armed conflict consumed the nation, so men and women, young and old, also had to be persuaded to participate. Coercion and propaganda went only so far: repression risked igniting unrest and patriotic fervor often waned (though battlefield demands did not). The US government estimated that it took six to ten workers to maintain one soldier in the field (Watkins 1920, 59). This workforce could extract concessions in exchange for its participation (Marwick 1974). The American Federation of Labor leveraged labor scarcity to gain support for collective bargaining during World War I (S. Shapiro 1971, 332). The civil rights community used the threat of tens of thousands of African Americans marching on the capital in 1941 to persuade Roosevelt to prohibit discrimination in federal and war industry jobs.

States also rely on promises for the future, especially as wars drag on and sacrifices mount. "The most effective strategy for generating mass loyalty is arguably to make promises of welfare reform after the war is ended" (Obinger, Petersen, and Starke 2018, 18). The population's commitment must be sustained, but additional concessions risk overtaxing the wartime economy. Promises of a better future allow officials to bolster support at little immediate cost. During World War I, Berlin issued public promises of social and political reform to sustain productivity (G. Craig 1964, 322). London promised India self-government in order to maintain access to the nearly 1.5 million Indian soldiers who fought for

Britain (Gerwarth and Manela 2014). Just as men had gained political, civil, and social rights through military service, total war allowed citizens and subjects to demand new rights. "Warfare in twentieth century Europe produced a definite flattening of the social pyramid," Andreski (1954, 28–29) claims.

The focus on bargaining in these arguments avoids the problems of the social solidarity and state capacity accounts. There is a pervasive sense of conflict. Actors leverage their control over resources to extract concessions from war-making elites. "White-hot bargaining forged rights and obligations of citizenship" (Tilly (1992b, 10). In these accounts, war does not dissolve class differences or enlighten an empowered state: it transforms the bargaining power of state and societal actors. Rights emerge only after attempts to extract resources ignite vehement resistance, and elites must concede at home or be defeated abroad. This emphasis on politics is important, but payback accounts cannot explain the inconsistent relationship between war and rights.

Democratic reforms sometimes follow wars that require heavy extraction. Britain, Austria, and Belgium broadened the franchise and many countries granted political rights to women after World War I. But these correlations often do not hold up to empirical scrutiny (Rubio-Marín 2014). While electoral reforms sometimes occur after a war, they are often unrelated to any bargain struck during the war.[10] In addition, there are multiple examples where even the most demanding wars do not lead to reform. Over seventy-five thousand Indian soldiers were killed during World War I, and Britain heavily taxed India to pay for the war, but instead of self-government, Britain "rewarded" India with repressive legislation that gave Britain extraordinary powers to quell "sedition" against imperial rule. Officials even hedged on the modest promise to "Indianize" the Indian Army officer corps.

Indians were subjects (not citizens), but it is not the absence of electoral punishment that allows wartime elites to escape their commitments. Democracies also renege on wartime promises for reform. As the following chapters detail, the demands placed on British citizens during World War I were enormous, and official promises for a better world were great. The payback was not. Expectations for democratic reform were also dashed in the United States after 1918. Organized labor made some of its greatest gains during the war, and it was determined to retain them in peacetime (Wynn 1986, 197). Yet most wartime reforms did not survive demobilization. As one historian notes, "By 1920 there was little left from wartime social reform except prohibition, immigration restriction, and racist hysteria" (Davis 1967, 533). American labor did no better from its support for World War II. More antilabor legislation was passed toward the end of the war and through 1947 than at any other period in US history (Johnson 2000, 344).

The disparity between participation, promises, and payback is especially stark for African Americans. Du Bois urged the Black community in 1917 to "close ranks" and support the war, assuming—as did many of his contemporaries—that war would provide opportunities to harness the power of the federal government to the cause of civil rights (Ellis 1992, 105–20). Yet Blacks made little progress during the war. Discrimination in the military and the civil service endured. The newly nationalized railroad enforced Jim Crow in southern states, segregating soldiers in uniform and officials traveling on federal war business. The postwar record was even worse. African Americans lost the economic gains they had made during the war, and there was no progress in civil or political rights (Klinkner and Smith 1999, 112–14). Appeals to make lynching a federal crime went nowhere. The war's "main accomplishment was to excite false hopes" (Scheiber and Scheiber 1969, 449). Du Bois bitterly remarked that he had not realized war's "wide impotence as a method of social reform" (quoted in Wynn 1986, 49). The highest-ranking African American in the Wilson administration agreed: "As one who recalls the assurance of 1917 and 1918, I confess personally a deep sense of disappointment, of poignant pain that a great country in time of need should promise so much and afterward perform so little" (quoted in Scheiber and Scheiber 1969, 458). In fact, World War I did more to inflame American racism than to address it. Images of Black soldiers expecting compensation for their service fueled white fears, contributed to the Klan's revival, and helped ignite racist violence across the country. Ten of the eighty-three Blacks lynched in 1919 were soldiers, some still in uniform, and one was burned at the stake while wearing his uniform (Mikkelsen 2009, 466; Wynn 1977, 49).

A focus on timing might rescue payback accounts and explain why war-making elites fail to uphold their promises. Societal actors lose their leverage once the war ends. In this sense, the Black community's World War I slogan, "First your country, then your rights," reflects a misguided hope that the community corrects the next time its country marches off to war. The "Double V campaign" during World War II stood for victory against Fascism abroad *simultaneously* with equal rights at home. Most African Americans agreed that their community should "not soft pedal on demands for complete freedom and citizenship" during the war (quoted in Wynn 2010, 76). However, many of the democratic reforms that scholars highlight in payback accounts endure long past wartime mobilization, or they are adopted after the war ends and society's leverage is gone. Neither pattern fits the payback argument. Rights should coincide with the need for resources and endure as long as the demand for resources remains.

Tilly (1993, 29) notes that institutions built in war are sometimes hijacked for other purposes after the war. Once the state had such power, "large segments of the population made claims on it for their own (mostly nonmilitary) ends." Tilly notes that this stronger state came to be used to provide benefits, such as education and welfare. But he neglects the extent that state actors use their newfound power to retract wartime gains and to crush peacetime demands. In fact, the focus on state power and bargaining in payback accounts means rights should be especially fragile once the war ends. Societal actors have lost their leverage and war has strengthened the state (and especially its coercive power). This newly empowered state has little reason to fulfill wartime promises, and it has the power to retract wartime concessions. Czar Nicholas II used his returning troops in 1905 to restore the absolutist regime and to roll back political concessions that he made during the Russo-Japanese War (Skocpol 1979, 94–96). A similar reversal occurred in Prussia while it was fighting Poland and France in the mid-1600s (Downing 1998, 16–17). The Chinese Communist Party was "mass regarding" during the revolution—it needed to build and maintain mass loyalty and extract resources from society—but its authoritarian structure reemerged upon victory in 1949 (Womack 1987).

Democracies are not immune from this problem. Democratically elected leaders also rely on war-empowered states to renege on wartime promises. Ottawa used its wartime state to repress labor radicals after World War I (Kealey 1992, 281–93). Canada's neighbor did something similar. The US Congress passed the Espionage and Sedition Acts to monitor radicals and antiwar activity during World War I. The federal government also created, almost from scratch, its intelligence apparatus: the Bureau of Intelligence, the US Army's Military Intelligence Division, and the Office of Naval Intelligence. These new agencies moved forcefully into domestic surveillance during the war, and they "skipped nary a beat in making a transition" to crusade against domestic reformers after the war (Kornweibel 1998, 9). Employers and officials used this newly empowered state during the Red Scare (1919–20) to undo labor's wartime gains and to break the power of organized labor (R. Schmidt 2000, 25–40). They also used these repressive institutions against the civil rights community. This new network of intelligence agencies investigated Black activists, infiltrated their organizations, and intimidated their audiences. Just as the ratchet failed to prevent a rollback, the payback became a "take-back."

Payback arguments miss an additional source of state power that restrains the demand for rights. Payback accounts are purely material. They assume a calculated exchange where actors (sometimes violently) bargain for advantage. Putting wartime politics front and center strengthens these explanations, but this narrow conception of interests ignores a potent source of state power: patriotism. Citizens sometimes contribute willingly to the war effort. They may expect to be rewarded for their sacrifices, but there is no explicit quid pro quo—citizens do not always bargain hard.

US officials knew they needed African American support to prosecute World War I. "The cooperation of this large element of our population in all civilian and military activities is of vital importance," a US intelligence agency reported. "The alienation, or worse, of eleven million people would be a serious menace to the successful prosecution of the war" (quoted in Scheiber and Scheiber 1969, 440). However, the Black community did not exploit its leverage during the national emergency. Some activists questioned the wisdom of loyally supporting a country that denied their community basic rights. But on the whole, African Americans rallied to the flag, volunteered for the military, bought Liberty Bonds, and organized loyalty parades. Late in his life Du Bois lamented that he, too, had been "swept into the national maelstrom" during the war and against his better judgment (quoted in Ellis 1992, 123).[11] Even if activists can resist patriotism's allure, there is often little room for maneuver. Disenfranchised groups risk repression and charges of disloyalty if they appear to privilege the pursuit of equal rights at home over support for the conflict abroad.

Payback arguments capture the politicized environment of wartime emergencies, but this approach cannot explain how leverage in war translates into political power (and rights) in peace. It cannot explain why wars, and especially large-scale ones, are rarely good for democracy. We do not know whether (and how) wartime bargains are important to postwar democratic reform. Most important, because payback accounts focus on the bargaining power of actors with fixed and material preferences, they neglect how wartime mobilization can alter what actors want, and what they think is possible. In particular, they neglect how the experience of war affects organized labor, a vital actor in democracy's advance. It is this wartime development of labor's interests, identity, and attitudes about the state that helps explain war's effect on democracy.

A Crucial Role for Justice

Mobilization for war has the potential to transform postwar politics, sometimes strengthening democracy and sometimes undermining it. Unraveling that process does not mean a wholesale rejection of conventional accounts. But explaining this link requires an indirect approach that engages research in sociology and political science on organized labor's role in democratization. It also means shifting the focus in two important ways. The first is to analyze the *type* of mobilization (not just its scale). Most conventional accounts stress mass mobilization: the greater the demands placed on society, the greater the growth in state capacity; the greater the extraction of resources, the more likely is democratic reform. Scale *is* important—weak actors gain leverage during total wars. The US secretary of the interior summarized labor's wartime power in 1943: "There are not enough jails in the country to hold these men and if there were, I must point out that a jailed miner produces no more coal" (quoted in Bondi 1995, 239). However, fixating on scale misses other essential variations in wartime mobilization. States use different strategies to gain labor's compliance. The variation in these mobilization strategies—and especially the extent of procedural justice—shapes labor's wartime development and the prospects for democratic reform.

The second shift in focus—especially compared with payback accounts—is to examine how war transforms the beliefs and aspirations of societal actors. Wars do create temporary alterations in the bargaining power of state and societal actors (as payback arguments stress), but wars also transform the bargainers themselves. Scholars note these war-inspired changes in belief. Elisabeth Jean Wood (2003) argues that participation in El Salvador's civil war promoted a political culture that embraced political action and redistributive claims. Historians refer to World War I as a "transformative moment" that created "new aspirations" and "surging consciousness" in the Black community (Lentz-Smith 2009, 4–9; Spero and Harris 1931, 387–88). Christopher Parker (2009) argues that service in the US military during World War II generated a political ideology among Black veterans that encouraged them to challenge white supremacy.[12] This potential for change is equally true of the working class. The experience of war shapes organized labor's political beliefs. Mobilization strategies can strengthen the bonds between labor and the state. They can enhance nationalist sentiment and commitment to state goals. Mobilization strategies can also alienate labor from the state and create distrust of state intentions. Mobilization for war shapes labor's collective identity, influencing its understanding of its interests and the best way to achieve them. And it does so systematically.

Gaining Labor's Compliance with the War Effort

Modern states cannot effectively wage total wars without labor's cooperation. "Twentieth-century warfare demands that the blood of the soldier must be mingled with three to five parts of the sweat of the man in the factories, mills, mines, and fields of the nation-in-arms," an American industrialist remarked in 1916 (quoted in Harries and Harries 1997, 55–56). States adopt different policies to address this common challenge. I draw on research on social justice to identify critical distinctions in these mobilization strategies. I then use that research, as well as studies of compliance in organizations and the development of organized labor, to consider how variations in mobilization transform the labor movement.

Research on social justice emerged in the 1960s and has evolved into a vast, multidisciplinary literature that examines how individuals assess fairness and the implications of those assessments for their attitudes, feelings, and behavior. For three reasons, this research is well suited to explaining how labor reacts to wartime mobilization. First, social justice research is highly generalizable. Researchers test these arguments in legal, political, educational, and managerial settings, and across local, state, and national groups. They confirm that perceptions of justice matter in "almost all settings in which people interact with one another, either as individuals or in groups" (Tyler et al. 1997, 9). Second, this literature explores the role of fairness in situations that closely resemble labor's position in wartime. Social justice researchers examine how average employees determine whether they are fairly treated in their jobs and their reactions to those assessments (Blader and Tyler 2015, 361). The "workplace" is larger in wartime, but state and society are forced together in what amounts to a single national firm waging war. State officials often become the employer, directly intervening on the shop floor and setting pay and working conditions. Finally, this research is well established. My hypotheses are not based on intuition, "common sense," or a few empirical tests. Social justice scholars have spent decades debating and testing (both in the field and in experimental studies) how perceptions of justice influence belief and action.

TYPES OF MOBILIZATION

State strategies to mobilize labor vary along two dimensions. The first is *outcome*, or the extent that labor is fairly compensated for its contributions to the war effort in both absolute and relative terms. The second is *process*, or the extent that labor is included in decision making and treated with respect. Research on distributive and procedural justice helps identify the criteria for each.

States often use increased wages and benefits, or other material rewards, to gain labor's compliance with the war effort. The US labor leader Samuel Gompers ensured that the working class profited from World War I. The Wilson administration required that companies supplying military uniforms pay minimum wages, maintain eight-hour workdays, and permit inspections of sanitary facilities. During 1917 alone, eleven states passed stricter child labor laws, six approved compulsory education bills, and five instituted pensions for mothers. World War I also saw the first US experimentation with public housing and the endorsement of forms of health insurance (Davis 1967).

But remuneration is not just about what individuals gain (is it favorable?). It is also about how individuals fare relative to others (is it fair?). The earliest social psychological research on justice sought to understand worker dissatisfaction with wages and promotions. Scholars concluded that distributive justice is key (Ambrose and Kulik 1999).[13] A sense of injustice derives not from how much one receives but from a belief that others contribute less and gain more. This comparison is horizontal and vertical: machinists compare their contributions and rewards with those of other machinists and with those of their supervisors. States often recognize the importance of distributive justice in wartime. Immediately following the German invasion of Poland, Prime Minister Neville Chamberlain stressed that measures to control profits in the arms industry would accompany the introduction of military conscription.[14] When Churchill assumed power eight months later, his government imposed a 100 percent tax rate on excess corporate profits (Leff 1991, 1314). Yet other states do little to promote a sense of shared sacrifice. During World War II, and despite high inflation, French officials froze wages and heavily taxed overtime pay but imposed few additional taxes on employers (Imlay 2003, 285).

Social justice research shifted in the 1970s from a focus on outcomes to a concern with the fairness of the decision-making process, or procedural justice.[15] This is the second dimension on which mobilization strategies differ. Justice theorists initially examined the *formal* aspects of procedures. Are people allowed to present evidence before a decision is made, and do they have a say in the rendering of the decision? Also important are whether procedures are consistently applied and without bias, and whether there are opportunities to modify and reverse them (G. Leventhal 1980; Thibaut and Walker 1975). Researchers initially assumed that this concern about procedures was instrumental, but later research found that individuals care about the process itself, regardless of their ability to influence outcomes.[16] "Having one's say" increases the perception of justice even when that "voice" occurs after the decision has been made (Emery, Matthews, and Kitzmann 1994). Scholars also realized that individuals care about the *informal* aspects of procedures, which is how formal structures are enacted. Being treated with dignity and respect and receiving clear and adequate explanations for decisions shape perceptions of justice (Bies and Moag 1986).[17]

Mobilization strategies vary in the extent they embrace the formal and informal aspects of procedural justice in both economic and political forums. The German Auxiliary Service Law of 1916 forced employers to accept trade unionists as legitimate partners on factory committees (Feldman 1966). The Wilson administration also increased labor's voice in economic decision making. It encouraged companies in war-related industries to voluntarily recognize unions and to sign collective bargaining agreements. The federal government created a vast propaganda machine to explain why the war (and labor's sacrifices) was important. Officials developed specialized pamphlets for dissemination in the labor press, and they trained thousands of volunteers to speak at public events, including trade union meetings (Creel 1920, 1, 17). Within months of the outbreak of World War II, British officials reached out to trade union leaders to inform them of decisions affecting their members. Churchill later attached the minority Labour Party to his governing coalition, and he enlisted Britain's top union leader as minister of labor. Yet some governments provide little procedural justice during wartime.

Austria-Hungary eliminated independent union activities and stripped workers of their rights during World War I (Beneš 2016). The French government reacted similarly during World War II, excluding labor from economic and political decision making. "Dictation, not collaboration, marked [French] wartime industrial relations" (Imlay 2003, 285). Gone was the cross-party regime that governed France during World War I.

HYPOTHESES ON LABOR'S WARTIME DEVELOPMENT

Historians and political scientists have noted the importance of distributive justice in wartime.[18] Individuals may accept inequity as the result of an impersonal market, but total war transforms inequity into injustice. State officials exhort labor to prioritize the collectivity, and labor expects all citizens to do the same. "No feature of World War II . . . has been more striking," John Kenneth Galbraith noted, "than the scrutiny which each of the several economic groups brings to bear upon what the others are getting." Perceptions of shared sacrifice promote labor satisfaction. The British labor leader Ernest Bevin remarked in 1940 that the excess-profits tax would make "labour throw itself heart and soul into the war effort" (quoted in Leff 1991, 1301, 1315). Evidence of profiteering generates dissatisfaction. Knowledge of immense wartime profits and the inequality of sacrifice—reflected in rumors that the German crown princess bathed in milk while working-class families went hungry—provoked some of the most intense labor unrest in Germany during World War I (Sirianni 1980, 37).

Research on shared sacrifice identifies when labor is likely to be dissatisfied with allocation decisions. But what is less well understood among historians and political scientists, and is arguably more important, is labor's reactions to procedural justice. Social justice researchers find that individuals often care more about procedural than about distributive justice (Messick et al. 1985). But there is a more noteworthy reason to focus on procedural justice: perceptions of distributive and procedural justice have different consequences. Assessments of distributive justice have narrow implications. They predict attitudes toward specific outcomes, such as pay satisfaction. Perceptions of procedural justice have broader effects. They predict attitudes and behavior toward authorities or the system as a whole (Beugre and Baron 2001).[19] A study of courtroom fairness found that perceptions of procedure influenced defendants' evaluations of the judicial system, while unfavorable verdicts (or outcomes) did not (Tyler 1984). These assessments extend broadly. Perceptions of the fairness of judicial procedures influence individuals' evaluations of the political system as a whole (Tyler, Casper, and Fisher 1989). People focus on distributive issues when responding to a single decision, but they attend to the process when taking a long-term perspective on their membership in groups.

Research on procedural justice is especially useful in explaining how strategies to mobilize labor influence its wartime development. I deduce hypotheses from this literature to predict how labor's interests and identity change, and how the experience of war transforms labor's attitudes about the state. These hypotheses explain an important yet seemingly elusive consequence of war: ideational change. Many of the most important political attitudes that individuals exhibit in groups—such as allegiance to, or alienation from, the state—are linked to judgments about fairness. Perceptions of procedural justice also influence behavior that is key to organizational success. This includes positive activity, such as compliance with authorities, as well as the "dark side" of organizational life, such as defiance of authority's decisions and the desire for revenge. William Sewell Jr. (1996) argues that big events matter. I argue that they matter in predictable ways, as my three hypotheses discuss (and as summarized in table 1).

First, mobilization for war is likely to influence the labor movement's conception of its interests. *Hypothesis 1 expects procedurally unjust strategies to encourage radical demands and procedurally just strategies to encourage reformist demands.* State intervention in the economy and high levels of public ownership tend to foster a politically conscious labor movement (Geary 1981, 138; Poole 1986, 70). Fighting a total war intensifies this reaction. Even the most economically liberal states discard their principles as state officials intervene in industrial affairs. However, the direction of labor's politicization depends on how officials try to gain labor's compliance with the war effort. *Radical* and *reformist* goals differ based on whether actors perceive the political and economic systems as legitimate; whether they assume they can pursue their goals within existing structures; and whether they believe that conventional political and economic activity is sufficient to achieve their objectives.

I derive these expectations about labor's interests from research on labor and social justice. Labor scholars find that the more repressive the state, the more radical the labor movement.[20] Whereas the autocratic czarist state radicalized labor, Britain's liberal nineteenth-century institutions encouraged reformist goals. The logic is simple. When the state oppresses labor and denies it access to power, labor will view structural change as the only way to realize its interests. Findings in social justice research reinforce this expectation. Perceptions of procedural justice (and not outcome favorability) are central to attitudes about the authority's legitimacy (K. Kaiser and Holtfreter 2015; Tyler 1990).[21] One study found that assessments of how courts reach decisions—not agreement with the decisions—influence the court's legitimacy (Tyler and Mitchell 1994). Procedurally just strategies to mobilize labor will encourage reformist goals. In these cases, labor is likely to assume that it can pursue its interests within the existing order. In contrast, unjust procedures will undermine the state's legitimacy in labor's eyes and increase the appeal of radical demands.

Second, mobilization strategies are likely to influence labor's identity, or the degree of working-class *solidarity*, which is a feeling of unity based on a shared sense of purpose, interest, or sympathy. *Hypothesis 2 expects procedurally unjust strategies to encourage labor solidarity and procedurally just strategies to encourage labor fragmentation.* Research on labor finds that repression acts as a leveler. It narrows differences among workers. Excluded from decision-making forums, workers suffering the same fate band together to form their own normative system (Marks 1989, 14). Amitai Etzioni's (1975) finding that coercion breeds hostility toward the authority while simultaneously developing cohesion among organizational members supports this expectation. In contrast, procedurally just strategies reinforce labor fragmentation: regular interaction with employers and state officials helps bridge class divides. Including labor leaders in decision making also undermines solidarity between union leaders and the rank and file. Workers lose confidence in representatives who are pulled into state councils and whom they see as "overly cooperative." German officials understood that labor was critical to their winning World War I, and they consulted labor leaders about industrial mobilization. The entry of union leaders into official forums separated them from union members. As the war continued, local (factory floor) stewards displaced union leaders in organizing work stoppages (Geary 1981, 141). The inclusion of African American leaders in the US war effort had a similarly divisive effect on the Black community (Ellis 1992, 113–21).

Third, the strategies states use to mobilize labor are likely to influence two important attitudes that labor holds about the state: its identification with the state and its trust in it. *Hypothesis 3 expect procedurally unjust strategies to build labor's distrust in the state and alienation from it, and procedurally just strategies to build labor's trust in the state and allegiance to it.* Trust refers to labor's confidence in the state's intentions. Labor's identification with the state ranges from allegiance through indifference to alienation. Political allegiance is a positive feeling that leads people to want their state to do well. *Indifference* means no marked feeling for or against the state. *Alienation* refers to estrangement from the politics of one's society—that "this government is not my government." It implies rejection, not just disinterest (Lane 1962, 161–62).

Social justice researchers find that fair processes increase identification with the organization (Tyler and Blader 2013).[22] Outcome favorability and distributive justice do not have the same effect (Viswesvaran and Ones 2002). "When people are evaluating the extent to which they will be loyal to a group or relationship, people focus on the manner in which group decisions are made," two leading social justice researchers explain. "If they believe that such decisions are made fairly, then group members are more inclined to accept a long-term commitment to the group" (Lind and Tyler 1988, 225–26). The implications are clear: the more the state includes labor in decision making, and the more that officials treat labor with dignity and respect, the more the state can strengthen labor's identification with it. Procedural justice is a powerful commitment mechanism. A just process can persuade workers with little allegiance to the state to become committed, whereas unfair procedures undermine labor's identification with the state.

Perceptions of procedural justice also shape labor's trust in the state. Studies show that procedural (but not distributive) justice predicts trust in the organization's authority (Tyler, Rasinski, and Spodick 1985).[23] The more that individuals perceive that processes are fair, the more confident they are in the organization's good intentions (Brockner and Siegel 1996). Fair procedures communicate the authority's intent, and they signal that the authority's "heart is in the right place." The strengthening of an individual's identification also makes trust more likely. Group members who identify with the group tend to attribute favorable traits, such as trustworthiness, to that group (Brewer 2008; R. Kramer, Brewer, and Hanna 1996). The perception of procedural injustice—both formal and informal—has the opposite effect. It creates distrust and alienation. Mobilization strategies that treat labor with disrespect and that exclude it from decision making will aggravate labor's affective ties to the state, breeding alienation and generating distrust of state intentions.

There are two additional points about hypothesis 3. First, the links between fair procedures, on the one hand, and trust and commitment, on the other, hold even in the face of bad outcomes. Scholars examining how individuals combine information about process and outcome discovered the "fair process" effect. Individuals will view an undesirable outcome as more acceptable if they perceive as procedurally fair the process that led to the decision. They are likely to continue to identify with and trust in the authority responsible for that bad outcome (Brockner 2010; Colquitt et al. 2001). They are also more like to comply with the authority.[24] Second, the beneficial effects of procedural justice occur regardless of whether individuals can influence outcomes. Being treated with respect and receiving explanations for decisions are sufficient to generate trust in, and commitment to, the authority (Korsgaard and Roberson 1995; Tyler and Degoey 1995). Indeed, some researchers find that commitment and trust are more strongly linked to treatment with dignity and respect than with the ability to influence outcomes (Fuller and Hester 2001; Robbins et al. 2000). Respectful treatment is also sufficient to generate a belief that the process is fair (Goldman 2003).

TABLE 1 Wartime mobilization and the transformation of organized labor

---

Hypothesis 1: Interests—radical or reformist?
Procedurally *un*just strategies encourage radical demands; procedurally just strategies
encourage reformist demands.

Hypothesis 2: Identity—fragmented or united?
Procedurally *un*just strategies encourage labor solidarity; procedurally just strategies encourage
labor fragmentation.

Hypothesis 3: Attitudes about the state—allegiance and trust?
Procedurally *un*just strategies build labor's distrust in the state and alienation from it; procedurally just strategies build labor's trust in the state and allegiance to it.

How the Politics of War Explains the Politics of Peace

My argument relies on generalizable hypotheses about the influence of wartime mobilization on societal actors that democratic theorists posit as central to democracy's advance. I explain when labor will adopt radical or reformist goals, which policies encourage working-class solidarity, and whether labor will identify with, and have faith in, the state's good intentions. These wartime transformations help to explain whether, and why, war sometimes promotes democracy. Italy's postwar descent into Fascism is inexplicable without understanding how Rome's mobilization shaped what labor wanted, how it felt about the state, and how it hoped to achieve its goals. Wartime mobilization also influenced British labor, and many assumed that labor would benefit from its support for the war. But London's mobilization shaped labor's political attitudes in ways that ultimately limited the paybacks labor received. Recognizing that the politics of war do not end with the armistice provides an opportunity to better understand prospects for democratic reform.

In exploring how war-induced changes in the labor movement affect postwar democracy, I use a broad conception of democracy—social democracy—that encompasses civil, political, *and* social rights (i.e., health, education, and welfare). This definition, and not a procedural minimum that presumes civil rights, free and fair elections, and full suffrage, is useful for two reasons. First, conventional explanations linking war to democracy often use a broad definition of democracy. This is true of early literature on the origins of the British welfare state and recent research on progressive taxation. Second, a broad conception of democracy reflects the practicalities of democratic citizenship. Education and a basic level of socioeconomic well-being are necessary for the effective exercise of civil and political rights (Marshall 1950). Full citizenship also depends on sustained implementation of these rights. Democratic reforms that appear in the flush of victory but disappear within a few years confuse the politics of war with its consequences.

An advantage of drawing on the social justice research is that these arguments do not depend on specific contexts. Research on small groups can lead to theoretical insights about the same phenomena in larger units, such as states in times of war. Indeed, studying the same phenomena in different types of empirical units advances theory development. But there is a conundrum. Although my hypotheses on labor are generalizable, their consequences for democracy are not. Tilly (1995, 1601) captures this problem: "The regularities in political life are very broad, indeed transhistorical, but they do not operate in the form of recurrent structures and processes at a large scale." Instead, the regularities in political life "consist of recurrent causes which in different circumstances and sequences compound into highly variable but nonetheless explicable effects." Strategies to mobilize labor predictably influence the development of labor's political beliefs, but how these transformations then influence democracy depends on their interaction with other conditions and processes. My hypotheses are generalizable and testable, and they make the results explicable, but the history—the circumstances and sequences—creates synergies that defy a priori predictions about democracy's fate.

Bringing the politics of war into the politics of peace does not mean that long-term trends are irrelevant, or that war (or labor) always figures in explanations of democracy. But understanding "normal" politics, and especially its origins, sometimes requires exploring large-scale events. It is important that we examine how some of the greatest political upheavals of the twentieth century restructured some of society's most critical actors in the creation, consolidation, or downfall of democracy.

British and Italian Mobilization for the Great War

I assess my hypotheses and conventional explanations in Britain and Italy during the Great War. These cases are useful for four reasons. First, they provide variation in state mobilization strategies. Mass mobilization for World War I confronted states with similar problems, but Britain and Italy chose very different strategies to gain labor's compliance with the war effort, especially in the extent of procedural justice. This variation provides a good test of my hypotheses. Second, these cases should be easy for conventional arguments linking war to democratic reform. Mobilization for war expanded British and Italian state capacity, exposed chronic social problems, and required an unprecedented participation in the war effort. Never before had Britain and Italy asked so much from their citizens, and never before had their citizens given so much in return. If there was a time when egalitarian norms would develop, when the state would develop the capacity for reform, or when organized labor could extract concessions from the state, this was it. State survival hung in the balance and unemployment vanished.

The longer the war lasted and the more sacrifices piled up, the greater the expectations (and official promises) for democratic reform.

Third, Britain and Italy are important in a crucial period in the history of democracy. The Great War was a turning point for political regimes across Europe. Some survived the tragedy relatively unscathed while others collapsed into chaos and, ultimately, fascist or communist regimes. It is important to understand when organized labor helps further democracy, when it plays a destabilizing role in that process, and how wartime mobilization influences these trajectories. The contrasting fates of British and Italian democracy after World War I provide lessons for democratizers today, and especially about how perceptions of procedural justice influence political developments. Fourth, historical scrutiny of these cases makes it possible to establish the integrity of my causal variables. Assessing my argument requires a deep dive into what might seem like minutiae—such as disciplinary regimes in munitions factories. The depth of historical research on Italy and Britain makes it possible to reconstruct these strategies and to trace their possible effects on labor.

British and Italian labor were not in comparable positions in 1914. They had different histories and organized within different political regimes. I cannot evaluate war's purported effects on the labor movement without considering these differences. I must establish organized labor's prewar interests, identity, and attitudes about the state before assessing whether wartime mobilization reshaped them. However, I am not explaining the overall development of Italian and British democracy or their labor movements. Nor am I claiming that only war shapes these developments. Rather, my objective is more specific: to assess how the experience of war affects each labor movement *given the position of each when the war began*. Did the British and Italian mobilization strategies significantly restructure organized labor? And by extension, would the prospects for British and Italian democracy have differed if labor's wartime experience had been different, or if the war had not occurred at all? Can we understand how democratic each regime was several years after the war without understanding each labor movement's experience of that war?

Chapters 2 and 3 describe Italy's and Britain's strategies to gain labor's compliance. The Italian government imposed procedurally unjust strategies on its rural and urban workforce. Officials turned industrial policy over to army officers who supervised an arbitrary military code in war-related factories. The Italian high command imposed an equally unjust disciplinary regime on its peasant conscripts. In contrast, the British armed services played no role in the domestic wartime economy. Civilians oversaw Britain's industrial mobilization, and they adopted a procedurally just strategy to gain labor's cooperation. Both states used material rewards to gain labor's compliance, but neither adequately addressed calls for shared sacrifice.

Chapter 4 considers the origins of mobilization strategies to address a key counterfactual: Were other mobilization strategies possible? If prewar conditions—such as the strength of the Italian economy or the nature of its democracy—determine the type of mobilization, then these strategies become more of a consequence than a cause. Mobilization strategies would reflect the prewar economic and political structures, not choices made after the war began. But there was nothing inevitable about Italy's decision for war or its procedurally unjust mobilization. Leaders with different political orientations could have governed Italy during the war, and they were likely to have made different choices about how to best mobilize labor for war. The counterfactual gains additional strength with the realization that Italian policy makers based their mobilization strategies on assumptions other Italian leaders knew at the time to be false.

Chapters 5 and 6 take another deep dive into history to examine the effect of Italian and British mobilization on labor's wartime development. Italy's unjust strategies unified, radicalized, and alienated workers and conscripts. Whether it was in the Italian Socialist Party or the industrial or rural workforce, the shift to the left was dramatic. Italian labor emerged from the war primed for revolution. While large-scale wars often strengthen nationalism, Italy's unjust mobilization transformed a resigned acceptance of the state and its war into an angry rejection of both. The Italian government had squandered an opportunity to use the national emergency to build an "imagined community" that crossed regional and class divides. Mobilization for total war also politicized British labor, but London's relatively just strategy generated a different response. British labor remained reformist, and it continued to see its future within Britain's parliamentary regime. But organized labor's political attitudes did not stand still. The experience of procedural justice created space for ideas that were previously minority ones within the labor movement, underpinned them with socialist principles, and made them the touchstone for the Labour Party's vision for the future.

Chapters 7 and 8 discuss how Italian and British labor's experiences during the war shaped political developments (and democracy) after the war. Chapter 7 explains how mobilization-induced transformations of Italian and British labor influenced their postwar trajectories. Strike waves swept both countries as labor took to the streets to demand compensation for wartime sacrifices. British labor received little of what it thought its due, and what it had been promised, but the unrest subsided. In contrast, despite the enactment of extensive reform legislation, Italian popular protest intensified and provoked the Fascist reaction that destroyed the liberal regime. Chapter 8 then assesses how conventional arguments linking war to democracy fare in the British and Italian cases. It also describes how mobilization-induced transformations of British labor undercut prospects for postwar reform.

The concluding chapter draws broader lessons about the importance of justice in the politics of war and peace. Attending to concerns about justice highlights the role of process and affect in explaining how political actors respond to their experiences. It also contributes new understandings about the origins and consequences of political attitudes important to democracy, including nationalism, political trust, and the nature of civil society. Although we should not invest hope in, or give much causal weight to, war as a democratizer, there is a ray of hope. The *belief* in a link between war and democracy may dampen armed conflict. Policy makers who fear that large-scale wars will lead to democratic reform are reluctant to start and continue wars that might precipitate change they deem undesirable. If this fear of war-induced democracy is common, the anticipated but unintended (and typically unrealized) consequences of war may decrease the frequency and duration of wars.

DISCIPLINING ITALIAN LABOR

Nine months after World War I began, Italy entered the war in alliance with France and Britain. Prime Minister Antonio Salandra rapidly created the bureaucratic and regulatory structure—the Istituto della Mobilitazione Industriale (MI)—that ran Italy's industrial mobilization. The Ministry of War oversaw MI, and Salandra appointed General Alfredo Dallolio to direct this new agency. Generals and admirals chaired MI's Central Committee, as well as its seven (later eleven) regional committees. This structure was based on the French model, but Italy's regional committees were military bureaucracies, and not part of the Chamber of Commerce as in France. The military's direction of industrial mobilization had no counterpart in Britain, France, or Germany. It signaled Italy's militarization of industrial relations. The state would use unjust procedures to gain labor's compliance with the war effort. Explaining how the experience of war transformed Italian labor requires understanding the nature of this mobilization.

Italy's policies evolved, but officials remained convinced that the best way to manage industrial labor was to delegate extensive and repressive powers to the military. They saw no reason to give the working class a voice in decision making or to explain why its sacrifices were necessary. Officials simply imposed their decisions on labor. The remuneration labor received improved during the war, but Rome paid little attention to the perception of shared sacrifice. The Italian army's treatment of its conscripts mirrored the treatment of industrial workers. The high command imposed disciplinary terror on the rank and file. Army regulations were astonishingly unjust, even for the early twentieth-century, and the high command was uninterested in soldier morale. It made halting and belated efforts to inspire soldiers and to explain why they were fighting and dying. Remuneration was poor and distributively unjust.

Militarization of the Factories

MI's authority was vast. It managed war production, controlled trade, regulated the distribution of energy and raw materials, and promoted vital sectors of the economy (Galassi and Harrison 2005, 284–85). Its regional committees supervised ordnance factories and implemented MI directives in private companies deemed crucial to the war effort. These "auxiliary firms" were central to the war effort because unlike Britain, Italy did not significantly expand state-owned armament production (Forsyth 1993, 83). MI initially declared about two hundred factories as auxiliary, and their numbers rapidly grew to include most large industries regardless of their involvement in war production (Tomassini 1991, 66). Almost two thousand factories—the vast majority in northern Italy—were under military supervision and military law by the war's end (Toniolo 1990, 127). The ordnance factories and auxiliary firms together employed close to one million workers (Clark 2014, 231). One industrial worker in three was under MI's strict disciplinary regime by 1918.

Procedural Injustice (Formal)

Italian efforts to mobilize labor focused on imposing an unjust disciplinary regime while giving employers a relatively free hand (Tomassini 1990, 181). This "cardinal principle" to control labor but not capital meant that employees labored under an arbitrary, biased, and punitive military code. The formal decision-making procedures gave labor little voice in the design and implementation of policies that affected it. The working class and its representatives—the Socialist Party (Partito Socialista Italiano; PSI) and trade unions—were shut out of governance and industrial relations.

NO VOICE IN POLITICAL OR ECONOMIC FORUMS

The PSI had deputies in Parliament, and it met during the war, but what had been a limited democracy before 1915 no longer functioned. "A war government cannot be a free government," Salandra declared in May 1916 (quoted in Bosworth 2005, 61). Wartime centralization is common, but unlike in France and Britain, the Parliament was kept virtually in abeyance (F. Adler 1995, 93–94). "The governing powers had in fact suppressed the action of the Italian Parliament in a way that had no parallel in other allied countries," a prominent politician remarked (quoted in Giuliano Procacci 1968, 334). Deputies were ignorant of Salandra's negotiations with France and Britain to enter the war, and they played no role in the design of Italy's mobilization. The cabinet and administrative offices issued the decrees that created MI without consulting Parliament or union officials (Tomassini 1991, 60).[1] Parliament had no authority over MI, the "war dictator." MI ruled by executive fiat and kept few records (Corner 1997, 265; Galassi and Harrison 2005, 284).[2] This typified the formal structure of Italian wartime decision making, and especially organized labor's exclusion from it. Each of Italy's three wartime governments gave labor little voice.

Italy was also unusual in the composition of its wartime governments. There was no "national unity" government equivalent to the inclusion of Socialists in the French cabinet or the outreach to members of the Labour Party in Britain. Salandra refused to open his cabinet to all but a narrow group of conservative liberals. He preferred to "emulate the governments of the Central Powers whose successes he attributed in part to rule by a few 'superior wills'" (Saladino 1970, 151). Salandra rebuffed the indirect support of reformist Socialists who privately offered their support, and he declined the direct support of left-wing interventionists (De Grand 1989, 29). Even after Salandra's baseless hope for a quick victory evaporated, he rejected suggestions to include reformist Socialists in his government (Haywood 1999, 449). The two subsequent wartime governments were broader than Salandra's, but neither Paolo Boselli (June 1916–October 1917) nor Vittorio Emanuele Orlando (October 2017–June 1919) invited Socialists to join his government (Bosworth 2005, 63).

The working class was also excluded from decisions about industrial relations. While the heads of leading arms manufacturers sat on the Central Committee, labor representatives were initially excluded from it (Clark 1977, 14). High-ranking military officers, two to three employer representatives, two to three worker representatives, and several civilian experts served on MI's governing bodies. But firm executives (not the unions) chose labor's "representatives" (Clark 1977, 14; Galassi and Harrison 2005, 285). Unlike their counterparts in Allied and belligerent states, Italian unions had no legally recognized representative within the factories themselves (F. Adler 1995, 106). Dallolio did involve some reformist unions in wage negotiations as the war continued. Union representatives were included in the arbitral system in mid-1916, and from mid-1917 they sat in MI's Central Committee. The government also legalized worker commissions in factories in early 1918 (Giovanna Procacci 1989, 50; 1992, 158, 165; Tomassini 1990, 182–83).

Despite these formal changes, industrialists disproportionately influenced industrial relations. The employer and employee representatives on the Central Committee and the regional committees were advisory in name, but the industrialists' close ties to civilians on the committee, and the military's reluctance to challenge employers' advice, ensured that employers dominated committee deliberations (Forsyth 1993, 83). The industrialists also became their own regulators. MI's regional committee in Milan granted the head of the Pirelli tire company the responsibility for the production of rubber goods (Galassi and Harrison 2005, 286, 293–95).

ARBITRARY AND BIASED CONTROL

The official designation of a firm as "auxiliary" drastically altered the management of it. Employers lost much of their control, but they often welcomed this status, as it eased access to credit, raw materials, transportation, and energy. Auxiliary status also ensured employers a stable workforce and the enforcement of military discipline on the shop floor. Dallolio succeeded in what he saw as one of MI's main objectives: "to bind labor to the factories" (quoted in Tomassini 1990, 181). As in Britain, the workforce in auxiliary firms lost the right to strike, and they could not leave their jobs to take better ones elsewhere (Giovanna Procacci 1992, 155). But there the apparent similarities with Britain end. Military officers directed Italy's industrial relations. Workers did not live in barracks or wear uniforms, but they were subject to military regulations and military discipline. "The factories . . . became veritable armed camps surrounded by troops and controlled internally through a network of informers and spies," one historian observes (Cardoza 1982, 236).

Military officers enforced the military penal code in the auxiliary firms. They determined the punishments for infractions, including whether workers would be sent to a military court or directly to the front. Officers regularly imposed heavy fines and long prison terms for minor offenses, such as being late for work or arguing with a colleague. Employees who "disobeyed" a civilian official were treated as if they were soldiers. They could not refuse to obey "orders," leave their "posts," or take time off for whatever reason (Tomassini 1990, 182–97). The exemption of auxiliary workers from military service gave these punitive measures an especially strong bite. The military code equated strikes with desertion, and those absent from work could be charged with desertion and sent to the front. Men suspected of union activity, political militancy, or "defeatist and unpatriotic activity," and those who failed to meet the required rate of production (even if due to poor health) could be stripped of their draft exemptions (Giovanna Procacci 1989, 38). These decisions were not subject to appeal, and punishment was widespread, especially during the last year of the war.

Military officers and employers dominated the MI committees in auxiliary firms that arbitrated disputes about pay and working conditions (and that replaced the right to strike). These processes favored employers, especially in the first years of the war. The military officers managing MI regularly accepted the employer's assessment when workers were accused of violating the disciplinary regime. MI's regional committees rarely granted workers' requests to change jobs if employers objected (Clark 1977, 25). A confusion of administrative authorities and the power accorded surveillance officers contributed to the arbitrary and unjust application of regulations. Skilled workers were often fined for defective products when the poor quality of the raw materials caused the problem. Local interests swayed the regional committees' arbitration decisions, which meant their inconsistent application from one firm to the next (Corner and Procacci 1997, 227). Although Dallolio eventually ended this practice, authorities often meted out collective punishments for individual infractions (Giovanna Procacci 1992, 156–57). State authorities also swiftly and brutally suppressed industrial unrest. The most severe example occurred when bread shortages sparked an insurrection in Turin in August 1917. Dallolio "characteristically" urged repression (Bosworth 2005, 86). More than eight hundred workers were arrested, and the army's actions led to over fifty deaths.

The militarization of the industrial workforce extended beyond male workers with military obligations. The entire workforce in auxiliary factories was subject to this procedurally unjust military code. Women, children, and the elderly could more easily strike because they were free from the threat of military service. But they were subject to military discipline and military courts (Giovanna Procacci 1992, 172). Rome also imposed martial law on large regions of Italy, thus removing their populations from civilian jurisdiction. The "war zones" were initially border regions, fortified harbors, and sections of the Adriatic coast, but after the Turin uprising in August 1917 and growing concern about social unrest, most of the north where industry was concentrated, as well as Reggio Calabria and Messina in the south, was put under martial law. Within these zones, army officers supervised about 650,000 laborers who assisted with logistical and defensive operations. Like their counterparts in auxiliary firms, they were subject to the military's unjust penal code (Ermacora 2017).

This widespread application of martial law meant that almost a third of the Italian population lived under direct military administration by the war's end (Haywood 1999, 459). A rigid military penal code replaced the civil one, and the army had absolute power, even over firms not under MI's jurisdiction or engaged in war work (Giovanna Procacci 1989, 49; Snowden 1986, 155). Officials harshly repressed any apparent dissent within these regions. There was no right to peacefully assemble or to engage in union activities. Even workers outside the auxiliary system lost their right to strike (Mead 2006, 135–36). It is hard to overstate the punitive nature of state-society relations. "Military justice is at the point of almost completely absorbing the judicial system of our country," the president of the Supreme Military Court observed (quoted in Giovanna Procacci 2013, 157).

Procedural Injustice (Informal)

Italy's mobilization also provided none of the informal aspects of procedural justice. The imposition of military control humiliated the urban workforce. MI's disciplinary regime returned the traditional working class to an earlier form of industrial control that challenged its personal dignity, its independence, and the rights that it felt were integral to its trade (Giovanna Procacci 1992, 171–72). Union leaders were always suspected of "defeatism." MI stationed armed troops within factories and planted spies on the shop floor to uncover "subversives" (F. Adler 1995, 105). Italy was engaged in a war of unprecedented proportions, but Rome's efforts to shape wartime opinion focused on repressing dissent, not persuading labor that its contributions were important. Workers were simply expected "to obey the laws, work hard, and fulfill their various tasks unquestionably" (Whittam 1975, 153). They needed to know neither why they were laboring long hours in the factories nor why their brothers, sons, and fathers were dying on the battlefield.

NO EXPLANATION FOR LABOR'S SACRIFICES

Advocates of Italian intervention hoped the war would forge a strong national identity, but officials did little to unite the country and to rally the working class. Antonio Salandra, Italy's premier until June 1916, was "anything but a politician for a mass age." He "steadfastly refused" to reach out to the masses (Whittam 1975, 152–53). Salandra and his foreign minister and leading political ally, Sidney Sonnino, hated public opinion and were indifferent to popular support. They were part of a traditional elite who believed in its right to rule and its subjects' blind obedience. Salandra was furious, for example, when the organizers of interventionist demonstrations—the "Radiant Days of May"—included the middle and lower classes in their rallies in *support* of his decision for war. Politics was the business of elites and nothing more (Mead 2006, 252). Officials never attempted to reach beyond their narrow circle to justify the war. As a leading democratic interventionists observed, "The Italian people never understood why there were persons who wanted to go to war" (Salvemini 1973, 104). The writer Carlo Levi reached the same conclusion during his exile to southern Italy in the 1930s. The village had lost nearly fifty men to the war, yet "it had nothing to do with their way of life" (quoted in M. Thompson 2008, 390).

The government initially outsourced propaganda to private middle-class groups. Officials hoped that each town would form a "patriotic" committee, but they left the initiative to individual town councils. A collection of associations, including religious bodies, mutual aid societies, and newly formed patriotic and irredentist groups, organized in cities and in central and northern Italy. They raised money for the war and produced material in support of Italy's irredentist claims. But these groups were bourgeois in their origins and orientation. They targeted their efforts at the middle class and made few appeals to labor (Corner and Procacci 1997, 228; Giovanna Procacci 1995, 11; Tomassini 1996, 583–84). State officials rarely canvassed public opinion, and they infrequently queried local authorities to gauge popular support (Bosworth 2005, 56, 74; Corner and Procacci 1997, 228). The government was also slow to organize the press and to use battlefield images for propaganda purposes. The army initially barred journalists from the front, and most officials never understood the value of front-line reporting. The high command dismissed journalists as "shirkers" and blamed them for battlefield reverses (Bosworth 2005, 74).

As the war continued, Rome recognized that it should not rely on middle-class voluntarism alone. This shift started after Boselli replaced Salandra as prime minister in June 1916. Boselli's new government created an agency to coordinate the voluntary organizations running Italy's propaganda campaigns. Boselli's actions marked an attempt to develop a modern propaganda machine, but this initiative remained "fragmentary and disorganized" (Bosworth 2005, 63). Most important, it focused on improving Italy's image abroad, not inspiring Italians at home (Wilcox 2016, 49). Another push for popular support occurred in fall 1917 because of rising industrial unrest and the military disaster at Caporetto. German and Austrian forces had broken through the front lines in October 1917 and foreign troops poured into northern Italy. Enemy forces now occupied much of area. Caporetto prompted Orlando's new government to adjust Italy's mobilization. Orlando took seriously the need for propaganda, and he sought to persuade Italians that the war was worth fighting. He created a new bureaucracy to organize appeals to factory workers and to distribute patriotic material throughout the country (Corner and Procacci 1997, 228). Although an improvement over prior programs, Orlando's efforts were limited and his enthusiasm for them quickly waned (Giovanna Procacci 1995, 11).

NO POSSIBILITY FOR DISSENT

In contrast to their tentative attempts at propaganda, officials spared no expense and never lapsed in their determination to squash dissent. Italy's wartime government destroyed civil liberties. New decrees gave officials control over the press and the authority to "safeguard public order." State officials disbanded political groups, forbade public assemblies, destroyed militant socialist and left-wing groups, and sent their leaders to the front or internment camps (Giovanna Procacci 1992, 165). These efforts accelerated as the war continued, and especially after Caporetto.

The rout of Italian forces in November 1917 confirmed the elite's worse fears about the working class. General Luigi Cadorna, the army chief of staff, blamed imaginary political subversives for orchestrating a "military strike" that caused the German and Austrian victory.[3] The middle class and segments of the press conducted defamatory campaigns against labor, depicting workers as immoral and as wasting their "wonderful salaries" on expensive clothing (Giovanna Procacci 1992, 159). They derided as "waste" the slight wartime increases in popular consumption of nonbasic commodities (Zamagni 1991, 143). These attacks intensified with news of Caporetto. Private patriotic groups conducting much of Italy's propaganda were especially acerbic. They struck out against the "internal (working-class) enemy," permitted anonymous allegations, and gave monetary awards to those who exposed "defeatists." Nationalists described those suspected of opposing the war as "traitors," as "backstabbers," and as being part of a "deadly contagion" (Mead 2006, 252–53). This contempt for the working class even extended to the depiction of Italian soldiers, whom they accused of cowardice and of despoiling Italy's honor. "Nothing will make up for the perennial curse on those renegers, those cowards of cowards, and no one will ever place flowers on the graves of those beasts," one woman wrote. "I have more hate for these unworthy 'brothers' than I do for the actual enemy" (quoted in Mead 2006, 248).

Dallolio had a similarly contemptuous reaction to Caporetto. Instead of capitalizing on the occupation of Italian territory to rally the masses and to explain why the war was worth fighting, Rome unleashed an intensified "hunt for the defeatist." Labor lost any remaining outlets to express its dissatisfaction with the war. A new series of decrees tightened censorship and imposed even harsher penalties for "unpatriotic" activities (Corner and Procacci 1997, 228; Tomassini 1996, 590). Behavior that had been prosecutable now became treasonous. Acts once considered lawful were now crimes. "Defeatists" could be imprisoned for up to ten years and fined the equivalent of a year of labor. Workers merely suspected of antiwar sentiments could be sent to the front (Giovanna Procacci 1992, 154–59). Officials fined and imprisoned a worker who explained that he did not buy a war bond because he "had never asked for war" (Mead 2006, 246). The vast majority of charges were for nothing more than expressing dissatisfaction with the war and the availability of basic foodstuffs. In the last ten months of the war, officials fined about a third of the workers in the auxiliary firms; more than twenty-five thousand were imprisoned (Ermacora 2017).

The government intensified its repression of workers, regardless of the workplace. A December 1917 decree mandated that workers outside the auxiliary system were also subject to military jurisdiction (Giovanna Procacci 2013, 159). The minister of justice reassured top officials that he worked hard to guarantee that "repression should be immediate and salutary" (quoted in Giovanna Procacci 1992, 154). The Ministries of War and Justice encouraged courts to impose punitive sentences (Knox 2007, 218).[4] Repression was especially severe in the war zones, where military tribunals convicted more than sixty thousand civilians for failing to support the war (Gibelli 2010, 471). The severity of Italy's policies had few rivals, even among the Central powers.

Material Rewards

Although Rome held fast on repressing any apparent dissent, its efforts to provide adequate remuneration improved as the war dragged on and unrest increased. Indeed, by some measures, working-class conditions were better during the war than in the prewar period. But labor's wartime compensation was neither favorable nor fair: wages scarcely addressed basic needs, and officials did little to create even a semblance of shared sacrifice.

MEAGER COMPENSATION

Inflation hit Italy harder than most belligerents, including Britain. Prices had shot up 50 percent by 1916 and increased further in the last two years of war.[5] Yet MI regulations initially froze wages at prewar levels, outlawed strikes, and prevented workers from moving to better-paid jobs. Dallolio soon recognized that something had to be done to stop the decline in real wages. MI directed subordinate agencies in fall 1916 not to blindly follow employers' advice. Officials should take an independent stance in wage disputes. MI also intervened to keep wages in line with inflation. Regional committees arbitrated disputes in the auxiliary plants, and their authority in these compulsory negotiations led to substantial increases in nominal wages (Tomassini 1991, 76–77). Officials initiated several additional policies to increase wage packages and maintain productivity (Pluviano and Guerrini 2000, 112). MI began regulating overtime pay in 1916, and it prevented employers from cutting wages for piecework. MI also created an unemployment compensation fund for workers temporarily laid off because of a shortage in raw materials or a power failure (Tomassini 1991, 81).

The most significant changes in Italy's remuneration occurred after the Russian Revolution and Caporetto. Officials developed a new interpretation of "equitable treatment" as outlined in MI's original documents. The state now recognized the need for a minimum standard. Workers must sacrifice for the war effort, but they should be guaranteed a basic subsistence. MI began granting temporary indemnities—or cost-of-living allowances—in 1917 that factored in inflation and the number of dependents. MI also instituted a sliding wage scale that automatically adjusted wage rates (Giovanna Procacci 1995, 22; Tomassini 1990, 189–91). Many employers reacted angrily to these new policies, but Dallolio sought to drive production to the maximum, "cost what it may" (quoted in Tomassini 1991, 82, 81–84).

Rome also encouraged the provision of welfare benefits to workers. Officials initially coordinated the activities of voluntary groups that provided welfare assistance, but MI created its own programs as the war continued. These included subsidies for soldiers' families and compulsory insurance against workplace accidents, disability, and old age for workers in auxiliary plants (Corner and Procacci 1997, 228; Giovanna Procacci 1992, 159; 1995, 15–22). Officials also paid some attention to safety and hygiene in the factories, especially for women and children (Tomassini 1991, 69–70).

Italy was spared the hunger and starvation that the British blockade imposed on Germany and Austria-Hungary. There were serious food shortages in urban centers, especially Milan and Turin in the spring and summer of 1917, but the elimination of unemployment helped increase the consumption of primary necessities, and especially food (Forsyth 1993, 89; Knox 2007, 211). High employment meant that some families could now depend on more than one salary, and price controls on basic foodstuffs and the introduction of rationing helped the working class gain access to basic necessities (Pluviano and Guerrini 2000, 111–12; Tomassini 1996, 581–90). Per capital consumption increased slightly compared with 1914, and average per capita food consumption rose from an index of 100 in 1913 to 116 in 1918. Working-class diets now included unusual products, such as sugar, coffee, and meat (Zamagni 1991, 143–48).

The industrial workforce's food consumption improved from the low prewar standard, but government policy did not relieve the hardship imposed on the working class. Families who lost their main breadwinner were especially hard hit, and inflation erased most of the wage increases (Seton-Watson 1967, 468). The new factory standards were modest and sporadically enforced. Overcrowded factories, long hours, and intense work rhythms led to deteriorating conditions and alarming accident rates (Ermacora 2017). Cities were teeming with munitions workers with limited access to public and private assistance. The increase in Italy's infant mortality rate outpaced that of other European belligerents (Giovanna Procacci 1992, 157–63).

DISTRIBUTIVE INJUSTICE

Industrialists played prominent roles in MI, and their working relationships with Dallolio and other military officers meant that the state rarely used its extensive and newly authorized power to rein in profits. A staggering degree of administrative confusion allowed officials to bypass public accounting procedures. It also allowed firms engaged in war production to set their own terms (Forsyth 1993, 81–82). The State Auditors' Department no longer examined contracts to private firms, officials often placed orders without written contracts, and poor record-keeping meant that the state could not assess a product's effective cost (Giovanna

Procacci 1992, 155; Toniolo 1990, 129; Zamagni 1993, 221). A postwar inquiry found several instances of multiple copies of the same contract that recorded vastly different prices. Officials accepted firm prices without question, and they granted employers huge depreciation allowances, massive cash advances, and generous tax exemptions on new equipment (F. Adler 1995, 103, 116; Galassi and Harrison 2005, 286). This bureaucratic disorder, lax oversight, advantageous war contracts, and a commitment to "production at any cost" led to unprecedently high profits (Clark 2014, 230). Wartime-declared corporate profits after taxes nearly tripled in steel and automobiles, and they doubled in the chemical industry. Profits in the province of Bologna sometimes surpassed 100 percent (Giovanna Procacci 1992, 164).

The government took measures to provide a minimum living standard, and the rationing of basic foodstuffs improved as the war continued (Zamagni 1991, 143). But these efforts did not address the glaring inequality (Giovanna Procacci 1992, 163; Tomassini 1996, 583). Labor knew that firms were making huge profits, and that many products were only available to the privileged few (Clark 2014, 232). Soaring profits ensured that the elite had access to a flourishing black market while the working class endured food shortages and faced dangerous factory and housing conditions. Unlike many belligerents, the government refused to use its fiscal power to force the wealthier sectors of society to pay their fair share. The poorest in Italy bore a disproportionate burden of the war costs. Income taxes covered 14 percent of German, 18 percent of British, and under 6 percent of Italian war costs. Rome relied—as it always had—on indirect taxes whose rates increased during the war (Corner 2002a, 280–81).

Officials did decree direct taxes on wartime profits. The most important—the Extraordinary War Profits Tax—was adopted in November 1915. It called for a 60 percent tax on all wartime profits above the established norm. However, lax oversight ensured that these stringent conditions were never met. Industrialists passed the cost back to the state in the form of higher prices, a practice that was so well known it was dubbed the "circle game" (Forsyth 1993, 4, 93). Italy's privileged classes were not forced to pay their fair share. It was only after the war (in 1919 and 1920) that the state imposed a capital levy and a high corporate tax rate on wartime profits (Galassi and Harrison 2005, 286; Zamagni 1993).

Terrorizing Peasant Conscripts

Understanding how mobilization for war transformed Italian labor also requires examining the rural workforce. Industrialization had reduced rural labor to a small portion of the population in most of Europe and especially in Britain, where it was 9 percent of the active population in 1901. But Italy was still an agrarian society in 1915. Almost 60 percent of the Italian workforce was agricultural at the turn of the century (Trebilcock 1981, 435). Even after the wartime surge in manufacturing, the majority of workers in industrial regions were agrarian (Knox 2007, 316). It was not until 1930 that the value of Italy's industrial production surpassed that of agriculture (Giuliano Procacci 1968, 312). The type of agricultural labor differed by region. Large commercial farms dominated the northern provinces. An army of day laborers (*braccianti*) worked these "factories in the fields." Employed when large enterprises needed labor and paid hourly wages or piece rates, these landless workers lived in overcrowded, unsanitary, and temporary "agrotowns." (Corner 1975, 2–3). Karl Marx disparaged peasants as "sacks of potatoes," but unlike most of Europe's rural workforce, the *braccianti* were organized in agricultural unions and were attracted to socialist ideas (Cardoza 1982, 23–27, 55; Pernicone 1974). Agriculture in the center and the south of Italy was different. Farming had not modernized, and traditional land tenure remained. Small tenants and sharecroppers dominated the center, and large landowners controlled much of the south.[6]

Regardless of his regional origin, the Italian peasant's experience of war was at the front. Given the small size of the industrial workforce and the need for skilled workers, conscripts came disproportionately from the countryside. Italy's army was almost entirely a conscript force, and peasants could not avoid military service. Over two and a half million men were conscripted from rural areas, and most front-line soldiers were southern peasants or agricultural workers. They suffered 94 percent of all casualties (Knox 2007, 200). Understanding these peasants' experience of military service is critical to understanding their wartime transformation.

Procedural Injustice

Militaries maintain stricter hierarchies than factories, but the challenges of mobilizing soldiers resemble those of mobilizing industrial labor. Military commanders seek to maximize compliance without eliciting unrest, and they use a range of strategies to achieve these goals. However, the Italian army was distinct in its rigid autocratic structure and its draconian and arbitrary measures. The high command sought to terrorize its troops into unflinching obedience. The first directive from General Cadorna, the head of the Italian army, stressed that discipline would be unrelenting. Commanders would be punished if they failed to use "extreme measures of coercion and repression." Cadorna regularly renewed calls for unfettered discipline. A fall 1915 directive declared that soldiers who attempted to surrender or retreat instead of "taking the way of honor that leads to victory or

MAP 1.   Italy and the Isonzo front in 1917

death" would be met with "the summary justice of the bullet" (both quoted in M. Thompson 2008, 262). Another instruction stressed that commanders should apply punishments with "lightning immediacy" (quoted in Gooch 2014, 135). After the war, the officer responsible for the judicial system concluded that most of Cadorna's directives were illegal (M. Thompson 2008, 274).

ARBITRARY AND BIASED PROCESSES

The Italian high command directed officers to convene a court-martial only if severe punishment were guaranteed. Most military infractions were swiftly discharged in the field without a military lawyer or the right to appeal (M. Thompson 2008, 262). Conscripts were harshly punished or killed without having their cases put before a military tribunal. As a result, punishments varied widely from one unit to the next (Wilcox 2005, 78). Depending on the location and the commander, the same action could result in a summary execution, capital punishment after a court-martial, a few months in prison, or a disciplinary sentence (Guerrini and Pluviano 2014, 186). "The chief characteristics of disciplinary enforcement were a lack of conformity and continual improvisation," a study of the Italian army concluded (Wilcox 2016, 72).

The Italian system was ruthlessly indiscriminate. Cadorna demanded that military tribunals apply "punitive justice." He insisted on summary executions for mildly mutinous behavior (*Le magazine de la Grande Guerre* 2005). One officer shot a soldier for saluting with a pipe in his mouth; another beat a soldier so badly (for dropping his rifle while training) that the man lost the use of a hand. Minor offenders were sometimes tied to posts within view of the enemy with the aim of "saving bullets," as one officer put it (quoted in M. Thompson 2008, 267, 227). Soldiers knew that an Italian offensive was imminent when they saw Carabinieri (elite military police) with machine guns take up positions behind the lines. The prevalence of this practice is unknown, though one historian noted the matter-of-fact way an Italian doctor reported that he had treated eighty casualties of enemy fire and twenty-five wounded by Carabinieri. No other army on the western front deployed military police to shoot soldiers who failed to advance (Rochat 2010, 92).

The Italian army never punished an officer for excessive brutality (O'Brien 2006, 356). To the contrary, officers quickly learned that their advancement depended on their application of draconian and arbitrary discipline. Many of the officers Cadorna demoted or relieved of command were being punished for leniency or apparent weakness (Wilcox 2016, 73–76). In 1917, a regiment that had sustained heavy losses and fought for a long time without leave refused to advance. Its commanding officer calmly persuaded the soldiers to return to their line. The division commander became incensed when he learned of this incident, and especially that no one had been shot. "That's bad, very bad," he snapped (quoted in Wilcox 2016, 73). He then relieved the regiment's commander and ordered his replacement to immediately execute five soldiers chosen at random. By the time subsequent inquiries were complete, twenty-nine soldiers had been executed, although the incident had been resolved and there was no evidence of the men's culpability.

Desertion was a capital crime across Europe, and deserters received a high proportion of the death sentences in the military during the war. However, what counted as desertion and the punishment imposed varied across military codes. In Germany, first-time desertion was not a capital offense, and convictions required proof of intent to desert. The French army imposed death sentences only on those who deserted to the enemy. Repeated desertions and desertions to the interior or in a war zone carried harsh penalties, but they were not capital crimes (L. Smith 1991, 49; Welch 2014). The British army had a broad definition of desertion, but intent was permitted as a defense. In Italy, it was simple: being absent from one's unit was sufficient for a charge of desertion. Most Italian "deserters" were conscripts returning late from leave. The Italian military code initially sanctioned death sentences after five days of unauthorized leave; it was reduced to three days in April 1917 and down to twenty-four hours three months later (M. Thompson 2008, 258, 268–70). Italian soldiers who "deserted" were sometimes shot on sight. Returning from leave one day late could lead to a summary execution (Guerrini and Pluviano 2014, 186).

The number of summary executions in the Italian army is unknown, but most estimates are in the hundreds.[7] These were not cases of rogue officers taking the law into their own hands and acting contrary to the military code or general expectations within the army. Cadorna demanded, and the army legalized, rough justice. The military criminal code obligated officers to use violence to prevent mutiny, theft, or pillage. The "Rules of Combat" called on any officer present to execute anyone "exert[ing] a harmful influence on the courage of his comrades or subordinates" (quoted in Guerrini and Pluviano 2014, 180). Cadorna's two wartime decrees reminded officers of the need to enforce summary justice. He explained in 1915, "Every soldier . . . must be persuaded that his superior has the sacred power to immediately shoot reluctant and cowardly men. Everybody must know that if someone ignominiously tries to surrender or retreat, bullets from the rear lines or from the Carabinieri posted at the rear will hit him before he brings shame on himself, provided that his officers' bullets have not shot him dead" (quoted in Guerrini and Pluviano 2014, 181). The "everybody must know" is important. Cadorna believed that news of these executions would terrorize soldiers into compliance. The high command widely publicized their occurrence, often exaggerating the facts to reinforce the deterrent effect and to encourage officers to assume the "correct" attitude. There was no equivalent abroad. Summary executions occurred in other armies, but in contrast to Italy, their penal codes explicitly prohibited them, their high commands did not approve them, and they were not an accepted practice. Extrajudicial executions were rare in the French, British, German, and Austro-Hungarian armies (Guerrini and Pluviano 2014, 180, 187).[8]

The most shocking illustration of arbitrary military injustice was the Italian army's use of decimation, the ancient Roman custom of killing every tenth member of a mutinous legion. This practice guaranteed the death of innocent men. Cadorna revived decimation early in the war, and he encouraged its use. He sent a telegram in November 1916 to every commander, extolling the disciplinary power of summary executions and calling for a random shooting if the guilty could not be found (Guerrini and Pluviano 2014, 182). In the summer of 1917, a soldier whose tour had again been extended wrote that his unit would surrender unless its leave was granted. The commander was unable to identify the offender so he had four randomly chosen men shot on the spot (M. Thompson 2008, 266). In another case, a commander had two randomly selected men executed after an unknown soldier threw rocks at an officer. Cadorna congratulated this commander for his action, and he often referred to this incident as an example for others to emulate (Wilcox 2005, 82).

The absence of due process is arresting. There was no protection from arbitrary and despotic procedures, and the army was indifferent to the rights of the accused, both in regulations and in practice. In one sense this is not unusual. All military codes in World War I favored discipline over justice, and speed over deliberation. But the Italian system stood apart. Witnesses and expert testimony could be excluded, and commanders could proceed without judicial process or oversight (Mead 2006, 92; Giovanna Procacci 2013, 158). There was no possibility of appeal, even for death sentences. Most executions were carried out within twenty-four hours (Oram 2003, 24).

The French army court-martialed and executed soldiers who mutinied in the spring of 1917. But French sentences were reached through due process. French regulations required courts-martial before the use of capital punishment. Even relatively minor offenses had to be administered through the military's judicial system (Wilcox 2005, 80). French sentences were also subject to appeal. To ensure a measure of civilian oversight and to check the military's interest in discipline, the French president had to approve each death sentence (L. Smith 1991, 50). Discipline in the British army was harsh—especially compared with France and Germany—but there was nonetheless due process.[9] Summary punishments that exceeded twenty-eight days of imprisonment were prohibited (M. Thompson 2008, 269). All British capital sentences were also reviewed. They were sent up the command, through the accused's commanding officer, through the brigade, division, and corps levels, and up to the commander in chief, who could confirm or commute the sentence based on the comments submitted at various levels (M. Thompson 2008, 274; Welch 2014).

The Italian high command resorted to execution more than its western allies and adversaries. If the victims of summary justice are added to those executed after a trial, over a thousand Italian soldiers were victims of capital punishment. Summary executions caused at least a third of these deaths. This was the highest number among the belligerents. It was three times the number executed in the British army (known for its faith in the deterrent power of death sentences). It was twenty-three times the number of German soldiers executed (Welch 2014). These comparisons are especially telling given that the Italian army fought for a shorter period and mobilized an equal or smaller number of men. The Italian army was also more likely to carry out its death sentences. Three-quarters of the Italian ones were imposed as compared with one-tenth in the British army (Guerrini and Pluviano 2014, 186–88; M. Thompson 2008, 6, 258). The Italian army executed 15 per 100,000 soldiers after trial compared with 0.4, 5.4, and 8.9 soldiers per 100,000 in the longer-serving German, British, and French armies, respectively (Knox 2007, 203; Rochat 2010, 92). There were miscarriages of justice in the British army, and historians debate the fairness of British capital courts-martial (Rubin 2013). But here again the comparison is telling. There can be no debate about the fairness of Italian military "justice." An official report later referred to Cadorna's command as "mystical sadism" (quoted in Absalom 1995, 91).

In many European armies the quality of judicial proceeding improved, and the severity of the penalties declined as the war continued. The British army provided legal advisers to the accused beginning in 1917 (Welch 2014). There was a downward trend in the number of executions in the French and British armies. In fact, the French army executed more soldiers during the first year of the war despite the large-scale mutinies in spring 1917. The opposite occurred in Italy's army. The number of executions increased from one year to the next (Guerrini and Pluviano 2014, 188). For the Italian soldier there was no escape from this unjust disciplinary regime.

NO EXPLANATION, ONLY REPRESSION

Alone among European armies, the Italian high command saw no need for patriotic instruction. General Cadorna shared Salandra's view of the limited value of propaganda, which the army chief thought "distasteful and lacking in military seriousness" (Absalom 1995, 91). Cadorna did not see the army as a "school of the nation," and he gave little thought to the problem of morale. He saw no reason to either explain the war's aims to the peasant conscripts or try to justify their sacrifices (Whittam 1975, 153). Severe discipline was the only method that worked with "uneducated masses," as Cadorna called them. "Obedience was a beautifully simple requirement, not to be contaminated with notions of education or motivation," one historian explains. "The soldiers did not need to reason; they merely had to do and die" (M. Thompson 2008, 274–75). Cadorna's morale-building efforts never amounted to more than allowing chaplains back in the army and providing grappa—or as soldiers dubbed it, *benzina* (motor fuel)—to front-line troops (Absalom 1995, 94). Cadorna sought "passive faithfulness unto death, not ideological fervor or cohesion" (Knox 2007, 201–2).

The average conscript was twenty or twenty-one years old. He had never left his local community, and he had little connection with Italy as a nation-state. Most important, he knew little about why he was called to the front (M. Thompson 2008, 95). Yet under Cadorna's command, and in contrast to other western armies, the army produced little propaganda for the rank and file. The Italian army did not create a "trench newspaper" or similar material that would engage soldiers and help them make sense of why they were fighting and dying (Snowden 1986, 150). What was done to instill a sense of mission came from independent initiatives, without the Supreme Command's support, and often only after overcoming its resistance (Wilcox 2005, 78). Officers who tried to provide patriotic instruction had received no training, and their efforts were often poorly conceived (Wilcox 2016, 45–47). The high command prohibited the distribution of propaganda within the forces, even from strident supporters of the war.

Officers frequently noted that soldiers did not know why Italy was at war. Letters home revealed that the men knew little of why they were in uniform (Mead 2006, 115, 219). After the defeat at Caporetto, an internal report found that there was no organized antiwar activity in the army. But there was also no sense among conscripts of why they were fighting or that victory was important (M. Thompson 2008, 331, 390; Wilcox 2014). "We understood nothing," one soldier recalled. "We only tried not to die. We did not care about killing Austrians, but we had to kill them because if they came forward they killed you" (quoted in Duggan 2008, 397). Soldiers were confused about Italy's war aims. "I did not know why there was a war at all," a veteran explained. "For that matter they didn't let the troops in on anything. You had to find your reasons for yourself, on the spot" (quoted in M. Thompson 2008, 95).

After Caporetto, General Armando Diaz replaced Cadorna as the army chief of staff and supreme commander. Diaz belonged to a new generation of World War I officers, and he introduced important reforms. He created a new tactical system, and he ended decimations and summary executions. He also recognized the importance of morale. Diaz had won the affection and respect of his regiment during the Libya war, and his first statement to the troops on assuming command in November 1917 was to encourage them "to fight for their land, home, family and honour" (quoted in M. Thompson 2008, 323). Diaz created a propaganda and education section—the "P Service"—to figure out what soldiers thought and to spread "the conviction of the absolute necessity of our war among the troops" (quoted in M. Thompson 2008, 331–32; Wilcox 2016, 48–49). The army now paid attention to the production of "trench newspapers" and its propaganda section disseminated posters, leaflets, and films as part of its morale-boosting campaign. It also organized theatrical productions and meetings at the front lines where military personnel—and especially badly wounded veterans—gave patriotic speeches (Gooch 2014, 256–59; Rochat 2010). Officials began stressing that the war was worth fighting, and that a more just society would emerge in its wake. There would be "land to the peasants" when soldiers returned home from the war.

Diaz's new propaganda office was about more than patriotic appeals. It was also a surveillance service that was networked with societal actors, and that aimed to purge any signs of "defeatism" within the army (M. Thompson 2008, 270, 332). Military censors scoured soldiers' letters to identify critics of the war, and the army harshly punished all offenders.

A Mixed Record on Compensation

The Italian army's pay and benefits to soldiers (and their families) were meager when compared with those of other belligerents. British and French soldiers were better clothed, were better fed, and had access to better medical facilities than their Italian counterparts (Snowden 1989, 38). Italian conscripts were allocated only half the leave of French soldiers and even then, they often did not receive it. Whereas the German army sought to minimize how long recruits were in battle, front-line service in the Italian army could continue for months (Knox 2007, 218). The Italian soldier's basic pay, plus supplements for his family, did not keep pace with inflation. Diseases such as typhus, cholera, malaria, and trench foot were rampant, killing proportionally three times as many Italian as German soldiers (Knox 2007, 201; Snowden 1986, 152). Hundreds of Italian soldiers froze to death in the harsh alpine conditions (Bosworth 2005, 71).

The Italian soldier's living standards were, however, often better than his prewar condition, and standards improved after Diaz replaced Cadorna as supreme commander in November 1917. Diaz explained to his commanders that soldiers had to be "personally concerned that we are caring for them, that their well-being, their needs, their sacrifices are recognized" (quoted in Gooch 2014, 259). Troops now had better clothing, annual leaves were extended, and rations were augmented. The caloric value of rations rose from about 3,000 in November 1917 to 3,500 in June 1918. Although the amount delivered varied during the war, the army's allocated rations were an advance (both nutritionally and calorically) on the peasant conscript's peacetime consumption (Forsyth 1993, 89; Pluviano and Guerrini 2000, 107). The initial army allocation of meat or fish had seemed "luxurious." Even after its reduction at the end of 1916, the meat rations were an "undreamed of luxury" for soldiers who might have eaten meat or fish once or twice a year in peacetime (Wilcox 2016, 105–6). As the war continued, the government also increased conscript pay, provided free life insurance, and introduced programs to assist widows, orphans, and the wounded. Officials expedited the payment of death benefits (Giovanna Procacci 1992, 159; M. Thompson 2008, 323, 330–32).

Despite the loss of more than half of the rural male workforce to the front, agricultural production almost matched its prewar output (Clark 2014, 233). In this respect, Italy's endemic prewar rural underemployment served it well. However, the economic conditions of the agricultural workforce (or the families of the peasant conscripts) varied according to the land tenure system. The landowning peasantry prospered most, and its ranks expanded thanks to wartime inflation (Knox 2007, 225). Tenant farmers and sharecroppers who were paid a share of the harvest also benefited from the rise in farm prices (C. Schmidt 1938, 26). It was the *braccianti* who were especially hard hit. They were paid in monetary wages so the sharp rise in food prices cut into their already miserable existence. The socialist agricultural leagues did gain substantial wage increases for the *braccianti* during the war, but employers often evaded their obligations (Cardoza 1982, 230–31).

State efforts to bridge the gap between inflation and the meager wages of farm workers were not sufficient to meet the need (Quine 2002, 102). The government funded mutual societies that provided disability benefits to returning soldiers, and it directly subsidized the families of soldiers, and especially those who were dead or wounded. Officials also introduced compulsory accident insurance for agricultural workers (Ferrera 2018, 105). But only a modicum of welfare assistance was available. Local communes (townships or municipalities) had been largely responsible for public services before the war, and with greatly reduced budgets they could not maintain the support. Many of the policy initiatives were limited and unevenly applied. Others, such as rationing and rent and price controls, were only moderately effective. Rural housing, sanitation, public works, and education deteriorated during the war (Snowden 1989, 35–36). The peasant conscript (and his family) received inadequate compensation during Italy's war.

Inequitable Outcomes

Few soldiers were surprised that officers led comfortable lives that bore little resemblance to their own. British officers had separate quarters, dining facilities, cinemas, and even brothels. They ate well and were served with fine silver. British officers with shell shock received mental health treatment; soldiers suffering from it might be tried for cowardice or sent back to the front. The British army worked hard to reinforce these distinctions. Trench harmony between the British officer and the common soldier is a myth (DeGroot 1996, 166). Yet even compared with the British, distributive injustice in the Italian army was extreme. Italian officers ate as well as they might during peacetime holidays (Bosworth 2005, 70), and they enjoyed an afternoon siesta that astonished their British colleagues (Wilcox 2016, 107). While Italian conscripts often did not receive their (already short) leaves, officers' leaves were extremely generous. Some conscripts went two years without relief; generals received sixty days a year (Wilcox 2016, 60).

The fate of Italian conscripts who became prisoners of war (POWs) exemplifies the distributive injustice in the Italian army. Governments across Europe had prepared for a short war, and because of the British naval blockade, the Central powers were unable to adequately care for the influx of POWs. France, Britain, and many belligerent states subsidized aid for their interned nationals. By mid-1915, local committees were sending six ten-pound packages to each British POW every month (Wilson 1986, 159). Italy refused to follow suit, despite the Red Cross's persistent and desperate appeals. Because the Italian high command "knew" that most Italian POWs were deserters, they believed that publicizing the severe hardship conscripts would face if they "allowed themselves" to be taken captive would deter "cowardice." During the cold winter of 1917–18, the government did nothing as hundreds of Italian prisoners died every day (M. Thompson 2008, 351–52). It was only that summer, and under harsh international condemnation, that Orlando allowed a small shipment of food to be sent to Italian POWs. It arrived after the war ended (Gorgolini 2015).

This policy of refusing aid to its own nationals was unique to Italy, and its consequences were dire. Close to 20 percent of Italian conscripts who were POWs (or one hundred thousand soldiers) died in captivity. This rate was far higher than any other country. It was nine times the rate of Austrian prisoners in Italian camps, and five times the rate of French prisoners who were often interned for longer. Even Russian POWs had a better chance of surviving than the Italians (O'Brien 2006, 354). In fact, it was more dangerous to be an Italian POW than to serve in the front-line infantry of the Italian army. Italian officers who became POWs did not share this danger. Rome allowed officers in POW camps to receive packages of food, clothing, and medical supplies. Not surprisingly, Italian officers were much more likely than conscripts to survive their internment. Three percent of Italian officers died in captivity as compared with 16 percent of the Italian soldiers (Gorgolini 2015; M. Thompson 2008, 351–52). This ratio would have been even higher if soldiers from other nations had not provided handouts to Italian conscripts serving in POW camps with them.

Officers received favorable treatment in all military codes during World War I. Across Europe, proportionately fewer officers were brought before military tribunals and found guilty than the rank and file. But unlike other European armies, the Italian army had no permanent court with jurisdiction over officers (Oram 2003, 23). Few Italian officers were brought before a court-martial and fewer still were convicted. Just over 1 percent of the officers were court-martialed compared with 6 percent of the conscripts; a third of the officers were found guilty compared with two-thirds of the conscripts (O'Brien 2006, 356). The Italian army's preference for "field justice" reinforced this disproportionate punishment. While an officer could justify his absence as necessary for family reasons, a conscript might be shot for returning late from leave (Guerrini and Pluviano 2014, 186). Many officers used claims of mental illness to escape a guilty sentence, a defense unavailable to "simple" soldiers, who were assumed capable of handling difficult field conditions. Officers did not completely escape summary execution—three were shot—but the numbers pale in comparison with the rank and file (Bianchi 2013, 167, 174).

Even casualty rates on the battlefield disproportionately hit Italian conscripts. Italian officers died at just under half the rate of the rank and file. This ratio is *not* par for the course. As a proportion of those serving, regular officers in the German army died at more than three times the rate of Italian officers (Knox 2007, 205). Even officers in the class-ridden British army died at a higher rate than their Italian counterparts (Winter 1985a, 83–99).

The distributive injustice between conscripts and their officers stretched home to the countryside (and to soldiers' families), where the government did little to promote shared sacrifice. While the economic position of the families of many conscripts deteriorated, rural elites grew wealthy under the war economy. Soaring agricultural prices and bonuses for planting (or not planting) certain crops meant that even more than in peacetime, the costs and benefits of rural life were dramatically skewed (Snowden 1989, 34). The real incomes of large commercial leaseholders in the Po Valley more than quintupled during the war while inflation cut day laborers' wages. As with their industrial counterparts, the rural elite's enormous war profits were relatively free from taxation (Cardoza 1982, 232). While peasants made up the bulk of the Italian front line, rural elites largely avoided mandatory military service. Under emergency directives to maintain agricultural yields (and because of government favoritism), large landowners monopolized the military exemptions available to agricultural workers (Cardoza 1982, 233). Salandra did not even bother to conceal that his three sons were able to evade front-line service (Bosworth 2005, 62).

Conclusion: An Unjust Mobilization

Italian labor's wartime experiences were procedurally unjust. Industrial relations had reverted to the social control typical of the reactionary politics of the nineteenth century. Conscripts fought under an equally unjust military code. Indeed, Italy's policies often went beyond those of its autocratic adversaries in Central Europe. Austrian women were never subjected to militarization; the German army was never present in firms; German labor retained some job mobility; and German repression of dissent was less severe than in Italy. Even Dallolio's turn to remuneration did not displace Italy's harsh policies. Labor unrest prompted ever more repression. Rome made no attempt to provide even an illusion of procedural or distributive justice.

Did Italy's astonishingly unjust mobilization strategy change Italian labor's interests, identity, and attitudes about the state, as my hypotheses predict? I explore that question in chapter 5, but I first detail how the British government reacted to the demands of total war. They, too, needed to gain labor's compliance with the war effort, but the British took a radically different approach, and one that had very different consequences for labor's wartime transformation.

3

MANAGING BRITISH LABOR

British officials initially followed a "business as usual" strategy. They assumed that Britain would limit its contribution to naval operations and the deployment of a small professional army to the continent. Other than assuming control of the railroads and guaranteeing the food supply, the government did not foresee extensive intervention in the economy (Broadberry and Howlett 2005, 223). The Committee of Imperial Defense's *War Book* contained eleven detailed chapters, but there were no plans for industrial mobilization. There was no manpower registry, no survey of industrial resources, and no plans for an administrative apparatus to manage the home front (Burk 1982, 2; Simmonds 2012, 37). To the extent that officials anticipated labor problems, they sought to minimize the unemployment they assumed the national crisis would cause (Commons 1922, 704).

The realities of modern warfare quickly upended these assumptions. The British army always needed more men and material, and firms faced severe shortages of skilled labor as vast numbers of volunteers joined the army. The engineering trades, the iron and steel industry, the mines, and the explosives trade lost 20 percent of their workforce by June 1915 (R. Adams 1978, 72). Government ministers recognized the need to tackle manpower problems, and officials reached a series of agreements with organized labor to structure industrial mobilization. These policies were adjusted over time, but whatever the changes, British mobilization shared few features with the Italian approach. While Rome charged the military with industrial mobilization and imposed unjust procedures on labor, British civilians managed the home front and adopted procedurally just policies to gain labor's compliance. Officials treated organized labor as a junior partner in Britain's mobilization for war. They felt it important to reach out to labor to explain why its sacrifices were necessary. Officials also sought to maintain labor's standard of living, but they reneged on their promises to ensure comparative sacrifice.

Negotiating British Mobilization

The government negotiated two important agreements with unions and employers to resolve manpower problems and increase productivity. Officials brokered the Shells and Fuses Agreement with the Engineering Employers Federation and the engineering unions in early March 1915. Later that month, they negotiated the Treasury Agreement with the principal trade unions involved in war production (except mining). These voluntary agreements were designed to minimize strikes and to allow dilution, which is the breaking down of craft procedures into operations that unskilled workers can perform. Diluting skill requirements threatens the status and wages of skilled workers. In exchange, the government promised that skilled workers' wages would not be cut, and that trade union practices would be restored in peacetime. Officials also reassured labor that the government would restrict profits in war industries (R. Adams 1978, 79; Simmonds 2012, 86–87; Wrigley 1987a, 24–25).

The "Shell Scandal" erupted in May 1915. Newspapers declared that the "need for shells" had caused the defeat of a British offensive earlier that month.[1] The ensuing political storm, along with the resignation of Admiral Lord Fisher following the Dardanelles disaster, led to the downfall of Herbert Asquith's Liberal government. The Treasury Agreement had failed. It had neither contained industrial unrest nor produced the necessary war material. Asquith's new coalition government (May 1915–December 1916) sought to strengthen official control over munitions production. It introduced two critical changes to British mobilization. First, it created the Ministry of Munitions, which was the first and the most important of the new war ministries. Asquith appointed the Liberal politician David Lloyd George to run it. Second, Asquith gained Parliament's approval to give the voluntary Treasury Agreement legislative force as the Munitions of War Act.

The Munitions of War Act was the most important legislation on Britain's wartime industrial relations.[2] Lloyd George was just the politician to take advantage of its extensive powers. He championed an interventionist approach, and he assumed that nothing should stand in the way of production. Even a "perfectly democratic State," Lloyd George claimed, has the "right to commandeer every resource, every power, life, limb, wealth and everything else for the interest of the State" (quoted in R. Adams 1978, 83, 43). The Ministry of Munitions ran Britain's industrial mobilization. It had broad powers, and it controlled large and critical sectors of the domestic economy, as well as imports and essential raw materials. The ministry was "like an octopus with its tentacles reaching out into the whole economy" (Wrigley 1982a, 46). By the summer of 1916, it supervised almost the entire process of munitions production, from research and development to the supply of arms to the War Office. It ensured the massive supply of materials for the Somme offensive in July 1916 (Wrigley 1976, 72).

The Munitions of War Act contained three important provisions designed to control labor and to minimize interruptions in war production. First, the unions agreed to suspend the right to strike and to refer disputes to the Committee of Production for compulsory arbitration. Second, unions agreed to suspend traditional workshop practices, thereby opening the door to dilution (and the shop floor to unskilled or semiskilled labor, including women). Third, a system of "leaving certificates"—the infamous Clause 7—curtailed labor mobility. Workers engaged in war production could only change jobs if they obtained a certificate from their employer testifying that they were not needed. Failure to acquire a certificate meant six weeks of unemployment, a penalty few could afford. Workers could appeal to the munitions tribunal if employers denied their request, but better pay and conditions were not grounds for a job transfer (A. Reid 1985a, 54).

Labor's concessions were significant. These provisions weakened its ability to take advantage of full employment, and they threatened the "aristocracy of labor's" privileges. In exchange, the government reiterated its pledges from the Treasury Agreement. It would introduce a tax on excess profits to ensure that everyone paid their fair share. It guaranteed that the wages of skilled workers would be maintained despite changes in shop procedures (and that officials would consult union officials before any changes in procedures). Finally, the government promised that it would help secure the restoration of restrictive trade union practices after the war ended.

Some of these provisions may sound familiar. Italian labor in the auxiliary factories also lost the right to strike and to change jobs. These resemblances are misleading. First, the Italian government imposed these provisions on labor; British labor agreed to these restrictions in negotiations with state officials. Second, Italian officials harshly punished workers who violated IM regulations; British penalties were mild and seldom enforced. Just over one-fifth of 1 percent of British workers who participated in illegal work stoppages were convicted in the first year of the war. The fines they paid were minimal: they came to less than one-sixteenth of 1 percent of the statutory maximum. Even then, officials occasionally waived the fines or allowed others to pay them (Rubin 1979, 267–68). When officials harshly reacted to industrial unrest, the government focused on punishing leaders (and placating the rank and file). A shop stewards' strike broke out in the engineering works on the Red Clydeside, a militant shipbuilding center in

Glasgow, in March 1916. Industrial unrest erupted the following spring and spread to over two hundred thousand men, causing the loss of 1.3 million working days (Bourne 1989, 209). In both cases, the government punished union leaders as stipulated in the Defence of the Realm Act (DORA), emergency legislation that gave the government sweeping powers to subject citizens to military law, and to restrict information.[3] Several union leaders were arrested and imprisoned, and several more were deported to other parts of Britain without trial, as allowed under DORA (Brown 1983, 90–91; A. Reid 1985a, 58; Wrigley, 1976, 122). But unlike in Italy, the British government could not send "troublesome" trade unionists to the front, and it rarely punished the rank and file for violating wartime regulations (Commons 1922, 706).

Restrictions on job mobility are the final (apparent) similarity between Italian and British regulations. Intended to ensure uninterrupted production and to prevent skilled workers from taking private work, the leaving certificate became a major grievance in British firms producing for the war effort. Trade unionists dubbed it "the Slavery Act" (Wrigley 1987a, 29–31). However, while Italian labor never regained the wartime right to change jobs, the leaving certificate lasted two years. Following protracted labor negotiations, the government first weakened Clause 7 in January 1916 and abandoned it altogether following an engineering strike in 1917 (Rubin 1977, 152). Officials decided that it was better to concede to one of the strikers' important demands than to wield the provisions in the Munitions of War Act against illegally striking workers.

The War Office initially resisted expanding munitions production beyond state-owned factories and private firms on the "War Office List." But as head of the new Ministry of Munitions, Lloyd George quickly shifted course. He was convinced that the War Office was incapable of producing the material necessary to defeat Germany (Bourne 1989, 190). He encouraged a variety of firms—from jewelers to car manufacturers—to convert to war production (R. Adams 1978, 2, 57). The Ministry of War had the authority to designate any private company producing munitions a "controlled" establishment, thus bringing the firm and its employers under the provisions of the Munitions of War Act. The definition of "munitions work" was initially broad, and legislative amendments and a judicial decision further widened it. By the end of the war, around twenty thousand firms were designated as controlled. Workers in these factories were essentially state employees. Their representatives directly negotiated with officials over wages, working conditions, and state-mandated welfare.

The British state was also an employer in its own right. The Ministry of Munitions built many factories during the war, and it took control of the railroads, shipping, mining, and flourmills, as well as over 125 privately owned firms. It had the authority to require companies to produce war material and to transfer skilled labor and machinery to state-owned factories (Bourne 1989, 189). Over 250 national factories, mines, and quarries were under ministry supervision by 1918 (Simmonds 2012, 74). Firms that were subject to some form of wartime regulation employed about two-thirds of the labor force (Tawney 1943, 3). The Ministry of Munitions had over sixty-five thousand employees and was the largest employer by the war's end (Noel Whiteside 1992, 110). It also set up co-ordination committees for industries, such as cotton and wool, that were not under its direct supervision (Gerber 2005, 32–36).

The final significant development in the organization of the British war economy came when Lloyd George replaced Asquith as prime minister in December 1916. Lloyd George created four new ministries—shipping, labor, food, and national service—to broaden the state's management of the war economy.

Procedural Justice: From the Factory Floor to the War Cabinet

The British government's support for procedural justice is impressive, whether compared with the policies of its Italian ally or the prior treatment of British labor. Officials accorded the working class a degree of respect that had previously eluded it and that would have shocked its Italian counterpart. British officials regularly met with labor leaders and included them in economic and political forums. They also worked hard to persuade workers of the war's importance and their vital role in Britain's ultimate victory.

FORMAL JUSTICE

The Liberal Party had been in office for almost a decade by 1914. Labour had emerged as a separate party, but it was not a serious candidate for power. The Conservatives were the only other party capable of aspiring to office. Asquith's all-Liberal government remained in power for the first nine months of the war. Asquith dismissed suggestions that he include opposition members in the government. But following the Shell Scandal and Fisher's resignation, Asquith formed the first coalition government in British history (May 1915–December 1916). He appointed Conservatives to it and, as another first in British history, also included Labour Party members. Asquith appointed Arthur Henderson, the chair of the Parliamentary Labour Party, as the president of the Board of Education. Despite his job title, Henderson primarily served as an unofficial adviser on labor affairs. He brought the voice of organized labor into the heart of the British government. Asquith also appointed two additional Labour MPs to minor cabinet offices. Asquith's government was not a genuine government of national unity—that would come later—but he had already gone further than any wartime Italian government.

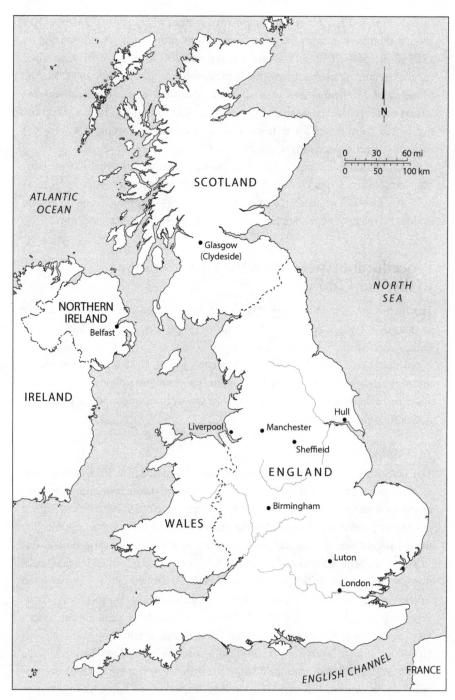

MAP 2. United Kingdom

Lloyd George's government (December 1916–January 1919) gave labor an unprecedented seat at the table. Conservatives dominated his cabinet, with the exception of the premiership (Lloyd George was a Liberal). But eight Labour members entered the new government, almost tripling the number in Asquith's coalition. Lloyd George reappointed Henderson, and he included this Labour leader as one of five members of his major administrative innovation, the War Cabinet.[4] Henderson served alongside some of the leading lights in British politics, including Andrew Bonar Law, the head of the Conservative Party, and Lord Milner and Lord Curzon, two major supporters of imperialism. Lloyd George led the War Cabinet. It had central direction of the war and met almost daily. Lloyd George also appointed trade unionists to two of his newly created ministries. John Hodge of the Steel Smelters' Association became the minister of labor, and George Barnes of the Typographical Association became the minister of pensions. Lloyd George invited additional labor representatives to serve in junior posts.

The inclusion of labor leaders in the cabinet was the tip of the iceberg. Officials negotiated the framework for Britain's mobilization with union leaders whose industries were critical to the war effort—engineering, shipbuilding, iron and steel, the metal trades, and many others. They did not impose the Treasury Agreement on labor or develop it in consultation with employer-chosen labor "representatives," as occurred in Italy. The government placed union officials on committees concerned with production, relief, and the distribution of food and fuel. Officials also encouraged labor's participation in the implementation of policies of particular concern to it. Lloyd George appointed Henderson to head the committee tasked with executing the Treasury Agreement. Officials reached out to labor leaders for assistance when skilled workers resisted dilution (Hardach 1977, 194; Wrigley 1987a, 55–57). A similar pattern occurred with regard to military conscription. Britain relied on voluntary enlistment until January 1916. Decisions about how to "comb out" men from the factories (or whom to exempt from military service) were contentious, but the decisions were made in consultation with, or sometimes even at the direction of, organized labor. Government officials involved union leaders in early discussions about military service, and they placed labor representatives on national and local bodies that organized recruiting and the lists of exempted men (Noel Whiteside 1992, 111; Wrigley 1987a, 44–46).

Officials increasingly enlisted labor's support as the demand for soldiers and skilled labor continued unabated. There were never enough men to go around. The War Office had unrestricted access to whoever enlisted for the first six months of the war, regardless of whether the shop floor was adequately manned (Wrigley 1987a, 24). Later in the war, the War Office accused the factories of starving the armed services of necessary manpower. The government reached an agreement with the Amalgamated Society of Engineers (ASE) in November 1916 in hopes of partially addressing this problem. Angry over the number of skilled workers called into military service, munitions workers in Sheffield had gone out on strike. Officials granted the ASE the authority to certify if one of its members qualified as a skilled worker (and was thus exempt from military service). Lloyd George took the lead in extending similar "trade card" schemes to thirty-two unions (Simmonds 2012, 87; Turner 1992, 128–29). The government later abolished these plans—they were unworkable—but officials had practically handed over to unions the power to determine which workers would serve in the military.

Officials consulted union representatives at every administrative level. Lloyd George frequently met with leaders of key trade unions. The Ministry of Munitions kept communication open with labor in its respective sectors. The director of one department explained that his strategy included "the exercise of considerable tact, very great patience, numerous meetings . . . and a very full knowledge . . . of the workman's point of view" (quoted in A. Reid 1985a, 66). The Trades Union Congress (TUC)—the federation of trade unions—provided the government with the names of unionists to serve on various official bodies, including joint industrial committees (A. Reid 1988b, 22–23; Wrigley 1987a, 55–57). The government also relied on local trade councils to administer war emergency regulations. These committees managed the allocation of pensions, food distribution, and local prices (Bush 1992, 127). Officials regularly engaged union leaders about the implementation of industrial legislation and changes in production methods. Official guidelines stressed that managers should consult labor and discuss the details of any change in shop-floor practices before proceeding with dilution (R. Adams 1978, 43).[5]

Although many employers had bargained with unions before the war, many others had refused (Gospel 1987, 163). The Munitions of War Act broke down much of this resistance. The government would only award contracts to firms that recognized unions and that could enter into joint committees of employers and employees (Wrigley 1976, 132). Previously recalcitrant employers in engineering, coal mining, and port transportation were now sitting down with labor. The shipping and railroad industries fully recognized unions during the war. A leading official brokered a deal in March 1916 with mine owners who agreed that union membership would be a condition for wartime employment (Wrigley 1987a, 23, 37, 58). An amendment to the Munitions Act in August 1917 made it illegal to fire employees because they belonged to a union or participated in a labor dispute (Rubin 1984, 324). Numerous other wartime initiatives encouraged unionization, augmented the legitimacy of unions, and increased labor's voice in decision making. Following a government report on the causes of the engineering strikes in May 1917, the Whitley Committee recommended the creation of industrial councils composed of employee and employer representatives.[6] This proposal, as well as government support for national wage bargaining, encouraged trade union growth among unskilled workers in industries where collective bargaining was not well established, and in relatively unorganized sectors of the economy that were peripheral to the war effort (Noel Whiteside 1992, 114–16).

Officials also designed the munitions tribunals to ensure worker participation. Each tribunal comprised a chair (a barrister or solicitor) and two assessors, one that workers chose and one that employers chose (R. Adams 1978, 88). These tribunals supported union rights. In a widely reported case, a tribunal ruled against an employer of a controlled establishment who fired an employee for joining a union. The employee had signed a company statement renouncing union membership, but the tribunal decreed that the employer's actions were illegal (Rubin 1984, 323–24). The government had initially assumed that ordinary criminal courts would hold these proceedings, but officials instead used specially constituted tribunals modeled after (less intimidating) unemployment insurance panels (Rubin 1979, 265). Officials preferred settings that would signal the tribunals' separation from the traditional judicial system. A high-ranking ministry official explained that it was important that the working man be put at ease (Rubin 1979, 266).

Some historians dismiss the British government's "consultations" with labor as a way to convey policy decisions and to pass down unwelcome news. Labor was often not involved in drafting policy that it helped to implement, and labor's inclusion in administrative agencies did not necessarily mean any real transfer of power (Gerber 2005, 36; Noel Whiteside 1992, 116–21). Lloyd George brought Henderson into his War Cabinet because of Henderson's standing in the labor movement, not because he planned to give the Labour leader real responsibility (Winter 1974, 240–41). Historians skeptical of British intentions to engage labor are especially critical of Lloyd George's creation of the Ministry of Labour in December 1916.

The Ministry of Labour was important to the labor movement. The TUC had demanded its creation since 1904, and the Labour Party had introduced multiple resolutions calling for one before the war. Yet this new ministry's promise went unfulfilled. It lacked an effective staff, and the proliferation of wartime agencies created confusion about overlapping authority. The Ministry of Labour shared responsibilities with the Ministry of Munitions and the War Office about issues where it should have had authority, and it competed with the Ministry of National Service, another new ministry whose separate existence was difficult to justify (Lowe 1982, 108–14). All this added up to a weak ministry that did not begin to have the authority Ernest Bevin enjoyed as head of the Ministry of Labour during World War II. "We hardly ever have to bat on any but a spoiled wicket," a ministry official grumbled during the war (quoted in Turner 1992, 376).[7]

The Ministry of Labour was the Cinderella service in Whitehall. Lloyd George created it "as a sop to organized labor" (Noel Whiteside 1992, 115). But to dismiss the ministry (and other official efforts to reach out to labor) as window dressing designed to provide an illusion of labor power (or an illusion of fair procedures) misunderstands how individuals assess procedural justice. Formal procedures *are* important: individuals care whether they have a say in decisions that affect them. But they also care about the informal aspects of decision making. Being treated with dignity and respect—being included where one was once excluded—increases the perception of procedural justice even when that "voice" has no effect on decisions.

Labor's representatives were often unable to influence British policy, but their voices were heard, and they had a seat at the table. Lloyd George's inclusion of Henderson in his War Cabinet symbolized the government's recognition of the working class. The socialist reformers Sidney and Beatrice Webb could reasonably claim that labor had gained a foothold in governing: "Trade Unionism has . . . won its recognition by Parliament and the Government, by law and by custom, as a separate element in the community, entitled to distinct recognition as a part of the social machinery of the State, its members being thus allowed to give . . . not only their votes as citizens, but also their concurrence as an order or estate" (quoted in Wrigley 1982b, 81). By 1916, union officials assumed that their members were justified in ignoring government policy if they had not been consulted about it (Noelle Whiteside 1980, 864, 873). The president of the Board of Trade noted in a parliamentary speech in 1917, "We have passed through a lot of history in dealing with the labour question during the war. We began in old Board of Trade spirit in which you govern labour for the good of labour on behalf of labour but keep labour at a distance" (quoted in Charles 1973, 78). Now labor was incorporated in government and regularly consulted.

INFORMAL JUSTICE

The British government had little organizational capacity for managing the public sphere when the war began (Bourne 1989, 200–202). Propaganda efforts developed during the war, with a collection of official and unofficial bodies explaining to ever-broader sectors of society why the country needed its support. Officials were persuaded that it was vital that labor understand why its sacrifices were important.

For the first two years of the war, the major propaganda efforts came from what historians term "self-mobilization," or more accurately, government-assisted self-mobilization. Intellectuals, artists, religious groups, commercial advertisers, and patriotic organizations worked tirelessly to support the war. They organized meetings, printed pamphlets, and directed campaigns to encourage food economy and voluntary enlistment in the armed services (Horne 2010, 282). The government sought to both limit and obscure its involvement in these activities; officials created an illusion of voluntarism while working hard in support of these efforts. The Parliamentary Recruiting Committee, a bipartisan and quasi-governmental organization formed in August 1914, cooperated with other departments and received guidance from the War Office. It led major campaigns to fill the volunteer army, and it organized rallies and distributed posters calling on men to enlist. Whatever the major initiative—whether to recruit soldiers or promote war bonds—the government worked behind the scenes to support the efforts of private groups, feeding them pamphlets, books, and financial support (DeGroot 1996, 177). State agencies distributed reports of German atrocities and printed material for private groups to circulate (Monger 2012, 25–26).

As with many aspects of Britain's home-front mobilization, Lloyd George's accession to power in December 1916 altered the government's role. The new prime minister was not content to have officials take a back seat in private or semiofficial efforts. At his first War Cabinet meeting, Lloyd George stressed that propaganda was vital to the war effort. He was unable to overcome cabinet opposition to the creation of a full ministry of information (though he created it a year later), but he restructured the ad hoc, decentralized, and overlapping propaganda efforts into a sophisticated state machine designed to elicit mass support (Messinger 1992, 11–16, 47; Monger 2012, 17–24).

Italian officials had been uninterested in propaganda, and they believed that the best response to "defeatist" attitudes was to prevent their expression. British officials responded differently, especially under Lloyd George's direction. The government intensified patriotic campaigns as war weariness increased. Following strikes in May 1917, and facing long casualty lists, inflation, high taxes, and fuel and food shortages, London initiated a major effort to justify the war and to combat calls for a negotiated settlement. The War Cabinet created the parliamentary cross-party National War Aims Committee (NWAC) in June 1917 to counteract the pacifist movement and to mobilize support for outright victory (Horne 1997, 199–200).

Three shifts in focus—toward the home front, the working class, and broad appeals—accompanied these organizational developments and increased budgetary support. First, the War Cabinet granted the new Department of Information the authority to target domestic audiences (Messinger 1992, 91). The government had been involved in propaganda at home since the war began, but the campaign concentrated on strategically important Allied and neutral countries, and especially the United States. With US entry into the war (and official apprehension about war weariness), officials now directed that propaganda efforts focus at home (Horne 1997, 198–99). The second shift was to expand the understanding of what constituted public opinion. Although the government had promoted the distribution of anti-German cartoons at a trade union conference in late 1915, official propaganda initially targeted the "thinking classes." Officials tended to dismiss mass opinion as irrational and sectarian (Monger 2012, 25). This changed. The government increasingly took working-class attitudes seriously.

The third shift was to address civilian morale in general (Bourne 1989, 201–3). Before the creation of the NWAC, the government targeted specific goals, such as voluntary enlistment. The NWAC continued these campaigns. It produced masses of posters, pamphlets, and illustrated periodicals heralding the sacrifice and heroism of British soldiers, and it often relied on private actors, such as newsagents, to distribute the materials (DeGroot 1996, 179; Wilson 1986, 734–39). As the NWAC expanded into mass propaganda, it also exploited populist mediums to shape the public's understanding of the war and its participation in it (Messinger 1992, 39–50; Searle 2004, 768). Officials saw film as the best vehicle for this outreach. They commissioned *The Battle of the Somme*, which included actual footage of the battle and of British dead and wounded. The film was a sensation. It opened in thirty-four theaters in August 1916, and it played to packed audiences hundreds of times in the first few months. Over ten million people saw it (Simmonds 2012, 242–43). Officials produced over seven hundred films by the war's end. Most were nonfiction and relied on newsreels of military operations, the royal family, and women engaged in war work. Officials also arranged for messages from the prime minister to be delivered in movie theaters and music halls (Horne 1997, 206).

British officials spent time and effort explaining why sacrifice was important. Half of the six objectives in the NWAC's founding document emphasized this goal: propaganda should stress "the gravity of the crisis" and "the momentous issues at stake." The NWAC's messages should convey "a living sense of their [the public's] responsibility and share in the great task" of defeating Germany (quoted in Monger 2012, 33). "The chief need," a leading official in the Ministry of Labour noted, "is for a better education of the working-classes as to the actual military situation and needs, the aims of the Allies so far as it is possible to define them, and the results that would inevitably follow from an inclusive peace" (quoted in Monger 2012, 27). Appeals made in London would be insufficient, he noted. Labour MPs and local trade unionists should take this message across the country and to the factory floor. They should ensure that the messages resonated with workers. The NWAC enlisted prominent trade unionists to write pamphlets explaining why Prussian militarism had to be destroyed (DeGroot 1996, 179).

Official efforts to justify wartime policy began with the adoption of dilution. Officials explained to skilled workers why this threat to their livelihood was necessary. They did not simply impose dilution on them. On assuming his post as minister of munitions in June 1915, Lloyd George traveled the country giving major speeches in industrial centers. He told munitions workers that his message was the most urgent one ever given to a Manchester audience. Britain's future was their future, and British victory hinged on their willingness to suspend union practices. Echoing Tennyson's famous poem "The Charge of the Light Brigade," Lloyd George declared, "[German victories were] not because of the superior valor of her soldiers, but by pouring in showers of shot and shell." He then appealed for each worker's support: "The State needs the help of each of you."[8] A few months later Lloyd George requested an audience at the September 1915 meeting of the TUC—the first large gathering of trade unionists during the war. He again wanted to explain why dilution was critical to defeating Germany (Wrigley 1987a, 56). Lloyd George stressed that the war would be won or lost in the factories: this war was "an engineer's war." A week later, he met with leaders of the most important engineering union to drive home the necessity of dilution (R. Adams 1978, 43). Five months later, Lloyd George followed the advice of trade union leaders and spoke at a shop stewards' meeting in Glasgow. That a government minister was willing to travel to Scotland to meet with embittered opponents of dilution led the American labor economist John Commons (1922, 712) to comment that this gesture must have brought labor to the government's side.

NWAC officials believed that face-to-face interaction was the most effective way to reach the public. They consulted with local constituency organizations to identify speakers and to cater the message to local conditions. Sometimes they organized large meetings that featured a major public figure, such as Lloyd George, and included a band marching through the town with Boy Scouts handing out pamphlets and planes dropping leaflets. Most NWAC meetings were smaller. They included a few speeches, usually a Conservative and a Liberal Party member, a specially trained NWAC staff member, and sometimes an army or navy "eyewitness" (Monger 2012, 32, 42–49). Altogether, the NWAC organized about one hundred thousand meetings during the war (DeGroot 1996, 178–79). These public rallies were initially in large cities and holiday resorts, but knowledge of local conditions allowed officials to focus on industrial areas in response to, or in anticipation of, strikes and declines in productivity (Bourne 1989, 203; Wilson 1986, 734). Lloyd George thought this activity sufficiently important that he enlisted well-known individuals, such as Emmeline Pankhurst (a founder of the suffragette movement), Ben Tillett (a prominent labor leader), and leaders of the Church of England, to speak to munition workers (Wrigley 1976, 136). The NWAC also organized groups of workers to visit front lines in Western Europe (Simmonds 2012, 240–47).

London had become uneasy about the war effort by the end of 1917. Russia had opened peace negotiations with Germany, Italy had suffered a major defeat at Caporetto, and France was exhausted. Officials worried that labor might be willing to settle for a negotiated end to the conflict. The Reichstag had passed a resolution calling for a negotiated peace, and a prominent Conservative had published a letter in the *Daily Telegraph* calling for the same. Persuaded that he must address war weariness in the country, Lloyd George—renowned for his rhetorical skills—gave his most significant speech on British war aims (Simmonds 2012, 246; Wrigley 1982b, 91–92). He addressed trade union leaders, not members of

Parliament or other elites, and he used language tailored to them. If additional workers had to be sent to the front despite earlier pledges to the contrary, Lloyd George felt it important that labor understand why the change was necessary. His efforts would have puzzled his Italian counterparts.

Lloyd George's actions were typical. British officials relied on consultation and persuasion—not their compulsory powers—to gain labor's support (Noel Whiteside 1992, 120). DORA gave the government the authority to limit freedom of the press, but officials had no need for this authority in most cases. Fleet Street patriotically supported the war. Editors observed War Office instructions about topics to avoid and they voluntarily submitted articles that they feared might include sensitive material (DeGroot 1996, 183). But not everyone was so compliant. The Home Office prosecuted many pacifists during the first two years of war. It ordered the seizure of pacifist material and conducted police raids of the offices of pacifist newspapers. Officials became especially concerned about this material as the war continued and the idea of a negotiated settlement with Germany gained traction. The Home Office noted in 1917 that one of the most important pacifist newspapers, the *Labour Leader*, had "considerable [power], and its influence is far reaching amongst the laboring classes" (quoted in Hopkin 1970, 160, 161–64).

One might expect officials to double down on repression (as Italy had done) in reaction to news that pacifism was gaining ground among the working class. The opposite occurred. The number of prosecutions of pacifists sharply declined in 1917 even though the number of potential cases had increased. The police commander in the Welsh county with the largest continuous coalfield in Britain recommended forty prosecutions in the first nine months of 1917 (he had recommended fifty-four during the previous two and a half years). London chose to prosecute one of these forty cases. Officials decided that it was better to launch a countercampaign to persuade British workers that the war was worth fighting than to repress antiwar sentiments (Hopkin 1970, 166–68). The government used surveillance of "labor papers" not to ferret out "defeatists" but to better understand how to pitch their response to pacifist campaigning (Monger 2012, 59–60).

British officials not only sought to justify their policies, they also treated labor with newfound respect. Prime Minister Asquith accorded Henderson, the first Labour Party member to serve in a British cabinet (and a former iron molder and "illegitimate" son of a domestic servant), respect and consideration (F. Leventhal 1989, 60; Riddell 1999, 43). Ben Tillett, a leading trade unionist, commented that the war had created a "new relationship between the classes, a closer bond of fairer, sweeter human ties of friendship" (quoted in Cronin and Weiler 1991, 52). The inclusion of British labor had prewar precedents, but the depth and the nature of this involvement at the local and national level were new (Wrigley 1976, 23). It marked a (temporary) transformation of British politics.

Lloyd George's account of a meeting in 1915 between the former prime minister Arthur Balfour and union leaders in a Treasury room containing an eighteenth-century gilt throne illustrates the novelty of labor's presence in high councils of government. Lloyd George describes Balfour's "quizzical and embarrassed wonder" at conversing with workmen. Balfour had spoken to groups of workers, but "so far he had only talked to them; now he was talked to by them." Lloyd George surmised that Balfour was wary of this new experience, and he noted that Balfour was surprised "to find the workmen's representatives talked so well." Lloyd George concluded that a new era had begun: "Those stalwart artisans [were] leaning against and sitting on the steps of the throne of the dead Queen, and on equal terms negotiating conditions with the government of the day upon a question that vitally affected the conduct of a great war. Queen Anne was indeed dead" (Lloyd George 1933, 259–60).

Remuneration: Favorable Yet Unfair Outcomes

Many states used material rewards to gain labor's compliance with the war effort. Britain was no different. It developed an array of policies to provide the working class with favorable outcomes, including improved wages and welfare facilities in factories. The British government also understood the importance of comparative sacrifice. Labor cared not only how much it received but also whether others worked less and received more. The Treasury Agreement and the Munitions of War Act included a commitment to restrict wartime profits. Officials knew that skilled workers would resist dilution unless they were assured that employers would also do their part. Yet the government failed to deliver on its promises for an equality of sacrifice for all.

WAGES AND WELFARE

The Ministry of Munitions pioneered the spread of welfare in the controlled establishments (Charles 1973, 92). Officials encouraged employers to view better working conditions as patriotic, and as a good business practice (Wrigley 1987b, 3). They distributed studies showing that long workweeks hurt productivity (Commons 1922, 720; Searle 2004, 804, 816). Officials also tried to improve working conditions, which had become overcrowded and increasingly unsanitary under the pace of wartime production (Bourne 1989, 190). The government set mandatory standards for heating, lighting, machine design, and ventilation, and they required factories engaged in war work to provide medical clinics and canteens (R. Adams 1978, 126–29; Wrigley 1987b, 6). The influx of women into factories had encouraged these policies. The number of medical centers for mothers and infants doubled during the war, but their reach went much further (Pope 1991, 62). Over a million workers could eat cheap hot meals at over nine hundred government-subsidized canteens by the war's end.

The wartime suspension of Treasury control of budgetary and tax policy facilitated the provision of welfare benefits to industrial workers. The Ministry of Munitions subsidized 75 percent of the cost of workplace nurseries. The Local Government Board underwrote half the cost of maternal centers (Searle 2004, 816–17). The ministry also underwrote measures to promote healthy working conditions. Firms could deduct the cost of food, medical services, welfare superintendents, and recreational facilities from their taxes (Wrigley 1987b, 3). Progressive firms had instituted some of these policies before the war, but wartime mobilization spread them much further. The government also built a limited number of homes for munitions workers during the war, including the picturesque "garden city" at the Royal Arsenal outside London. But the most significant policy affecting working-class housing was the Rent Restriction Act. In response to rent strikes in London, Birmingham, Luton, and Manchester, and especially on the Red Clydeside, Parliament rushed through legislation in November 1915 that ensured security of tenure and fixed rents at prewar levels for working-class housing (Searle 2004, 804, 816; Simmonds 2012, 181–82).

The Munitions of War Act outlawed strikes, required arbitration of industrial disputes, and detailed punishments for those who failed to comply. But as discussed earlier, officials made limited use of its authority to punish strikers. Indeed, official participation in wage negotiations often assisted workers (Noel Whiteside 1992, 111–16). Within two weeks of becoming law, more than two hundred thousand South Wales miners rejected the government's attempt at compulsory arbitration. They illegally struck over a pay dispute. Posters around the valley announced that strikers could be punished, but Lloyd George conceded to the miners' demands (Wrigley 1976, 122). This response was typical (Rubin 1987b, 247). The arbitration tribunals issued nearly eight thousand awards during the war. Official involvement in these negotiations improved labor's material well-being. Ministry officials rejected the conventional view that wages should be based on the value of the work done. They focused on the needs of workers and their families, and they based their assessments on inflation, which shot up during the war and hit working-class families hard (Lowe 1978a, 270; Simmonds 2012, 87).[9] Inflation rates determined wages in a wide range of industries by the war's end. Official arbitrators also awarded cost-of-living adjustments and bonuses to try to maintain labor's standard of living (Wrigley 1982b, 84).

The government took additional measures to support wages. Parliament extended minimum-wage protection to agriculture and a broad section of industries (Tanner 1990, 357; Noel Whiteside 1992, 116). The Munitions of War Act authorized the government to set wage rates of particular classes of workers, such as women and girls. After 1917, the government had the authority to extend an award to firms not party to the dispute but engaged in similar work.

Assessing the effect of government policy on British labor's standard of living is difficult. It depends on the sector, and some of the data are unavailable, controversial, or open to multiple interpretations (Bryder 1987; Simmonds 2012, 173; Wilson 1986, 151–52). The wages of skilled workers and "nonessential" employees did not keep up with inflation. And in general, the worse off a sector was before 1914, the more likely it maintained (or improved) its situation during the war. The wages of the semiskilled and unskilled often kept pace with, and sometimes exceeded, rising prices (Searle 2004, 803). Official cost-of-living adjustments, combined with controls on rent, food, and liquor and the availability of overtime pay and regular work for all family members (plus declining birth rates), meant that the most disadvantaged sector of the British working class was able to maintain, and sometimes improve, its food consumption during the war (Winter 1985a, 213–78).[10] Notably, Britain's infant mortality rate improved during the war, an advance no other European power could claim.

PROFITEERING AND THE DISTRIBUTION OF SACRIFICE

Lloyd George acknowledged that the "question of controlling private profits" was "vital to the whole issue of labour supply." But he also knew that profits in the munitions factories reached "unprecedented dimensions" (Lloyd George 1933, 263, 265). Indeed, many British firms did exceedingly well during the war. The average profit in coal, iron, engineering, and shipbuilding rose 32 percent above prewar levels by 1916. Some firm profits skyrocketed. One shipbuilder's profit rose almost 75 percent (Searle 2004, 797).

Wartime taxes on corporate profits took two forms. The munitions levy applied to firms that produced war material (the controlled establishments), and the Excess Profits Duty applied to all firms and businesses. This marked the first time in British history that firms (rather than individuals) were taxed (T. Adams 1922, 37–38; Charles 1973, 79). The Excess Profits Duty raised a lot of money— by war's end, it generated about one-third of total revenue (Broadberry and Howlett 2005, 217). But it did not fulfill the government's promises to make employers pay their fair share. The tax was not excessive. Its rate was based on the additional profits earned above prewar (trade boom) levels. The average tax rate was 63 percent (it rose to 80 percent for the last year of the war), which was significantly less than the 100 percent rate imposed during World War II. Whatever the rate, firms avoided much of the cost. They could deduct generous allowances for depreciation and capital expenditures, and there was room for creative book-keeping, fraud, and evasion (R. Adams 1978). The Treasury only collected about half of the excess profits (S. Pollard 1983, 31). A critic of this tax remarked that it did more to legitimize high profits than remove them (Searle 2004, 797). Nor did wartime income taxes change the perception of unequal sacrifice. Taxes were progressive during the war, but the rate imposed on the "supertax"-paying class was only marginally higher than what ordinary tax payers paid. There was no wartime increase in inheritance taxes (Balderston 1989, 234–35).

The difficulty gaining access to basic necessities reinforced the working class's perception of distributive injustice. Germany's campaign of unrestricted submarine warfare and Britain's heavy reliance on imported grain meant that food shortages arose, especially in the spring of 1915 when Britain had only six weeks of wheat remaining (and bread was the staple of most working-class diets). Officials made some symbolic gestures to address the problem, such as planting vegetables in the flower plots surrounding the Queen Victoria Memorial in front of Buckingham Palace. But only after a voluntary code failed did the government reluctantly adopt rationing (Pope 1991, 32). The rationing of meat, sugar, butter, margarine, and lard did not even begin until January 1918, and it was another six months before it was fully in place (DeGroot 1996, 90, 201–3).

Two factors further lessened any apparent message about shared sacrifice that rationing might have communicated. First, the government rationed food to districts on the basis of prior consumption patterns, thus allocating more food to the affluent (Monger 2012, 22). Second, a thriving black market reinforced the perception that the rich were secure from sacrifice. The labor newspaper the *Herald* regularly exposed the evasion of food rationing. It published a sensational front-page article (entitled "How They Starve at the Ritz") that mocked the "patriotic rich" who claim to have "tightened their belts."[11] The paper reproduced the Ritz dinner menu: lavish six-course meals of hors d'oeuvres, soup, fish, meat, vegetables, and dessert, and bottomless supplies of cream, cheese, and other luxuries. The article was republished and widely distributed in factories around the country. The *Economist* responded with an editorial decrying this "ignorant extravagance" that was fueling labor demands for (what the *Economist* saw as "inequitable") taxes on the rich.[12] The official in charge of the food supply conceded to Lloyd George that government policy had not created equitable outcomes: "Profiteering is rife in every commodity—bread, meat, tea, butter, and the masses are being exploited right and left" (quoted in DeGroot 1996, 119, 71).

The distribution of sacrifice favored the working class in one sense. A disproportionate number of the nearly three-quarters of a million British servicemen killed came from the upper classes. The vast majority of the officer corps were upper- and upper-middle-class men. Officers suffered disproportionately more casualties than the rank and file, although the ratio narrowed as the war continued.

About 7 percent of the officers and 4 percent of other ranks were killed in the last year of the war (Winter 1985a, 65–66). The average proportion of fatalities among recruits from elite private schools was around 20 percent and during 1916 was over 25 percent (Seldon and Walsh 2013, 240–41). Privilege did not equate with safety. While Antonio Salandra's sons spent the war in cushy billets far from the Italian front, the sons of the leaders of Britain's three main political parties all served (and suffered) at the front. Asquith of the Liberal Party and Henderson of the Labour Party each lost one son. The Conservative Bonar Law lost two.

Regardless of casualty rates (and perhaps because they were appalling whatever the ratio), soaring profits in industry and the inequitable distribution of scarce (but vital) commodities fed the perception of distributive injustice. A British commission on industrial unrest concluded in 1918 that a sense of "inequality of sacrifice" was widespread among the working class (Horne 1991, 299).

Conclusion: A Procedurally Just Strategy

While the military directed Italy's industrial mobilization, the British armed services played no role in the domestic economy. Lloyd George took control of the supply of military material away from the War Ministry. These structures and appointments were not symbolic. As in Italy, some British industrialists wanted the government to use the national emergency to repress labor. They hoped that the prewar practice of using the army to put down industrial unrest would continue.[13] And as in Italy, the wartime legislation—both the Munitions of War Act and DORA—gave the British government extensive powers. The British cabinet considered (but rejected) industrial conscription. Some leading Liberal and Conservative politicians urged its adoption, and as the newly appointed minister of munitions in June 1915, Lloyd George hinted at his support for this "Prussianist" policy (A. Reid 1985a, 62, 65). But for the most part (and unlike Italy), the British government avoided imposing decisions on labor.

Early historiography portrayed the British wartime state as a "servile state" attending to the interests of capital.[14] Business was booming, state contracts were huge, dilution threatened skilled workers, and Lloyd George hired prominent businessmen, the "men of push and go," to fill high-level positions (Simmonds 2012, 70–71). But the influx of businessmen in the Ministry of Munitions did not mean that the wartime state was a business state (Winter 1985b, 36). Industrialists were usually recruited for technical advice, not to formulate labor policy. Employers rarely participated in the design of labor policy after the initial months of the war (Whiteside 1992, 121). The civil servants who directed labor policy were progressive liberals or ex–trade unionists (A. Reid 1985a, 61–66). Many skilled workers did bitterly oppose dilution, and historians once depicted dilution as the work of a repressive state. However, leading unions both agreed to dilution in their negotiations with officials and participated in its implementation. Later research also found that dilution proceeded far less than had been assumed. Employers in the shipbuilding industry often did not want to dilute their workforce; employers were reluctant to hire unskilled women; and strikes to halt dilution often worked (S. Pollard 1983, 46; Tanner 1990, 354–57).[15] The government abandoned its decision to extend dilution to private work (Commons 1922, 712).

Unlike in Italy, there was no wartime offensive against British labor. But there was also no harmony of interest beyond the common desire to defeat Germany. There was serious friction between the government and labor, and there were illegal strikes during the war. Trade unionists resisted the spread of dilution, especially to private work. The shop stewards' movement also gained ground. The government created one commission after the other to study the sources of labor unrest and to provide guidance about how to address it.[16]

Yet ministry officials had become labor allies in workplace struggles. Lloyd George believed that total war meant restructuring state-society relations. Extensive consultations with trade unionists were necessary, and the national interest had priority over employer demands. Throughout the war, employers objected to what they saw as excessive government interference. They complained that Whitehall conceded far too much to labor during arbitration, and they protested their lack of control over the labor force (Cronin 1989, 468; A. Reid 1985a, 62–64). Frustrated by their exclusion from policy making, industrialists created their own association in 1916 to resist trade union influence on government policy. That many trade unionists preferred to work in government-regulated, controlled establishments that restricted trade union practices speaks to this new relationship between labor and the state (Rubin 1984, 317–19). The war years saw the beginning of the bridging of the "two nations" that had characterized Britain.[17]

The British government responded very differently from that of Italy to the demands of modern war. London reached out to labor and adopted a procedurally just strategy to gain its compliance. Chapter 6 assesses the effect of this mobilization strategy on British labor's wartime development. But first, chapter 4 addresses the question of the origins of these strategies. This issue is important. If Italy was too poor or if Italian labor was too radical for Rome to pursue a "British-like" mobilization, then one should focus not on Italy's mobilization strategy but on deeper economic and political constraints.

4

CHOOSING A MOBILIZATION STRATEGY: A COUNTERFACTUAL ANALYSIS

Claims about the *effect* of mobilization policies inevitably raise questions about their *origins*. How much choice was there? States face similar challenges when mobilizing for war, but they do not start in the same place. Britain was much stronger than Italy in 1914. British officials had the economic and political power to choose from a range of strategies to gain labor's compliance with the war effort. But Italy? As a late developer with a weak state, perhaps Rome was destined to adopt procedurally unjust policies that transformed Italian labor and ultimately undermined its fragile democracy. Prewar conditions might have determined Italy's mobilization and so (indirectly) the postwar outcomes themselves, which would make the type of mobilization less important in explaining postwar politics and Fascism's rise.

This chapter examines the origins of Italian policies to mobilize labor. I focus on Italy because it *was* more constrained than Britain. Italy was primarily an agricultural society with a weak democracy when the war began. But Antonio Salandra, Italy's premier in 1914, had choices. Italy's declaration of war was not inevitable. Most Italians supported neutrality and Italy had not been attacked. Most important, once the decision for war was made, Rome was not forced to impose procedurally unjust policies on labor. Counterfactual reasoning suggests that less conservative Italian politicians would have reacted very differently to the demands of total war. The Italian army also had choices in how it mobilized conscripts, as the change in policies following a wartime change in command suggests. Economic and political constraints are important, but mobilization strategies are not set in stone. Policy makers' choices reflect their political philosophies, their political agendas, and the constituents they serve.

Constraints on Italian Choices

The Italian economy had experienced its first "economic miracle" by 1914. The annual industrial growth rate averaged almost 7 percent from 1896 to 1908 (Giuliano Procacci 1968, 285). Modern industrial sectors in steel, engineering, and armaments developed in the industrial triangle around Milan, Turin, and Genoa. Indeed, Italy made the greatest relative economic advance of any major European state between 1901 and 1910 (Lyttelton 2004, 13). Yet Italy's economy lagged behind others in Europe, and especially Britain's. While British industrial workers outnumbered those in agriculture as early as 1815, the Italian rural labor force was still double that of industry on the eve of war (Malefakis 1993, 63–64). Italy's annual steel production—a critical ingredient of modern warfare—was an eighth of the British output (Gibelli 2010, 469; Zamagni 1993, 210).

The British state also had much greater capacity than the Italian one. Britain's strength partially stemmed from the consolidation of its democracy and the development of state institutions, but it was also due to strong ties between state and society. British workers saw themselves as part of a class or a local community, but they also identified with the nation as a whole. Italy had introduced near-universal male suffrage in 1912, and there was freedom of the press and assembly. But the Italian regime of 1915 is best depicted as a limited democracy or, as an Italian historian put it, as a "democracy in the making" (Salvemini 1973, 78). It lacked a functioning party system of government and opposition, and the practice of *trasformismo* (or the use of patronage rather than ideological solidarity to secure a stable parliamentary majority) meant that Parliament did not represent society. Italy also lacked a strong sense of national consciousness, especially among the working class. "*La patria*," explains the writer Curzio Malaparte, "was a conception beyond their power of understanding" (quoted in Whittam 1975, 154). Italian peasants and workers entered the war with little sense of belonging to a larger whole.[1]

Italy's comparatively weak economy and limited democracy did not, however, determine the decision for war or the design of its mobilization policies. Total war requires extensive state intervention, but states have latitude in how they attempt to gain labor's compliance.

Salandra's Choice for War

Refuting the first claim about the inevitability of Italy's intervention is easy. Italy could have avoided war, and it initially did. Italians from across the political spectrum greeted Salandra's declaration of neutrality in August 1914 with relief. Liberals, Socialists, Catholics, workers, peasants, and most deputies in Parliament were neutralist (Gibelli 2010, 466–67). Only a minority on the extreme left and right supported intervention. Attitudes had not appreciably changed when, nine months later, Italy entered the war on the side of the Triple Entente. Polling in April 1915 found widespread support for neutrality (Thayer 1964, 308). Italy was allied with Germany and Austria-Hungary when the war began, but treaty commitments had not required Italy's intervention. Vienna's failure to notify Rome of its decision to attack Serbia freed Italy of treaty obligations. Nor was war forced on Italy. To the contrary, it was Italy that attacked Austria in May 1915 in hopes of conquering territory. It was not until more than two years later, with the defeat at Caporetto in November 1917, that Italy was fighting a war of national defense.

Salandra and his foreign minister Sidney Sonnino engineered Italy's war of choice against the wishes of most Italian politicians and the country at large. Salandra knew the country opposed war, so instead of trying to persuade other politicians on the virtues of intervention, he conducted a "pre-fascist coup d'état" to impose his decision (F. Adler 1995, 92). "Salandra and his collaborators decided to trick them into war, to present them with a *fait accompli*" (Whittam 1975, 150). Salandra and Sonnino negotiated with Britain, France, and Russia about the conditions of Italy's entry without apprising Parliament of the treaty's terms or consulting with important sectors of society. Salandra only told his cabinet about these negotiations five days before committing Italy to war (M. Thompson 2008, 18). The regime did not send the text of the Treaty of London (the secret pact between the Triple Entente and Italy) to Parliament until after the war had ended, in March 1920 (Tasca 1938, 3).

Salandra's Choice for an Unjust Mobilization

The second and more important claim about the inevitability of Italy's choices—that Italy was bound to adopt procedurally unjust policies—requires addressing two questions. First, why did Salandra adopt these policies? Second, would other Italian politicians have made similar choices? The historical record (and counterfactual reasoning) makes clear that Salandra was not backed into a corner. Political preferences, not structural conditions, explain this conservative's decisions for war and an unjust mobilization. Salandra and his allies saw the war as an opportunity to impose policies that would bury Giovanni Giolitti's model of liberal reformism that had dominated Italian politics for much of the past decade. Other politicians, and especially Giolitti himself (who was likely to have governed Italy during the war), were unlikely to have adopted a similar strategy to gain labor's compliance.

A Catalyst for "National Rebirth"

The Salandra government chose mobilization policies that it hoped would advance its *domestic* agenda. Salandra was a wealthy landowner who represented the interests and outlook of the conservative Right. Sonnino had led the traditional Right since the end of the nineteenth century. Both men were anxious about recent developments in Italian politics. They feared the rise of socialism and they objected to the reformist policies of the preceding decade. They especially feared that the adoption of universal manhood suffrage in 1912 would encroach on elite privileges and undermine the status quo (Renzi 1988, 254). Salandra hoped to use the war to reverse the democratic gains of the preceding decade and to restore the dominance of conservative liberalism. Italy needed a war, a former foreign minister explained, "to purify herself politically" (quoted in Jones 1985, 161). The conflict would allow the regime to "effect a veritable revolution in the substance and conduct of domestic affairs" (Saladino 1970, 142).

The agrarian conservatives and industrial elites that Salandra's government represented were increasingly bitter about trends in labor relations before the war. They were hostile to Giolitti's efforts to "domesticate" labor by conceding some rights to it, and they objected to Giolitti's treatment of labor's demands as legitimate. Northern agriculturalists viewed with alarm reforms in Socialist municipalities (Cardoza 1982, 77, 184–85, 213, 220). Industrialists believed that Giolitti's labor policies and his neutrality in labor disputes came at the expense of their rights and interests. These rural and urban elites agreed on the need for a return to an authoritarian control of the workplace and protection from labor militancy (Giovanna Procacci 1992, 152–53). They concurred with Salandra and Sonnino that something had to be done.

These fears came to a head three weeks before the assassination of Archduke Franz Ferdinand. The killing of three workers in June 1914 sparked Red Week, the most significant strike wave in Italy since 1898, and one that required thousands of troops to restore order. This explosion of labor activism created panic within conservative circles and reinforced fears about the Left's growing power. It demonstrated to Sonnino that Giolitti's policies jeopardized the "entire edifice of liberty, civilization, and unity" (quoted in Cardoza 1982, 77).

In this context, the prospect of using war to strengthen conservative forces "proved irresistibly tempting" (Forsyth 1993, 64). One Bolognese explained that war was "an effective remedy against socialism which could be subdued in no other way" (quoted in Jones 1985, 165). It would purge the country of forces that threatened conservative liberalism. "The crisis caused by Red Week in June 1914 was formative for his [Salandra's] premiership, and the advent of the European war a few weeks later was an opportunity that he could not pass up" (M. Thompson 2008, 36). War would justify repressive legislation that would allow a decisive break with the past. The regime could use the war emergency to defeat its internal enemies and to revive the Right's fortunes (Haywood 1999, 409). It could undo the reforms of the prior decade, lessen Parliament's role, destroy the Socialist Party's local power structures, and curb urban and rural labor activism (Bosworth 1979, 378; Tasca 1938, 5). Salandra and his supporters imagined that war would unite the country and restore the army's and the monarchy's prestige. After a rapid victory, a conservative-liberal system would displace the distrusted Giolitti regime.

Historians concur that this domestic agenda was one reason, if not *the* reason, for Italy's entry into the war.[2] The prospect of completing Italian unification through territorial expansion was appealing. Victory would allow Italy to acquire its "unredeemed lands" (or Italian-speaking communities) in the Austrian Empire. But what pushed Salandra to intervene was his conviction that the wartime imposition of strict discipline would cripple the Socialists' and Giolitti's power. "For Salandra was not obsessed by territory. . . . His project was something else; he wanted to move Italian politics permanently to the right" (M. Thompson 2008, 36). A war would upend what Salandra saw as a decade of dangerous policies that had weakened the state and threatened to destroy the established order (Saladino 1970, 142). Salandra explained in his memoirs, "Only a war, with a phase of compulsory peace on the labor front and the militarization of society, would permit the hierarchical reorganisation of class relations" (quoted in M. Thompson 2008, 36). The interventionists who rallied in support of the war during the "Radiant Days of May" in 1915 cried out against an *internal* adversary: "viva la guerra, down with Giolitti, down with the traitors" (quoted in Cardoza 1982, 219). War was just the sort of anti-Giolittian and anti-Socialist strategy that could curb labor activism and reestablish authoritarian control.

The decision for war and the type of mobilization were inextricably linked. While the Catholic masses supported neutrality, the church hierarchy saw war as a way to reimpose discipline, reverse Socialist advances, and marginalize Giolitti from Italian politics (Giovanna Procacci 1992, 152; Webster 1960, 42, 50–52). Middle class support for the war stemmed, in part, from the hope that war would restore a conservative regime and forestall the rise of popular forces that universal manhood suffrage made increasingly likely (Haywood 1999, 430; Renzi 1988,

254; Tasca 1938, 4). The idea of leading his armies into battle appealed to King Vittorio Emanuele, especially as war "could rebut the cartoonists' image of him as a helmet with boots sticking out" (Bosworth 1979, 410). But the king also hoped that war could be used to restore order and discipline, renew the old hierarchies that the rise of popular classes had shaken, and counter the growing power of organized labor (Gibelli 2010, 467). Initially hesitant about intervention, the king changed course after Salandra persuaded him that the choice was either war with Austria-Hungary or revolution at home (M. Thompson 2008, 18). Italy's ambassador in Berlin agreed with Salandra's assessment: "The government now faces a choice between war or revolution, and naturally it will opt for the first to avoid the second" (quoted in Jones 1985, 162).[3]

Italy's unjust mobilization was not a strategy of last resort. It was not the last best choice of officials hemmed in by their state's political and economic weakness. It was Salandra and his conservative supporters' first choice. The war would serve as a catalyst for national rebirth.

How Would Giolitti Have Mobilized Labor?

Addressing the second claim about the inevitability of Italy's procedurally unjust mobilization requires engaging a counterfactual. Would other Italian politicians have reacted similarly to the demands of modern war? The answer is a resounding no. Italy could have met the challenge of World War I with a different political regime with a different domestic agenda. The political record and aspirations of other Italian politicians, and especially Giolitti, fundamentally differed from those of Salandra and his conservative allies. This counterfactual that replaces Salandra with Giolitti as premier during the war is plausible. It requires only a minimal rewrite of history (Tetlock and Belkin 1996). The period 1901–14 is commonly known as the "Giolittian era," when Giolitti was the undisputed leader of Italian politics. He served once as minister of the interior and four times as prime minister, and he wielded decisive influence as the leader of liberal forces in Parliament when out of office. Most observers (including Salandra) expected Giolitti to be governing Italy in August 1914 when war broke out (Saladino 1970, 137). Indeed, political analysts saw Giolitti's resignation in March 1914 as another of the "old fox's" strategic withdrawals. They assumed that Salandra's government was transitional, and that Giolitti would soon return to power (Haywood 1999, 395; Webster 1960, 40).[4]

It is unlikely that Giolitti would have declared war if he was governing Italy. His neutrality was widely known. He was criticized for his opposition to intervention during the "Radiant Days of May." Rumors circulated that the German ambassador had paid Giolitti millions of lire to keep Italy out of the war. The ardent interventionist Gabriele D'Annunzio denounced him and encouraged his supporters to attack Giolitti's home to punish him for not supporting intervention (Peck 1942, 5). Giolitti publicly and privately criticized Salandra's choice for war. He disputed a prominent politician's claim in November 1916 that he (Giolitti) would have entered the war: "Perhaps he did not realize that his statement was the most serious injury that one can inflict on a politician, judging him capable of counseling a policy different from that which he would have followed if he had been in government" (quoted in De Grand 2001b, 209; see also Clark 2014, 234). Giolitti stressed his opposition to war and his belief that Italy was too weak to fight a long war.

Even if Giolitti had chosen war, it stretches the imagination to assume he would have adopted Salandra's procedurally unjust mobilization. After all, Salandra designed his policies to reverse Giolitti's political legacy! Salandra and Sonnino's March 1914 government was the most conservative Italian government in years. It sought to unify liberal factions into a disciplined national party that would reverse socialism's rise and shift power away from Parliament and toward the monarchy and the executive. Repression of labor and leftist forces was integral to that program. Giolitti had endorsed a fundamentally different approach during his years leading Italy. He shared Salandra's understanding of the potential power of popular forces. But Giolitti was a pragmatic reformer who attempted to incorporate new political forces (not repress them). He sought to strengthen and stabilize the liberal regime (not reimpose an authoritarian one). Giolitti hoped that bringing Socialists and Catholics into the political mainstream would temper radical tendencies and avoid the polarization of politics.

One cannot know how Giolitti would have mobilized the economy if he had governed Italy during the war. But his political philosophy, his extensive record in politics, and his critique of Salandra's wartime mobilization provide substantial evidence that he would have eschewed Salandra's procedurally unjust approach. Giolitti understood the importance of procedural justice, even if he would not have used that term. He believed that the popular classes should be incorporated into the liberal order, and that the working class needed its own political and economic organizations. Had Giolitti led Italy during the war, it is unlikely that he would have done as Salandra and imposed labor's "representatives" on them. Nor is it likely that he would have excluded labor from participating in decisions that affected it. Giolitti saw labor as "an inevitable movement that no force will succeed in arresting" (quoted in Cardoza 1982, 69). This recognition of organized labor as a legitimate economic and political actor would have been especially likely during a total war, when labor's participation is key to military victory.

PRAGMATIC INCLUSION AND JUSTICE

Salandra's conviction that the liberal Right had an exclusive claim on power and his determination to use the war to restore an authoritarian regime ruled out the creation of cross-party coalitions. The two reformist leaders of the Socialist Party, Filippo Turati and Claudio Treves, had reached out to Salandra in May 1915. They offered to support his wartime government, and they suggested that their presence could help "rally the masses to the national cause" (quoted in Bosworth 2005, 60–61). Salandra spurned their offer even though this gesture might have broadened the weak popular support for the war. Salandra could not imagine a *union sacrée* as a necessary or legitimate way to govern Italy. In contrast, it is likely that Giolitti would have created a national unity government in wartime, as politicians in Paris and London had done.

Giolitti had a long record of pragmatic inclusion. He would reach out to whatever parliamentary group might work with him, including the Socialist Party. Giolitti had watched the rise of left-wing forces, and he had become convinced that socialism would play a role in Italian politics. After the PSI's formation in 1892, Socialists gained control over several important communes, and they increased their representation in Parliament. The key to managing these developments, Giolitti believed, was to give Socialists a stake in the constitutional order. Giolitti invited Socialists to accept positions in his government in 1903 and 1911 (Agócs 1971, 652; Salvemini 1973, 77). These efforts failed, but they signaled Giolitti's belief that Socialists were acceptable partners and legitimate representatives of their class. The PSI's parliamentary delegation supported three of Giolitti's governments, and Socialist deputies promoted, and sometimes helped draft, Giolitti's social legislation. Giolitti also gave the Socialist press more latitude than it had previously enjoyed (De Grand 1989, 17–19).

Giolitti's inclination to integrate popular forces extended to Catholics as well, who were also emerging as an important political force. Pope Pius IX had refused to recognize the newly formed Italian state, and he and his successors forbade Catholics from voting, as it would imply a recognition of the Italian Kingdom (which had seized the Papal States). The Vatican revised this policy in 1904 because it feared that Catholic electoral abstention could mean victory for the Socialist Left. Catholics could now vote to prevent the election of "subversives" (F. Adler 1995, 15). Giolitti reached out to this new electoral force. He especially welcomed the support of the Catholic masses when he hoped to use a liberal-Catholic alliance to counter gains that Socialists were likely to make after his 1912 electoral reform (Agócs 1971, 653; Forsyth 1993, 25). This legislation was the most significant piece of Giolitti's program of political "domestication" (and is additional evidence of Giolitti's support for procedural justice). Through his efforts, and despite vocal opposition from the Right, Giolitti enacted near-universal male suffrage six years before it came to Britain. The 1912 act extended the vote to all men over twenty-one who had completed military service and all men over thirty regardless of property or literacy. It tripled the size of the electorate, enfranchising industrial workers and most peasants and rural laborers.

Giolitti rejected the conservative Right's view that labor unions were inherently subversive. "The workers' organizations have a right to be represented in the same way as the industrialists and merchants," Giolitti declared before Parliament in 1901 (quoted in Hilton-Young 1949, 54). Labor unions were "a very noble intermediary between capital and labor," he noted a decade later. If the labor movement had appeared otherwise, Giolitti reasoned, this was because "they felt themselves systematically persecuted" (quoted in Cardoza 1982, 69). Giolitti saw unions as legitimate vehicles to realize working-class interests, and he protected collective bargaining rights. During a parliamentary debate about a proposal to outlaw strikes, Giolitti chided one of the bill's sponsors that he should know better. It was almost impossible "to walk a horse backwards" and even more difficult to "walk the world backwards" (quoted in Agócs 1971, 642).

Giolitti approached the labor movement through conciliation, not force (De Grand 1989, 5). He believed that preventing economic grievances from becoming dangerous political ones required settlements that recognized the validity of labor's claims. He rejected as counterproductive prior governments' almost automatic repression of leftist forces. He believed that repression failed to address the source of the unrest and it helped unite the socialist movement and fuel radical tendencies (Agócs 1971, 642; Pernicone 1974). "I believe we have got to make the capitalist and the worker equal before the law," Giolitti explained to fellow parliamentarians in 1901. "The friends of order have a duty to persuade the working class, and to persuade them with deeds, not words, that they have more to hope from the present order than from dreams of the future" (quoted in Hilton-Young 1949, 54).

Giolitti adopted a new approach to labor from the start of his first premiership in 1892. He refused to dispatch security forces to crush a series of unprecedentedly large strikes by Sicilian miners and rural laborers. Giolitti saw their actions to improve their living conditions as legitimate. And he stuck to his policy despite "mounting conservative hysteria" in Parliament, and the knowledge that it might lead to his government's collapse (Agócs 1971, 641). Giolitti dealt harshly with public employees, and he would repress violent labor unrest (De Grand 2001a, 63; Forsyth 1993, 19, 25). But as long as he was in power, private employers could no longer rely on Carabinieri to settle peaceful labor disputes. Giolitti argued that using armed force to put down strikes was "illegal, impolitic, and impossible" (quoted in Hilton-Young 1949, 51). He announced in 1901 that his government would remain neutral in economic disputes between labor and management, effectively assuming an unprecedented stance that favored the working class. Giolitti ordered a prefect in Emilia-Romagna in 1906 to "make the agrarians understand that the government cannot aid them in unjust actions. . . . I do not intend to provoke conflicts in order to reinforce the excessive demands of the agrarians" (quoted in Cardoza 1982, 114).

Giolitti persisted in his refusal to side with employers and to use force against labor. He dismissed calls for repression as "illegal and politically unwise" during a large strike wave of industrial and agricultural workers in the north and center of Italy in 1910. He criticized what he saw as employers' shortsighted resistance to labor's reasonable demands. He neither jailed the strike leaders nor crushed local Socialist organizations, which prompted a Socialist official to comment that Giolitti was not "attempting as others before him, to suffocate [unions] in the cradle" (quoted in Cardoza 1982, 72). Giolitti again supported striking workers in 1913, leading an analyst to note that his tenure marked "a fundamental turning point in Italian history" (Riley 2010, 25). Giolitti's stance on labor disputes so enraged industrial elites that they organized the first business association to defend their interests (F. Adler 1995, 29).

Giolitti's record provides ample evidence that he was likely to have adopted procedurally just policies if he had been responsible for mobilizing Italy's economy for war. He likely would have included labor and its representatives in decision making and demonstrated respect for the working class. Giolitti felt that labor's organizations had the right to a seat at the table. But he never appeared to have understood the new era of mass politics, which raises doubts about whether he would have developed policies to explain to workers why their sacrifices were necessary. Unlike Salandra, Giolitti understood that intervention would require the total mobilization of Italian resources. This recognition might have inclined him to develop policies to persuade the Italian masses that the war was worth fighting. But that supposition takes us beyond the historical record. "[Giolitti] regarded politics as a game to be played by a select few through backstage deals and considered the masses, at best, manipulated extras on the political scene" (Agócs 1971, 653). Perhaps the latter view would have encouraged Giolitti to develop a meaningful propaganda program to manipulate those extras, but there is little evidence from Giolitti's political career that supports this claim. However, his record on other aspects of procedural justice is overwhelming.

FAVORABLE AND FAIR OUTCOMES

Giolitti coupled his conviction that repressing labor would not work to a belief that economic concessions would. He believed that satisfying reasonable economic demands would avoid the politicization of workplace disputes. Concessions would isolate radicals and strengthen the liberal regime. Indeed, Giolitti was often exasperated with industrial and rural elites' resistance to what he saw as sensible economic reforms to improve the lives of the poor, which he insisted was one of the government's main tasks (Agócs 1971). "The State could have no interest" in restraining wage growth, Giolitti explained (quoted in Horowitz 1963, 48). He encouraged employers to develop an enlightened self-interest that could help persuade the masses that the government served more than the privileged few. "In this way, he hoped to edge Marx off the political stage" (D. Smith 1969, 217, 50).

Giolitti's support for collective bargaining encouraged the growth of labor organizations. Unions, rural leagues, and cooperatives spread rapidly during the decade before the war (Neufeld 1961, 321–55). Giolitti's neutrality in labor disputes also unleashed a wave of industrial and agricultural strikes. The labor movement could now act without fear of government repression. More than a thousand strikes involving close to two hundred thousand industrial workers occurred in 1901; no more than a few thousand workers had struck in the preceding years. The number of strikes in the countryside exploded as well, outpacing industrial strikes and stretching from northern commercial farms to southern Italy (Neufeld 1961, 547; Giuliano Procacci 1968, 208, 309, 317). All this organization and activism paid off. Organized labor won concessions during the Giolittian era that would have been unimaginable just a few years earlier. The real wages of industrial workers rose by about 40 percent between 1900 and 1913 (Corner 2002b, 23; Lyttelton 2002, 2).

Giolitti also promoted progressive reforms that laid the foundation for the Italian welfare state. While infuriating conservative liberals, he declared that he would adopt "whatever was reasonable in the socialist program" (quoted in Agócs 1971, 652). Giolitti's introduction of a life insurance bill (originally a Socialist proposal) prompted a leading industrialist to quip, "Our Giolitti had become for the moment Comrade Giolitti" (quoted in De Grand 2001b, 177). Giolitti supported moderate policies that he hoped would preempt the development of anti-regime forces. These policies included limited accident and disability insurance, the regulation of female and child labor, shorter working hours, a mandatory twenty-four-hour weekly holiday, and sickness and retirement insurance. Giolitti increased spending on public works by 50 percent between 1900 and 1907, helping to reduce unemployment (Duggan 2008, 363). His government also established the Worker's Inspectorate to supervise the application of labor laws, the Labor Office to gain a better understanding of labor conditions, the Council on Labor to draft social legislation, and agencies to address the needs of the unemployed and disabled (De Grand 1989, 15–19; Forsyth 1993, 25; Miller 1990, 27). Unsurprisingly, Salandra renounced these policies as "unjustified negation[s] of the fundamental principles of liberalism and the frank acceptance of the postulates of socialism" (quoted in Cardoza 1982, 195).

Early in the war, Giolitti criticized Salandra's mobilization policies and called for a new approach. He believed that the government should adopt policies that would "develop production which would boost working-class morale . . . [by] . . . responding to the immediate needs of the proletariat" (quoted in D'Alonzo 2001, 35). These "immediate needs" are likely to have included the provision of distributive justice. Salandra assumed that an unequal distribution of wealth was natural and inevitable, and as premier during World War I, he was indifferent to whether his policies promoted a sense of shared sacrifice. But Giolitti recognized that government policies could prevent the perception of inequity that often sparked labor unrest. In a Senate speech in 1901, Giolitti referenced a prefect's report that argued that the perception of distributive injustice (landowners' incomes had increased while rural laborers' had not) had triggered a local strike. Giolitti supported the legalization of unions and the right of collective action in part to realize a more balanced distribution of the economy's wealth (Agócs 1971, 640–44).

Giolitti also sought to develop an equitable tax system. Taxes on consumption that weighed heavily on the working class were the principal source of state revenue (Webster 1960, xi). Giolitti described this situation as "a paradise for the rich who were taxed to the minimum while they exploited to the utmost the industrial and agricultural proletariat" (Agócs 1971, 639). Giolitti reduced the taxes on food after learning that salt was taxed at a much higher rate than alcohol and tobacco (D. Smith 1969, 250). He introduced proposals for death duties and a progressive income tax to shift some of the burden to industrial and rural elites. These efforts failed, but Giolitti's pursuit of a fairer tax system illustrates his recognition of the importance of distributive justice. It also suggests that he would have been attuned to this issue in wartime when demands for shared sacrifice are especially strong.

The Giolittian era had been a "remarkable period for Italy," one of significant political and economic reform (Forsyth 1993, 21). Giolitti deserves credit for the adoption of near-universal manhood suffrage, the refusal to repress labor, and the beginnings of a welfare state. But Giolitti was no angel. He excelled in the practice of *trasformismo*, and he tried his best to manipulate the electorate. Nonetheless, his prewar policies look so good partly because Salandra's wartime policies were so extreme. And that is the point. Salandra adopted one set of policies to mobilize Italy's economy for war. They may appear inevitable given conditions in prewar Italy, but that is an illusion of hindsight (Fischoff 1982). People often perceive historical events as having been more predictable than they were at the time. As Philip Tetlock and Aaron Belkin (1996, 15) remind us, counterfactuals are useful correctives to "creeping determinism."

How Diaz Mobilized Soldiers

Establishing that the Italian army was not destined to enforce its procedurally unjust policies does not require counterfactual reasoning. When the wartime leadership of the army changed, so did its policies. The Italian officer corps agreed about the value of frontal assaults (though Luigi Cadorna's faith in them was extreme), but the General Staff had not developed a clear philosophical concept of war. The General Staff and the Military Academy were weak institutions. Italian military thought changed often, and officers had flexibility in the field (Gooch 1986, 311–14). Operational success was due to an individual commander's ability, not guiding principles or central control (Gooch 2010, 171).

The Italian army was not fated to discipline its soldiers as Cadorna had. Other Italian officers, such as General Armando Diaz, had different ideas about how to gain conscripts' compliance with the war effort. There had been a lively debate in Italian military journals before the war about the value of different forms of discipline. The army's regulations from as early as 1872 stressed that obedience should be gained through "personal conviction" and "not through fear of punishment" (quoted in Wilcox 2016, 76, 65–69). Cadorna disagreed with this approach and, from September 1914, pushed for harsher regulations. He succeeded in creating his (but not the inevitable) disciplinary regime. The army's practices became "increasingly ferocious" under Cadorna's command (Gooch 2014, 80).

Diaz became the chief of staff after Cadorna was forced out following the Caporetto disaster in November 1917. "The new field Commander of the Italian armies was different in every way from his predecessor," a foremost historian on the Italian army concludes. Diaz introduced a "revolution in military affairs" to correct many of Cadorna's policies (Gooch 2014, 247). Diaz's new tactical system was important, as the army's success at Vittorio Veneto in 1918 illustrated (Gooch 1986, 315). But his greatest reforms came in the management of morale.[5] Like most modern officers, Diaz understood its importance. His decision to shift from coercing conscripts to act to persuading them of its importance was a "dramatic break from his predecessor's [Cadorna's] principles" (Wilcox 2016, 51). Diaz created the army's propaganda agency to inspire conscripts, and he improved living conditions. He also adjusted the army's disciplinary regime. He did not abolish harsh punishments. Indeed, in some cases, such as for desertion, punishments became more severe. But Diaz eliminated the most procedurally unjust practices (summary executions and decimation). He also returned the army's disciplinary system to its prewar (or pre-Cadorna) provisions. Diaz was concerned about due process, accountability, and proof of guilt (Wilcox 2016, 76–87). The army's disciplinary system was procedurally fairer under him than it had been under Cadorna.

Predicated on an Illusion
(and So Not Inevitable)

Any Italian leader would have faced the same constraints in 1915. Italy was a weak state, with a weak economy and a working class with little allegiance to the state. But these factors did not require the adoption of unjust policies on the home front or the battlefield. To the contrary, less repressive and more concessionary policies would have better suited the Italian context and the war Italy fought. Salandra and Cadorna remained set in their ways, but other politicians and military officers recognized the need for different policies. Indeed, the longer the war lasted, the more pressure the government felt to adapt its mobilization to the situation at hand. Officials increasingly recognized that Salandra's approach was unsustainable. They had to try something new. Rome never let up on its repression of "defeatists," but Salandra's successors began to include reformist unions in some decision-making bodies and to increase labor's compensation.

Italy's mobilization became untenable because it was based on a false assumption: the belief that the war would be short and require only partial mobilization. Salandra knew that the need for munitions would be great, but he assumed the demand would be temporary. When Italy intervened in May 1915, Salandra was confident that Italy's offensive into Austria would bring victory within months (Jones 1985, 165; Renzi 1988, 265). He saw no need to prepare a winter campaign or the mass mobilization of the nation's resources. His initial request for a loan from Britain would cover one month of war. Italy would fight a limited war that would realize Italy's territorial aims, destroy the Socialists and Giolittians, and restore the conservative Right's political dominance.

Believing in the possibility of lightening offensives in August 1914 was misguided. A series of conflicts had shown that the tactical advantage lay with defending forces. But this misperception was common. Most European capitals and their high commands expected the war to be short. But to continue to believe in a swift victory in the spring of 1915 was fantastical. Italy entered the war after nine months of grueling offensives had confirmed the bleak lesson that fire kills. Modern firepower had transformed the Battle of the Marne into a bloody stalemate, and the Allied offensives in spring 1915 had failed miserably. Despite thousands of casualties and an unquenchable thirst for munitions, the war was no closer to termination than when it had begun.

Many European leaders responded to these battlefield realities. They discarded illusions of quick victory and revised mobilization plans. By December 1914, most Whitehall officials understood that they were facing a long conflict. It would not be "business as usual" at home while the army's professional forces defeated Germany abroad. Salandra and his supporters could have done likewise. A glance at the western front should have alerted them to the enormous difficulties of advancing against modern firepower. But they could have revised their policies on the basis of more than newspaper accounts. The Italian government had detailed knowledge about how the war was being fought. From August 1914 to May 1915, Italian military attachés in Paris and Berlin regularly sent home reports that accurately described the strength of the defensive (Haywood 1999, 442). Yet Cadorna explained away these reports, asserting that conditions on the western front were unique and would rarely repeat themselves on the Italian front (Gooch 2010, 176–77). Salandra's and Cadorna's wishful thinking was all the more remarkable given that they were planning to attack on terrain that was among the most challenging in Europe. Italian troops would have to fight uphill across rocky, mountainous terrain. Predictably, these offensives led to 250,000 casualties (a quarter of the army) within six months but with no real progress (Absalom 1995, 89–90).

Sidney Sonnino later acknowledged that the war was more demanding than the government had anticipated, commenting that it was "completely different from those of the past." But he had no answer when he was then queried about why he had not grasped the nature of modern warfare during nine months of Italian neutrality (quoted in Haywood 1999, 442–43). Sonnino and his supporters held fast to the illusion that their war would be different. A short war was necessary for domestic political reasons, so they persuaded themselves a quick victory was likely. By force of will, their war would not degenerate into a bloody stalemate (Gooch 1986, 314).

Other Italian policy makers—including those without access to the military attachés' reports—understood the reality before them. They grasped that Italy would fight a long war, and they recognized its implications for the Italian economy. In November 1914 (six months before Italy's intervention), Giolitti argued that Italian offensives were likely to fail. He did not share Salandra's confidence that the Italian army would quickly move from Ljubljana to Trieste and then on to Vienna. Giolitti feared that intervention would lead to an Austrian offensive and the loss of Italian territory to foreign occupation, as Caporetto later confirmed (Renzi 1988, 247). The prominent politician Francesco Nitti also believed that a war would become protracted and that it would require the mass mobilization of the country's resources (Jones 1985, 165). Indeed, Antonino di San Giuliano, Italy's foreign minister in August 1914, argued for neutrality because he did not believe Italy could sustain a long war (Gooch 2010, 160).

Italy's unjust (and dysfunctional and unrealistic) mobilization was not inevitable. It was predicated on an illusion, not Italy's needs and constraints. Salandra and Cadorna designed mobilization policies for a war they wanted to fight, not the one that others knew Italy was likely to face. Those with a realistic appraisal of the war ahead of them, including Giolitti, were likely to adopted policies better suited to the strategic realities before them. These policies would not have been designed with the goal of undoing the prior decade of liberal policies. It takes more than a minimal rewrite to imagine Giolitti intentionally designing policies to reverse the very policies that he had spent more than ten years putting in place.

Conclusion: A "Strategy" of Choice Divorced from Reality

Policy makers must balance immediate and long-term interests. Industrial productivity is critical, but they are also thinking past the wartime emergency. Italy's leaders were extreme in their intention to use what they believed would be a short, victorious war to reconstruct their preferred peacetime state, but concerns about how wartime policies shape postwar politics are common. Politicians have different constituencies with different political goals. These differences persist in wartime, and they influence the design of mobilization policies.

Giolitti and Salandra were not alone in disagreeing about the role organized labor should play in the domestic political economy. How France mobilized for World War II also depended on which political faction was in power. The center-right and right-wing leaders governing France limited state intervention in part because they feared the implications of large-scale intervention for the postwar order. They sided with leading industrialists and endorsed laissez-faire policies "with the burden falling disproportionately on labor" (Imlay 2003, 244). In contrast, if the center-left and left had dominated French politics in 1939, France would have fought World War II with greater state intervention and with policies that were sympathetic to labor demands (Imlay 2003, 255–71). Structural constraints influence how states mobilize their economies, but they do not determine the response. Politics and political beliefs are fundamental to the problems one sees and the solutions one selects (Kier 1997).

However intentional a state's mobilization, the term *strategy* imposes an improbable degree of coordination. Sometimes these policies are divorced from reality, as illustrated by Salandra's insistence that Italy's war would be short and a total mobilization unnecessary. Italy lacked anything resembling a coordinated plan. The artillery, engineering corps, and air force were expected to implement policies that were also the responsibility of the Ministry of Industrial Mobilization. The regional committees often worked at cross-purposes with other government agencies. Even subunits within the same ministry failed to coordinate (F. Adler 1995, 111). An inquiry revealed that almost three hundred agencies reported to six different ministries that had the authority to allocate resources for the war. "Financial chaos" and "administrative confusion" typified Italy's economic mobilization (Corner and Procacci 1997, 227; Galassi and Harrison 2005, 280–86; Zamagni 1993).

Misguided and confused mobilizations are not peculiar to Italy or a product of its weak state. Berlin's plans to increase munitions production in 1916 bore no relationship to German resources. This mismatch between the Hindenburg Program and German power led Gerald Feldman (1966, 150), in his influential study of German mobilization, to refer to Berlin's plans as "representing the triumph, not of imagination, but of fantasy." In their desire to increase productivity, "Germany's leaders increasingly took refuge in a fantasy world that allowed them to ignore the constraints within which they had to operate" (Bessel 2000, 445; see also Hancock 1991, 12). British policy during World War I was more realistic, but London never developed coherent mobilization policies (French 1982, 25–26; Noel Whiteside 1992, 122). R. H. Tawney's (1943, 6) classic account of wartime control notes, "The system, if such it can be called, was only to a small extent the result of design, and, even at its zenith . . . was rarely, if ever, envisaged as a whole. . . . It was not deliberately constructed at all." The Ministry of Munitions, the Coal Controller, the Ministry of Shipping, the Railway Executive, and the Air Ministry all had authority over labor in the controlled establishments. A career civil servant in the Ministry of Labour noted, "The full story of the chaos and confusion over the wages policy in the First World War would never be told" (quoted in Corfield 1993, 21). There was not even a central authority over the vital manpower issue. The Ministry of National Service, the Admiralty, a variety of smaller administrative units, and the newly formed Ministries of Munitions and Labour all played a role (Turner 1992, 165–67; Noel Whiteside 1992, 122). The chair of the Committee of Production derided this situation: "In labour matters the Government had no policy, never gave signs of having a policy, and could not be induced to have a policy" (Askwith 1920, 443).

Some of this disorder was intentional. The Conservatives' unease about granting power to organized labor partially explains the overlapping authority in labor policy. The Tories knew that industrial conflict would reemerge after the war, and they sought to contain labor's power (Turner 1992, 195, 369). Britain's administrative confusion also stemmed from ideological resistance to an expansion in state authority and the novelty of a total war (DeGroot 1996, 80, 105–6). World War I was aptly (if prematurely) called the Great War. Policy makers had never experienced anything like it, and many officials learned from their experiences. To avoid the social unrest that erupted in Germany during World War I, Nazi officials sought to avoid the food shortages and profiteering that had plagued Berlin's first mobilization for total war (Hancock 1991, 12–14). British officials also improved their management of the economy from one war to the next. London refused to allow the military's manpower targets to drive planning after

1939 (Winter 1985a, 39). States also learn from one another. Britain sent a team of experts to Washington to advise the American war effort after US entry in 1917 (Hoague, Brown, and Marcus 1940, 54). National Socialist leaders in Germany also claimed to have learned the vital role of propaganda from British efforts during World War I.

Regardless of improvements from one war to the next, or learning from others, these mobilization strategies were not finely tuned, efficient, or, most important, determinate responses to structural constraints. Beyond the common goal of maintaining productivity, policy makers differ in their objectives and how they seek to achieve them. Many factors intrude between the goals that authorities pursue and the means they adopt to realize them. The Italian government chose its mobilization policies largely in response to its domestic agenda. Rome sought to use war to return to the conservative policies of the pre-Giolittian era. This strategy was poorly adapted to industrialized warfare, and it was one of many that Italian politicians could have adopted (and were likely to have adopted). But once chosen, this strategy had profound consequences for labor's wartime development. As the next chapter details, Italy's procedurally unjust mobilization transformed labor's interests, identity, and attitudes about the state in ways that dramatically altered the terms of postwar politics.

ITALIAN LABOR'S
REVOLUTIONARY SOCIALISM

Italy was a late developer. The state nationalized railroads, promoted protection-
ist policies, and was active in industrial development. Yet in the two decades before World War I, officials rarely intervened in industrial relations. Under the
leadership of Giovanni Giolitti, the government remained neutral in economic
disputes between labor and employers. Giolitti sought to prevent economic grievances from becoming political ones. Mobilization for war turned economic disputes into political ones. State officials intervened in industrial and agricultural
relations as never before. Military officers took charge of discipline in factories,
promoted modest reforms to improve factory conditions, and supplanted employers in negotiations over pay and working conditions. Massive state intervention also occurred in the rural economy, as the state requisitioned crops, set prices,
conscripted soldiers, and froze contracts. Across the board, mobilization increased
the state's presence in working-class life. It brought workers face-to-face with the
state on the factory floor, in farmers' fields, and on the front lines.

Officials had hoped that granting some economic concessions to labor would
forestall the emergence of political conflict, but the state's active role in the wartime economy politicized the working class.[1] This reaction was common across
Europe. World War I transformed the relationship between economic and political activity, and workers increasingly sought to influence wartime state agencies. Where Italy stands apart, especially compared with other victorious nations,
is the type of mobilization it developed, and how these policies influenced labor's
development.

Antonio Salandra's choice for procedurally unjust policies transformed what had been troubled industrial relations with pockets of radical and syndicalist demands into a revolutionary situation. Up and down the peninsula, and in cities and the countryside, Italy's mobilization radicalized labor, created an unprecedented level of labor solidarity, and alienated labor from the state. Whatever the organizational form—whether the PSI or rural and urban unions—Italian labor moved decisively to the left, and away from the liberal state. An opportunity had been lost. Whereas wars often strengthen society's allegiance to the state, Italian labor's wartime encounter with the state increased the divide. That the Great War did not "make" Italians is surprising. It was the type of war that often builds nationalism, and Italian leaders expected intervention to complete the nation-building process. But Italy's procedurally unjust mobilization transformed labor's indifference toward the state and acquiescence to its war into a furious denunciation of both. Italy's unforced error turned an opportunity into a crisis.

Assessing my three hypotheses requires detailing the Italian labor movement's interests, identity, and political attitudes before, during, and after the war. Identifying the extraordinary influence of the state's mobilization policies requires explaining how preferences form, how identities change, and why—contrary to conventional expectations—the war failed to build Italian nationalism. Chapter 7 then examines how labor's wartime transformation influenced postwar politics and led to Italy's descent into Fascism.

From Reform to Revolution: A Change of Interest

The PSI was born reformist in 1892. It had to contend with revolutionary and syndicalist factions, but the party and its affiliated industrial and rural unions were reformist before the war. This moderation persisted during the early years of the war, but the government's unjust mobilization radicalized the labor movement. This swing to the left emerged in the spring and summer of 1917 and it intensified in the last year of the war, peaking during the Red Years of 1919–20. This radicalization meant different things to different workers. For those in the Turin munitions industry, it meant worker control of the factories. For peasant leagues in the Po Valley and sharecroppers in Tuscany, it meant direct control of the workplace. For peasants in the south, it meant the division of estates among landless peasants. Each demand posed a revolutionary challenge, and together they confirm hypothesis 1: procedurally unjust mobilizations encourage radical demands.

Pragmatic Reformism: Socialism before the War

The PSI's first program in 1893 sought to correct the injustices of the current political and economic order. It outlined reformist goals, and the Socialist leader, Filippo Turati, adopted conventional methods to reform the state from within (Clough 1968, 252). The PSI agreed in 1895 that universal suffrage was its key objective, and five years later, it approved interclass alliances. The PSI cooperated with bourgeois parties to win economic, social, and political reforms, and it allied with the Radical and Republican Parties, especially in the south (Craver 1996, 203; De Grand 1989, 17, 23). With little resistance from competing leadership factions or the rank and file, Socialists supported Giuseppe Zanardelli's liberal government (1901–3). Turati considered but declined Giolitti's invitation to join the government in 1903.

Italy's socialist movement had a "maximalist" wing that fought reformists for control of the party.[2] These factions opposed seeking concessions through cooperation with the bourgeois state. They feared that reforms would lead to minimal improvements while domesticating labor and derailing a proletariat victory. This revolutionary wing was slow to emerge as a true competitor. The failure of the 1904 general strike halted its rise and confirmed the reformists' dominance. With support of the trade unions (and revolutionaries a minority), the moderate wing triumphed at the PSI congresses in 1908 and 1910 (Clough 1968, 261–90; De Grand 1989, 22–24). The 1908 congress declared syndicalism incompatible with the PSI, and two years later, the congress endorsed social insurance and salaries for deputies. Speaking in Parliament in 1911, Giolitti observed that the Socialists had "relegated Karl Marx to the attic" (quoted in Clough 1968, 279). Giolitti understood that the parliamentary group and party leaders embraced reformist goals. He was confident that his proposal for universal suffrage would not threaten the liberal regime (Horowitz 1963, 52–56).

Revolutionaries took advantage of controversy over war in Libya (1911) to push the PSI to the left. Moderates lost control of the party at the 1912 and 1914 congresses (De Grand 1989, 23–25). These developments did not mean that revolutionaries drove the PSI between 1912 and 1914. When they controlled the directorate (the party's executive committee), they were reluctant to endorse positions that would deprive Socialists of benefits that came from working with the liberal state (Horowitz 1963, 58). Most important, the directorate guided the PSI on paper, but in practice the parliamentary group and local party associations dominated party life. Both remained moderate. The PSI was a confederation of local and regional organizations, not a centrally controlled party. Socialists helped provide housing, health care, and other social services at the local level. They had little contact with Socialist organizations in other regions, and their link to the national level was through their parliamentary deputy, not the party direc-torate. The Socialist-controlled local governments—the mayors and council members in small and medium-size municipalities—were all reformists (Bertrand 1976, 106; Giuliano Procacci 1979, 29). Irrespective of who dominated the direc-torate, reformists controlled the parliamentary group (the other main focus of PSI activities), as well as the vast majority of trade unions (De Grand 1989, 19–25).

Historians remark on the growing conservatism of the labor movement that Giolitti's "domestication" engendered before the war (Horowitz 1963, 60). Rela-tively free from government repression, unions struck for higher wages, and union density (or the proportion of trade union members out of those legally eligible to join a union) increased. The syndicalist challenge never disappeared, but by 1905, and especially after the failure of the 1904 general strike, moderates dominated the trade union movement. Reformists continued to consolidate their hold (Horowitz 1963, 47–60). They created labor's principal representative in 1906—the General Confederation of Labor (Confederazione Generale di Lavoro; CGL)—which brought together most non-Catholic labor organizations. The CGL was affiliated with the PSI, but it saw its role as separate from politics: it focused on improving pay and working conditions (Horowitz 1963, 47–96). The extreme Left never threatened the CGL's moderate leadership (De Grand 1989, 20; Pernicone 1974). The CGL remained reformist (and more moderate than the PSI), and it had good working relationships with the bourgeois Radical and Republican Parties (Giuliano Procacci 1979, 39–41). Organized labor had, according to one historian, "succumbed to bourgeois materialism" (Roberts 1979, 89).

Giolitti's enlightened labor policies also led to an explosive growth in agricul-tural unions, especially in northern Italy, where commercial agriculture em-ployed a large rural proletariat. Created in 1901, the Socialist-led Federation of Agricultural Laborers (Federterra) organized landless workers (or day laborers, the *braccianti*) in the northern regions of Emilia-Romagna, Lombardy, Piedmont, and Veneto.[3] The Federterra became the largest organization of rural workers, and it had more members than any industrial or commercial union (Cardoza 1982, 7, 55–71). These agricultural leagues were affiliated with the CGL, and they were an important source of PSI's mass support. But the Federterra set its own policies and concentrated on representing the *braccianti*, running employment offices, and negotiating labor contracts. Despite the Federterra's refrain of "land to the peasants" and its long-term goal of radical change, it did not advocate land expropriation or collectivization. It focused on the immediate economic goal of improving the daily lives of agricultural workers (Cardoza 1991, 193; Sarti 2004, 272).

The Socialist Party's Wartime Radicalization

The PSI and the CGL adopted the slogan "Neither support nor sabotage" when Italy declared war in May 1915. This neutral stance meant that the government did not see the PSI as a threat to stability (Bertrand 1976, 106). This position also allowed the working class to express its antimilitarism while providing space for those who supported the war (Gibelli 2010, 466). For example, the CGL and local Socialist administrations organized war relief and assistance to soldiers' families (De Grand 1989, 28). The PSI endorsed a moderate program in spring 1917 when the CGL, the PSI directorate, and the parliamentary group adopted *Peace and the Postwar Period*. This program was a typical basket of reformist goals, such as universal suffrage, social insurance, and progressive taxation. It was a platform that could be pursued in coordination with bourgeois parties (Horowitz 1963, 129; Tasca 1938, 12–13). Pragmatic reformism appeared to have won the day. The PSI's "revolutionary vision had not yet crystalized" (De Grand 1989, 29).

Months of a relentlessly unjust mobilization radicalized Italian labor. By the fall of 1917, the formula "Neither support nor sabotage" could no longer contain divisions within the socialist movement (Lyttelton 2004, 26). Reformists in Parliament and at the local level encouraged labor to support Italy after the military disaster at Caporetto in November 1917. Turati and Claudio Treves, the PSI's reformist leaders, published an article calling on the working class to defend Italy. Turati declared in Parliament, "It is our Fatherland, too, that is fighting" (quoted in Hilton-Young 1949, 83; see also Seton-Watson 1967, 482–83). But the majority within the PSI disagreed (Knox 2007, 219). They refused to support the war or even a policy of inaction. It was time to fight *against* the war and *for* revolution (Bertrand 1976, 106, 114). The Socialist who had coined the slogan "Neither support nor sabotage" now chose the latter. He urged Socialist mayors to encourage conscripts to desert (Seton-Watson 1967, 470). Other Socialist leaders called on Italy's conscripts to turn their rifles on their officers and the government (Hilton-Young 1949, 83).

The balance of power within the PSI had shifted. Reformists were now marginalized. In April 1918, revolutionaries in the directorate forced the party's leading moderates to resign from a government commission on postwar reconstruction (De Grand 1989, 33). This radicalization became more pronounced at the PSI's September 1918 congress (the first since the war began). Revolutionary rhetoric drowned out any remnants of reformism. The congress opened with a "thunderous acclamation" to Vladimir Lenin. Maximalists (or revolutionaries) obtained a crushing majority, gaining three-quarters of the vote to the reformists' 13 percent (Farneti 1978, 11). "That victory confirmed the estrangement of the PSI's remaining reformists from their own party and from the masses" (Knox 2007, 219). The congress condemned interclass alliances and it rejected its wartime platform, *Peace and the Postwar Period*, as "far too feeble and reformist" (Tasca 1938, 14; see also Seton-Watson 1967, 512). The PSI no longer saw its future within the liberal state. Following the Russian lead appeared an increasingly plausible and desirable path to realizing party goals.

The PSI formally adopted its revolutionary agenda at its first postwar congress in October 1919. The majority dismissed the original (and reformist) 1893 program as "outmoded and insufficiently revolutionary" (Horowitz 1963, 134). The reformists (and their commitment to peaceful change within the existing system) were outvoted four to one, and the remaining reformist leaders were ousted from the party's executive committee (De Grand 1989, 37). The PSI announced its support for the violent seizure of power and a dictatorship of the proletariat. "The proletariat must resort to the use of violence to defend itself against bourgeois violence, to conquer power, and to consolidate revolutionary conquests," the congress proclaimed (quoted in Hilton-Young 1949, 101). Delegates enthusiastically endorsed Lenin's Third International (the only major Western socialist party to join), and the PSI sent a high-ranking delegation to its Moscow congress.[4] Turati questioned the party's new direction: "Who among you takes seriously this armed revolution which so many talk endlessly about? . . . This is a monstrous scam." But loud jeers met this call for moderation (quoted in McNally 2017, 320).

The PSI agreed to participate in parliamentary elections scheduled the following month (November 1919). This decision was not a concession to the reformist minority or evidence of a parliamentary strategy. The PSI's involvement in electoral politics was theater. The new Socialist program called on its members to "obstruct and paralyze the experiment of social democracy [and] the establishment of a bourgeois parliament." Socialists must "intensify and complete the preparation for the forcible overthrow of the bourgeois state" (quoted in Elazar 2001, 58). The PSI triumphed at the polls and became the largest party, but the majority rejected working through the liberal state to achieve concrete and piecemeal goals. Socialist deputies entered the chamber and announced their "intention of erecting a proletarian dictatorship on its ruins" (quoted in Knox 2007, 271). Many either walked out in a noisy protest when the king opened the session or never bothered to show up (D. Smith 1989, 242). There was no need. The revolution was coming (De Grand 1989, 37–38).

The Radicalization of the Labor Movement

The shift at the top of the PSI reflected broad changes within the working class. The impulse for a radical restructuring came from below. While reformists dominated the labor movement before the war, the tables turned as the war progressed. Industrial workers were subjected to MI's procedurally unjust policies, and peasant conscripts suffered under Luigi Cadorna's disciplinary terror. The moderate leadership of the PSI, the CGL, and the more traditional unions were now isolated from the rank and file. The party either marginalized reformists, or union leaders and local councilors assumed militant stances to retain their positions (Clark 2014, 254). In anticipation of the November 1919 election, moderate CGL leaders felt compelled to declare their support for the PSI's intention of "completely emancipating the proletariat from capitalist slavery" (quoted in Bosworth 2005, 104). Three years of a procedurally unjust mobilization had radicalized the labor movement.

Although MI regulations limited the number of strikes during the war, workers took an increasing number of radical disputes to MI arbitration (Tomassini 1990, 194). Popular protest directed at the prevailing order also became more intense and more frequent (Snowden 1986, 164). Revolutionary agitation grew among workers in the cities, and especially in Turin, the center of Italy's war production. Food shortages in August 1917 escalated into a revolutionary situation. The police repressed the unrest, but the ideals of left-wing Socialists remained and would later give rise to the factory council movement (Seton-Watson 1967, 470). Even the CGL, the most moderate sector of the socialist movement, swung to the left during the war. Revolutionaries gained control of the CGL in July 1918 and consolidated their dominance over the next eighteen months (Knox 2007, 218). Syndicalists gained over half of the votes and maximalists held more than a third by the end of 1920 (Farneti 1978, 11). Not every demand was radical—many workers clamored for an eight-hour day and higher wages. But the air was "electrified" with the expectation that "great change was fated to come" (Pernicone 1974, 208). Thousands of workers in munition factories in central and northern Italy eagerly anticipated the order to do "as in Russia." Revolution had become the idée fixe by 1919.

Mobilization for war also radicalized the rural masses. The countryside supplied the vast majority of conscripts, and these peasants returned home from Cadorna's disciplinary regime with new and militant demands. "The silence of the peasantry was over," one of many historians concludes (Snowden 1989, 41).[5] The experience of procedural injustice had eliminated traditional attitudes toward authority. Veterans "flowed back into the [socialist] movement" and contributed to the intense postwar unrest (Corner 1981, 410). This radicalization was apparent by mid-1917. Troops traveling back and forth to the front were no longer allowed to keep their rifles because of the frequency of violence en route, such as shooting Carabinieri (M. Thompson 2008, 275). During the retreat at Caporetto in November 1917, Italian soldiers surrounded a car carrying the king and General Cadorna and began to sing the Socialist anthem, "Internationale." Conforming to type, Cadorna turned to his deputy and snapped, "Why doesn't someone shoot them?" (quoted in M. Thompson 2008, 312).

Conservatives had hoped that newly formed veterans' associations, and especially those in the south, would deliver a conservative revival after the war. But
the peasant conscripts eschewed nationalist messages and a return to the status
quo (Salvemini 1973, 161). The rural workforce expected a new order that would
realize its aspirations for land. In regions where peasants and day laborers controlled veterans' associations, the groups adopted platforms similar to that of the
PSI (Snowden 1986, 183). They demanded the distribution of uncultivated lands
to veterans, the organization of a constituent assembly to draft a new constitution,
and the replacement of the Senate with councils that workers and management
would elect (Ledeen 1975, 109–110).

The rural Socialist leagues also shifted left. The national Federterra had initially complied with government appeals to support the war effort, but by 1918,
the Federterra and the *braccianti* it represented "aspired to revolution" (Snowden
1989, 71; see also Cardoza 1982, 123, 222). The Federterra announced its goal of
socializing land in early 1919, and it formally adopted a program "more Bolshevik than anything yet seen in Russia" later that spring (Knox 2007, 248; see also
De Grand 1989, 36). This new platform contained two provisions that were the
basis of the Federterra's postwar struggle: the *imponibile di mano d'opera* (unions
decide the number of laborers assigned to each acre) and the *collocamento di classe*
(a union-controlled roster of agricultural workers to guarantee an equal distribution of labor). These were radical demands. Together they would give Socialist
leagues control over the labor market and prevent employers from keeping wages
low and profits high (Cardoza 1982, 250; Corner 2002a, 289). Local Federterra
leaders hoped that slashing employers' incomes would lead to the overthrow of
the land tenure system (Cardoza 1991, 193).

The transformation of the Bolognese Federterra illustrates the radicalization
of rural labor. In the early 1890s, these Socialist leagues did not challenge managerial authority or the economic position of large commercial farmers. When war
broke out, this "reformist citadel" initially cooperated with the government. The
Bolognese Federterra entered into a government-mediated truce with agrarian
elites. It agreed to suspend strikes for the war's duration and to take workplace
disputes to arbitration. Local Federterra leaders also assisted the families of conscripts, and they worked with mobilization committees to regulate the provision
of basic foodstuffs (Cardoza 1982, 57, 97, 141, 222–23). The Bolognese Federterra's moderation did not last. Those who had cooperated with the government
lost control of the provincial body in September 1919 as the league "shifted decisively to the left" (Cardoza 1982, 265). Newly elected leaders denounced the war
and cross-class alliances. They heralded the coming of the dictatorship of the proletariat. In the winter of 1919–20, the Bolognese Federterra endorsed a platform
that was more radical than the one the national congress had adopted the prior

June. These policies would wrest control from employers as the first step toward collective leases and the "socialization of the land" (Cardoza 1982, 276–77).

Before the war, Catholic peasants tended to support conservative candidates against Socialists (or other anticlericals). Three years of a procedurally unjust mobilization upended this tradition. The newly created (1919) Catholic People's Party was not a conservative force. The Partito Populare Italiano (PPI) was split between orthodox Catholics, a Christian democratic center, and the newly radicalized militant Catholic peasant leagues in the north. The PPI refused to join anti-Socialist coalitions in government or in local elections, and it denounced imperialism, supported disarmament, and called for the partition of large estates and worker ownership of the means of production (Clark 2014, 254; Maier 1975, 133). Above all, Catholic peasants wanted "land for the peasants." Catholic agricultural unions of northern and north-central Italy now rivaled their Socialist counterparts in their militant tactics. Some rural Catholic unions were even more radical and violent than the Federterra. A Socialist noted that young supporters of the Lombardy Catholic leagues accepted the Socialists' tactics, program, and maximalist end (Foot 1997, 421). These developments troubled those who had hoped the PPI would serve as a bulwark against socialism. "The saddest thing was that the clergy of the countryside and of the small towns, usually coming from peasant or working-class stock, were quick to applaud this catholic socialism and align themselves against the bourgeois class," one conservative Catholic remarked (quoted in Salvemini 1973, 140n8). The pope condemned the Socialist rhetoric of Catholic peasants as "completely perverse from the christian spirit" (quoted in Foot 1997, 426).

The war also radicalized Tuscan sharecroppers (the *mezzadri*). Their postwar demands included reformist policies, but sharecroppers (whether affiliated with Catholics or Socialists) were now making claims as revolutionary as those of the *braccianti* in the Po Valley. They wanted equal rights in the management of estates and restrictions on evictions. They sought to undermine property relations and give sharecroppers and their leagues workplace control (Snowden 1989, 43–49, 72–74). The radicalization of rural labor was sharpest in the northern and central regions of Italy, but southern peasants also called for the upending of the traditional order. A study of the Apulia region repeatedly references the radicalization of the ex-combatants. Officials warily noted that farm workers seemed to expect the revolution to occur any day (Snowden 1986, 153, 164). Everywhere peasants were demanding radical change.

Revolution in the Air

After the industrial conflict in Turin in August 1917 (and despite government suppression of news about it), rumors spread that the revolution had arrived. Those in Emilia-Romagna thought it was under way in northern Italy. Sicilians believed the revolution was spreading from one city to the next. An official in the north noted in September 1917, "They talk about the revolution as if it were something that could happen from one minute to the next" (quoted in Giovanna Procacci 1992, 148). A government minister telegraphed the prime minister after Caporetto that the "revolutionary phase" had begun (Giovanna Procacci 1992, 146–47). The ruling class was wrong about Caporetto—it was not a conscript-led military strike intended to spread insurrection—but they correctly understood labor's revolutionary aspirations. This shift had not occurred overnight—it was an evolving process punctuated by critical events, such as the Russian Revolution and Caporetto. And it was not uniform. Some sectors of the rural workforce did not share this newfound militancy. This was especially true of tenant farmers and sharecroppers who benefited from the sharp rise in farm prices, and who had used their earnings to buy plots of land.[6] But the vast majority of Italian labor endorsed radical change.

The brutality of trench warfare along the Isonzo front does not explain this transformation. The conditions *were* horrendous: the Italian high command repeatedly launched suicidal attacks against heavily entrenched positions. But so did commanders along the western front. British and French soldiers endured months of bloody stalemate punctuated by terrifying frontal assaults that produced mountains of casualties. The names of the battles at the Somme and Verdun resonate as deeply with the British and the French as Isonzo and Carso do with Italians. Indeed, Italy's western allies fought for longer and suffered greater losses. French and British soldiers endured months in the trenches before Italy entered the war. French battle deaths were staggering—more than 3 percent of the population—but Britain also lost a greater proportion of soldiers than Italy (Obinger, Petersen, and Starke 2018, 25). What was distinctive about Italy was not the horrors of modern warfare but the type of mobilization. French and British soldiers did not endure the Italian army's unjust disciplinary regime. And they, unlike their Italian counterparts, did not return home with a burning desire for radical change.

The radicalization of Italian labor was also not a function of poor pay and working conditions, or the result of the state's failure to deliver a robust remunerative strategy. Economic deprivation was not new to the Italian masses, and for many soldiers, wartime food consumption was an improvement on prewar conditions. There is no easy correlation between economic deprivation and radicalization, as wartime developments among sharecroppers in Tuscany illustrate. Nowhere in Italy was the contrast between the prewar labor peace and postwar militancy more apparent. Economic hardship cannot explain it. Unlike the *braccianti*, whose wages and living standards were badly hit by inflation, the *mezzadri* did relatively well during the war. As sharecroppers with plots of land, they were paid a share of the harvest. They were protected from the sharp wartime rise in prices for farm commodities. Indeed, the *mezzadri* who produced for the market often profited from wartime inflation. Most were able to maintain their economic position, and many accumulated some savings or reduced their debts by the war's end (Cardoza 1982, 232; Snowden 1989, 33–42).[7] Yet these Tuscan sharecroppers (and peasant conscripts) emerged from the war with a radical set of demands that astonished even their most ardent supporters. A radical Socialist newspaper in Tuscany noted the peasants' wartime conversion: "Anyone who has followed the phase of the agrarian struggle in Tuscany . . . can only be amazed by the mental transformation of our peasants." Another Tuscan agreed: "It seems like a dream" (both quoted in Snowden 1989, 42).

Developments in Turin are the industrial equivalent. As in other cities in Italy's industrial triangle, the size of Turin's workforce exploded as firms converted to war production. Italy's manufacturing centers teemed with workers crowded into substandard housing. However, Turin stood apart in two ways. First, it had the highest concentration of workers under MI's direct authority (Levy 2002, 175–76). Second, wages were higher in Turin than in other cities. By the end of 1917, workers in Turin earned on average 25 percent more than in other industrial centers, such as Milan (Giovanna Procacci 1992, 157; Tomassini 1991, 80). But it was the relatively well-paid workers in Turin who swung dramatically to the left. The peak of revolutionary agitation during the war occurred in Turin in August 1917. What had begun as a bread strike quickly escalated into open rebellion against the war. It took the army and up to 250 casualties to restore order (Haywood 1999, 459). Turin had become the heart of the revolutionary left-wing faction of the PSI that became the Communist Party in 1921.

To argue that Italy's unjust mobilization radicalized labor does not mean that revolutionary positions were new to Italian labor. Many of these ideas dated from prior eras. But before World War I and the mobilization it entailed, the PSI had worked within Italy's institutions to reform the liberal state and to gain benefits for its constituents. The PSI had remained a member of the Second International, which represented socialist and social democratic parties in Europe and North America. The PSI's affiliated trade unions were even more moderate in the decade before war. Three years of a procedurally unjust mobilization transformed this political landscape. PSI documents after 1918 refer to representative institutions as "nothing else but enemy strongholds to be conquered and then destroyed" (Sabbatucci 1996, 49). Indeed, analysts warn against seeing labor radicalism as a permanent feature of Italian socialism because it prevents one from "fully grasping the novelty" of the maximalists' positions (Sabbatucci 1996, 48). Italian labor now rejected reformism. The rural and urban workforce wanted and expected a revolution.[8] This evidence supports hypothesis 1: years of a procedurally unjust mobilization radicalized Italian labor.

From Fragmentation to Solidarity: A Change of Identity

The labor movement flourished under Giolitti's enlightened policies. It organized without fear of government repression, and it rapidly grew in the decade before the war. But like most working-class movements, it could not overcome ideological, skill, and rural and urban divides. Catholic unions attracted artisans, the CGL enrolled skilled workers in the industrial north, and the syndicalists split from the CGL to form their own union. Rare were strikes that encompassed different strata of workers. The traditional division between rural and urban workers remained.[9]

Wartime economic expansion further divided the working class. Thousands of peasants, children, and women entered factories for the first time. As in Britain and other European states, skilled labor greeted this infusion of unskilled labor with hostility. The "aristocracy of labor" sought to protect its status, wages, and working conditions against the onslaught of wartime regulations, the demanding work rhythms, and the dilution of its skills (Giovanna Procacci 1989, 38–39; 1992, 167–72). Work stoppages were minor, spontaneous, localized, and limited to a single category of workers in one factory. The new unskilled workforce dominated this industrial unrest, with few skilled workers participating. However, the experience of war remade this fragmented and diverse workforce. As hypothesis 2 expects, Italy's procedurally unjust mobilization created an unusual degree of working-class solidarity.

The Rise of Urban Working-Class Solidarity

This solidarity first emerged during a strike wave in the winter of 1916–17 that bridged skill, workshop, and gender divides. Labor unrest was no longer contained within individual firms. Reports from MI officials, prefects, and the police noted this transformation in the auxiliary factories. Protests that unified workers and crossed factory and skill levels became the norm. Demands often focused on the needs of unskilled workers (not the protection of skilled ones) during the last year of war. Calls for minimum pay, egalitarian wages, and wage increases that were inversely proportionate to basic pay became common. Joint action among different categories of workers continued to multiply and involved thousands of workers as protests grew in size (Musso 1990, 231–38; Giovanna Procacci 1992, 169–73). "By 1918, the reunification of the working class had been realized," a leading historian of wartime Italy explains (Giovanna Procacci 1989, 52, 40–45). This newly reconstructed working class forwarded *memoriali unici* (single lists of demands) in the main metalworking areas. Solidarity strikes became common among steel and metal workers. Many protests in auxiliary firms during the spring and summer of 1918 involved the new and old working class (Giovanna Procacci 1992, 165, 173).[10]

Not all skilled workers supported this solidarity, but egalitarian claims continued to spread. These protests led to significant reductions in wage differentials in the immediate postwar years (Musso 1990, 232, 235). This solidarity also crossed the blue-collar line. Manual workers stood with the Fiat clerical staff in 1919 (Berta 1993, 113). Italy's unjust mobilization also temporarily narrowed the gap between skilled male workers and the female workforce. Men had initially seen women as interlopers threatening their wages and traditions. Yet links between the two developed (Giovanna Procacci 1992, 169). Women and men in the textile industry joined forces to protest excessive profits. A wave of female-led protests occurred in much of northern Italy in spring 1917. Thousands of women took to the streets of Milan to protest the shortage of food. At great personal risk (they could be dismissed and sent to the front), male factory workers supported these demonstrations, joining street protests and singing songs against the war (Foot 1996, 41–49; Tomassini 1996, 589).

This newfound solidarity among urban workers was *not* most pronounced in sectors where pay or conditions were the poorest or the composition of the working class most homogeneous (Giovanna Procacci 1992, 173). Instead, the solidarity was greatest where the disciplinary regime (or the experience of procedural injustice) was the harshest—in iron, steel, and metal production.

The Emergence of Rural Solidarity

Solidarity among peasants also increased during the war. The commercialization of agriculture before the war had undermined what little security sharecroppers in rural Tuscany had: their expenses increased while their living standards declined. Yet the *mezzadri* posed no threat to the landlords' power. They were isolated from each other and had no collective identity. The sharecropper "lived as if he were the only peasant in Italy" (Snowden 1989, 16, 3–23). While rural unrest hit other agricultural regions, Tuscan sharecroppers remained quiescent. This social peace disappeared after the war. Conscripts returned from the front (and the disciplinary terror) with a new collective consciousness. This transformation surprised (and pleased) those who had previously tried to organize this rural workforce. The Socialist paper in Tuscany remarked, "No one would ever have believed them [the sharecroppers] capable of a demonstration of strength, determination, and solidarity" (quoted Snowden 1989, 42, 33–36, 137).

Working-class solidarity also crossed the urban-rural divide. Economic mobilization increased interaction between industrial and agricultural workers. Rural workers filled unskilled positions within the armaments industry, and hundreds of small workshops sprang up outside cities or in the countryside (Snowden 1986, 161). Peasants joined forces with industrial workers in Lombardy in protracted protests during the war. Unrest on the outskirts of Milan in May 1917 linked urban and rural workers. This was a "magic moment of worker-peasant unity," and it continued into the postwar period (Foot 1996, 44).

Large numbers of this new working class moved back to the countryside within a year of the Armistice. Yet wartime solidarity remained. During a wave of postwar unrest, the rural and industrial workforce joined returning veterans in an unprecedented mobilization (Farneti 1978, 7–16). A general strike in July 1919 united industrial and agricultural workers, prompting the Socialist paper in Milan to congratulate the rural workforce: "Well done peasants! Your rough and worn hands unite with those of the urban workers, frighten the bosses and are a happy and secure guarantee for all the workers that the day of judgment is close at hand" (quoted in Foot 1999, 162). The following spring, unrest spread across the northern province of Piedmont. About three hundred thousand industrial and urban workers (including members of the public sector) and two hundred thousand rural day laborers joined the strike action (Foot 1999, 162–68). The war years also generated some solidarity between Catholics and Socialists. These unions were not natural allies. They organized different types of workers, and Socialists were skeptical of their clerical counterparts. Yet there were "moments" of Catholic-Socialist unity in the postwar era (Foot 1997).

Cooperation between different parts of the labor movement was in many cases sporadic, and differences between them remained. But Italy's mobilization had generated an unusual degree of working-class unity that would have taken, at best, years of organizing to develop. British labor also fought a long and difficult war and worked under a wartime regime that limited its ability to use industrial action to gain concessions from the state and employers. Yet the British working class left the war as fragmented as it had entered it. Italy's procedurally unjust mobilization explains Italian labor's unprecedented working-class solidarity, which supports hypothesis 2.

From Indifference to Alienation: A Change of Attitude about the State

A huge gathering in 1911 inaugurated a memorial celebrating Italy's fiftieth anniversary (Foot and Owen 2012, 264). Four years later, frenzied crowds called for

Italy's intervention in World War I. Yet these well-dressed crowds represented a minority of Italians. Middle- and upper-class Italians were attached to their nation, but patriotism was *not* a mass phenomenon.[11] Austrian prince Metternich's observation in 1847 that Italy was nothing but a "geographic expression" was true on the eve of war. The liberal state had failed to create a national identity that crossed class, regional, and political divides. The working class was more attached to local or class ties than to an imaginary Italian nation. Socialist and Catholic labor movements had built parallel organizations that reinforced their "separate belongings." In the years preceding the war, peasants in central Italy would say they were "going to Italy" when they left for military service (A. Kramer 2014, 23).

The Italian popular classes did not support intervention. Regional governors reported in spring 1915 that most Italians wanted to remain neutral (Thayer 1964, 307–8). Trent and Trieste—the Austrian lands with Italian-speaking populations that interventionists hoped to annex—meant little to peasants and workers. To them, the war was a misfortune that would pass. Prefects reported that the vast majority of Italians accepted their fate with "indifference and resignation." They were unenthusiastic about the state's adventure, but they would do as Rome decreed (Whittam 1975, 152). Prefects correctly predicted that if Italy went to war, working-class men would obey their mobilization notices. They would go to the front and fight (M. Thompson 2008, 31). However, by the war's end, labor's resigned acceptance of the state and its war was gone. The regime's procedural injustice—both at home and on the battlefield—transformed labor's attitudes about the state, as hypothesis 3 expects.

Hooray for Caporetto!

With the exception of a general strike in Turin, there was initially little active opposition to the war within the labor movement (Snowden 1986, 160–61). The working class and its representatives tacitly accepted Rome's decision for war. Representatives from the CGL met with parliamentary and local PSI leaders in May 1915 for a special session to discuss the war. Socialist deputies spoke of the need for Socialists to "do their duty" on the home front, and they opposed the youth federation's call for a general strike (Craver 1996, 225; De Grand 1989, 29). The reformist leaders of the PSI privately offered to support Salandra's government in May 1915. The PSI and its affiliated unions also collaborated with the government (though syndicalists refused). The Federterra organized war relief and worked with officials to contain rural unrest. The Socialist administration in Milan made "strenuous efforts" to support the war (Foot 1996, 43). Officials in Rome commended Bologna's Socialist mayor for developing programs to support the mobilization (Cardoza 1982, 222–23). The CGL also "willingly cooperated" with the wartime state, helping to implement MI regulations in auxiliary factories and providing aid to workers (Pernicone 1974, 207).

Months of procedural injustice transformed labor's political attitudes. Urban workers, Catholic rural masses, and peasant conscripts became increasingly alienated from the state and its war. Beginning in the winter of 1916–17, labor unrest often targeted the war and symbols of the state. Gatherings in southern villages to mark the departure of soldiers to the front often became violent protests involving much of the community. Some attacks focused on industrialists and rich families who supported the war. But the most violent actions struck at symbols of state authority and included the torching of town halls and assaults on Carabinieri barracks (Giovanna Procacci 1989, 42; 1992, 164; Snowden 1986, 160–61). Alienation also developed in the cities where the auxiliary factories were located. Employers in leading industrial regions reported that antiwar sentiments—not economic demands—drove the August 1917 labor unrest (Tomassini 1996, 589–90). Many Catholic peasant unions joined their Socialist counterparts in denouncing the war and rejecting Italy's participation in it (Bosworth 2005, 87).

The military disaster in November 1917 was the gravest threat to Italy since unification, but Caporetto did not generate patriotism within the working class. German and Austrian troops surged into northern Italy, forcing Italian soldiers to retreat deep into their territory. Thousands of Italian soldiers were killed, wounded, or taken prisoner. Thousands more were left wandering the countryside (Bosworth 2005, 64). The Italian army had disintegrated. Only half of its units remained intact, and it lost staggering amounts of equipment (D. Smith 1969, 312–13). Foreign forces now occupied fourteen thousand square kilometers of Italy and ruled over almost a million Italians (M. Thompson 2008, 294, 324). Some Italians reacted with alarm to this dire situation. The Vatican called on Catholics to resist the invasion (Mead 2006, 251–52; M. Thompson 2008, 332). Moderate Socialists argued that the party could not ignore what foreign occupation would mean for the working class. But the Italian popular classes disagreed. The majority of conscripts and workers spurned calls to support the war even though it had become a war of national defense (Knox 2007, 219). Their reaction captures the alienation that procedural injustice produces.

Most soldiers greeted with relief and sometimes joy the prospect of an end to the war—even if it meant the loss of significant territory to foreign occupation. From the second day of Caporetto, soldiers fell away from the front, discarding their rifles and shouting, "The war's over! We're going home! Up with the Pope! Up with Russia!" (quoted in M. Thompson 2008, 312). An officer noted that most soldiers were in "high spirits, as if they had found the solution to a difficult problem" (quoted in M. Thompson 2008, 316). Thousands of "weaponless and surprisingly good natured fugitives" fled invading forces (Knox 2007, 216). Some

Italian soldiers even cheered the foreign armies for, they thought, ending the war. A German officer recalled coming across an Italian brigade that, when forced to surrender, tossed its weapons aside and ran toward him: "In an instant, I was surrounded and hoisted on Italian soldiers. '*Evviva Germania!*' [Long live Germany] sounded from a thousand throats" (quoted in Duggan 2008, 392). Other soldiers expressed pride that their actions might hasten the war's end. A soldier was arrested in spring 1918 for suggesting that the real barbarians were not the Germans but Italian elites: "It would be better if the Germans did come as far as the Po" (quoted in Corner 1975, 39). A study of the Italian army after the defeat concluded that the conscripts saw no reason for war or bringing it to a victorious end (Wilcox 2014).

Many civilians had similar reactions. Rather than generating allegiance to the beleaguered state, many greeted news of Caporetto with relief. They hoped that foreign occupation would bring a better government that would address their basic needs (Giovanna Procacci 1989, 51). Prefects around the country reported similar reactions. There was little evidence in northeast Italy that the locals objected to Austrian occupation (Gilmour 2011, 289). Students protested when a teacher in Lombardy instructed them to write an essay about the need to fight to a victorious end. Why should those who oppose the war do the fighting? one student asked. While most Italians living in northern cities followed the army's retreat, the rural population stayed put (M. Thompson 2008, 334, 348). They were prepared to exchange the devil they knew for the devil they didn't know.[12] Several peasants were arrested for expressing the common belief that Italian soldiers were right to flee: "because you would be better off under the Germans than under the thieves in our government" (quoted in Corner 1975, 39). Four weeks into Caporetto, the new army chief of staff, General Armando Diaz, cautioned the prime minister that peasants in northern Italy opposed the war. The women were especially vocal, Diaz explained. They preferred Austrian occupation because they believed that the war would end, and "anyway everyone knows the Austrians treat people well" (quoted in M. Thompson 2008, 334). The only basis for their preference for Austrian and German rule was their alienation and distrust of their own government.

Some civilians even celebrated the military disaster (Corner 1975, 39; Giovanna Procacci 1992, 174; 1995, 22–23). A journalist in Milan reported that "in many areas they have prepared risotto and got drunk in order to celebrate the arrival of the Austrians in Italy—who have come, according to the peasants, to chop off the heads of the gentlemen who wanted the war, and then to help the poor" (quoted in Corner and Procacci 1997, 230). Celebrations broke out in rural Tuscany and southern Italy as people welcomed news of foreign occupation and the prospect of the war's end (Corner 1975, 39; M. Thompson 2008, 334).

The working class across Europe became disillusioned with the war, but they did not celebrate when their troops were thrown on the defensive. As the Italian army was desperately trying to halt the Austrian and German advance in northeastern Italy, Socialist deputies in Parliament shouted, "Down with the war! Up the revolution!" (quoted in Knox 2007, 219). Italian firms expressed their support after Caporetto, but it was owners—not employees—who signed these declarations. Labor unrest had declined since its height in the summer of 1917, but the level of activism that occurred simultaneously with the retreat of Italian forces belies claims that invasion rallied the urban workforce to Italy's defense (M. Thompson 2008, 333). The number of factory workers who were fined or imprisoned for declaring their opposition to the war *increased* after Caporetto (Ermacora 2017).

Compare these actions with British labor's reactions to the massive German offensive in March 1918. German forces crashed through British lines, advancing deep into Allied territory and leading to the largest breakthrough in three years of warfare along the western front. Panic swept the British line, and many Germans assumed the war was all but over. The first few days were so successful that Berlin declared March 24 a national holiday. British labor immediately responded to this military setback. Over forty thousand munitions workers volunteered for military service in the subsequent five weeks, in comparison with sixty-eight thousand in the last eight months of 1917 (Wilson 1986, 656). A shop steward in Sheffield recounted, "Men who had left jobs at twelve pounds a week and accepted others at thirty shillings a week in order to escape military service, were now anxious to join up" (quoted in Wilson 1986, 655–56). Even miners put their grievances aside. The Miners' Federation had resisted the "comb-out" of its members for military service before the German offensive. Yet these men were once again rushing to get to the front (Wilson 1986, 653–56).

This resurgence of British patriotism also occurred on the shop floor. Industrial unrest plummeted after the German assault. The ASE and the shop stewards' organization declared an industrial truce. The "combing out" of skilled men for military service had become increasingly contentious, but unions put aside their objections in the face of the German attack (Hardach 1977, 191). Even the more radical union leaders discouraged industrial action (Tanner 1990, 60). The Ministry of Munitions noted the "magical disappearance of labour opposition" in the wake of the German advance (quoted in Gregory 2008, 205). More than half a million days had been lost to strikes in the munitions industry the previous November. The total dropped to fifteen thousand days in the month following the German offensive (Waites 1987, 208, 323). In Glasgow alone, and despite a history of troubled industrial relations, over one hundred thousand men responded to official appeals to work over the Easter holiday. Many contributed their pay to a charitable fund (Gregory 2008, 204; Wilson 1986, 656). The German offensive also weakened what little working-class pacifism existed. The Ministry of Labour reported in April 1918, "The seriousness of the present position has rallied a large number of men who were previously tending toward pacifism" (quoted in Horne 1997, 210). An upsurge of unrest among engineers, railway men, and miners occurred later that summer, but only after the danger of a German breakthrough had passed.

This comparison with Caporetto is imperfect. The British had been at war for longer, they had lost more men, and most important, foreign troops had not invaded and occupied British soil. But that is the point. British failure to stop the Germans was a stunning failure, but Caporetto was a defeat of unprecedented proportions. Caporetto was the largest territorial reversal of any battle during the war, and it left foreign forces in control of large swaths of Italian territory. At one point, it looked as if Venice might be lost. But after months of a punishingly unjust mobilization, Italian labor accepted the news with equanimity and sometimes joy.

Deserters as Heroes

In most cases, and especially in the armies of Italy's democratic allies, rank-and-file discontent focused on the war's conduct. The situation in Italy was different. "English soldiers might want to murder Haig, but they did not (generally) put in question the fact of fighting for Britain. It was the development of anti-State feeling . . . which remained the distinctive factor in the Italian case" (Corner 1997, 267). Even the large-scale French mutinies in 1917 do not challenge this assessment. French conscripts objected to how the war was being fought. They were not rejecting France or calling for peace at any price (Horne 2010, 287; L. Smith 2010, 427–28). They wanted the leaves they were due, and they had lost confidence in the high command. They no longer wanted to launch suicidal offensives that served no military purpose. And they wanted peace. But unlike their Italian counterparts, French soldiers would not accept peace at any price. France must emerge victorious. Germany must return Alsace-Lorraine and pay reparations. Otherwise French soldiers would continue to fight.

Italians deserted at a higher rate than soldiers in other armies (M. Thompson 2008, 275). Even French desertions at the height of the mutinies in spring 1917 pale in comparison. Three times more Italian soldiers abandoned an army that was half France's size (Knox 2007, 209). Not all soldiers desert because they oppose the war. During Caporetto, many soldiers had no choice as their units collapsed under the Austro-German assault (Wilcox 2009, 35–37, 42). But for two reasons, these comparisons are suggestive of the depth of Italian soldiers' alienation. First, they faced more severe punishments for desertion than did French conscripts. Second, the Italian high command ensured that soldiers knew that Italian POWs died at a punitively high rate.

During the war, young British women would give a white feather—a symbol of cowardice—to men out of uniform to shame the "shirker" to enlist. The opposite occurred in Italy as alienation toward the state and its war grew. From mid-1917, and especially after Caporetto, Italian peasants began *shielding* deserters (Giovanna Procacci 1989, 51). These men helped with the harvest and were accepted into the community. They were not seen as traitors who had brought shame on themselves for abandoning their brothers-in-arms. To the contrary, these women regretted that their family members had not done the same. They saw the deserters as heroes and as "good people . . . who never did anyone any wrong" (Bravo 1989, 107, 111–12). These sentiments were widespread. Women in the south protested the dispatch of their men to the front. Those in central and northern Italy organized marches into town to encourage work stoppages in armament factories with cries of "We want our men back!" (quoted in Knox 2007, 213; see also Haywood 1999, 459). Women who were imprisoned for violating MI regulations hoped that their absence would help end the war. Others rejected government aid provided to soldiers' dependents (Giovanna Procacci 2013, 163).

Women in other countries also protested the war. They also wanted their men back. French seamstresses organized a protest for better pay and working conditions in spring 1917. The unrest quickly spread to the munitions factories, and it escalated into demands for peace. But like their husbands, brothers, and sons in the trenches, these protesters did not reject France or victory on French terms. The women waved the tricolor as they marched through the streets of Paris. Unlike their Italian counterparts, they had no intention of abandoning their war work (L. Smith 2010, 427–28).

Millions of French and British civilians poured into the streets when the Armistice was declared. "Conversation in the Strand [a main London thoroughfare] was impossible owing to the din of cheers, whistles, hooters, and fireworks," the *Daily Mirror* reported on November 12, 1918. There was relative silence in Rome. No popular gatherings greeted the war's end. Many Italians continued to denounce the war despite Italy's historic victory (Corner and Procacci 1997). Much of the working class stayed away from victory celebrations and instead celebrated the anniversary of the Russian Revolution three days later (Musso 1990). This denunciation of the state and its war continued. As the first anniversary of victory approached, officials canceled all festivities. They feared the events would provoke violence just before national elections (Knox 2007, 278–79). Military officers were ordered not to wear uniforms in public because of the insults it generated. A Socialist deputy was elected in November 1919 based largely on his record as a deserter (Hilton-

Young 1949, 103). Cremona—the capital of a northern province—elected a deserter as its mayor the following year (Foot 1997, 420).

The controversy over war memorials symbolizes the depth of labor's alienation. Police had to remove Socialist flyers posted across Rome before the internment of the Unknown Warrior in November 1921. The flyers explained that the best way to honor the soldier would be to do as he would do if he could rise from the dead: curse the war (M. Thompson 2008, 388). Socialist administrations often resisted attempts by local elites to construct war memorials in village squares. Local Socialist councils refused to allocate funds, boycotted the dedications, or built their own memorials that depicted a different war and that denounced the war effort. These alternate monuments were etched with statements that condemned the "futile slaughter," "the barbaric conflict," and the "agonizing waste of human life." The dead were "victims," not "the fallen." The war was "European," not "national." The men had died not "for the patria" but for the "greed of the rulers" and "jealousy of the powerful" (Foot 2009, 38; Mead 2006, 268–71; Ventrone 2011, 98). Some memorials even included the names of deserters among the war dead.

This controversy over war memorials had no counterpart among Italy's victorious allies. French and British victories were commemorated as national triumphs testifying to their soldiers' resilience and strength. The Royal Artillery Monument in Green Park (London) honors the artilleryman's character and resistance in the face of modern firepower. World War I monuments in French villages speak to French pride in their *poulu* (common soldier, literally "hairy one") who withstood the German assault. There was no constituency in Britain or France willing to honor deserters. Not until 2001 did Britain construct a monument to soldiers shot for cowardice or desertion, and only in 2006 did Britain issue posthumous pardons for these men. France has never done the latter. President Nicolas Sarkozy noted in 2008 that French deserters who were shot during World War I "were not dishonored, nor were they cowards," but he granted no pardons.[13]

While large-scale wars often generate strong nationalist responses, Italy's war had the opposite effect. The punitively unjust regime in the factories and the army generated alienation from the state and its war, which confirms hypothesis 3.

A Lost Opportunity for Nation Building

Scholars recognize that war sometimes fails to accomplish its historic mission of nation building. Anthony Smith (1981) stresses that war can divide a nation if it lacks a "core ethic." Lewis Coser (1956) emphasizes the degree of precrisis cohesion. Arthur Stein and Bruce Russett (1980) contend that war will fragment society if war costs are inequitably distributed. My argument is different. Rather than focusing on preexisting conditions or the distribution of resources, I examine how the state fights its war. What type of mobilization strategy does it use? Does the state adjudicate disputes and complaints with summary executions or with (at least the perception of) justice? Outcomes are not irrelevant—winning a war is better than losing one. But the Italian experience shows that victory is not sufficient. It matters *how* one wins the war. In some cases, process trumps outcome. How the Italian state fought the war explains why even victory did not produce patriotic celebrations or the nation Italy's leaders desired.

The conservatives and nationalists who supported intervention believed that war would finally create a united Italy, bound together in the crucible of war. They had seen the Libyan war (1911) increase national unity, and they expected this new war to forge a consensus around the king, the army, and the ruling class. War would bridge the divide between the "real Italy" of the masses and the "legal Italy" of the government and the state. For King Vittorio Emanuele, the war was a historic opportunity to strengthen allegiance to the Crown and the conservative regime (Gibelli 2010, 466). Sidney Sonnino, the foreign minister when Italy declared war, saw the same problem and the same solution: "The great majority of the people, over 90 percent . . . feel themselves outsiders in the state" (quoted in Jones 1985, 157; see also Duggan 2008, xviii). War would bring them into the national community, counteract the power of organized labor, and enhance the state's prestige. "Patriotism was to replace poverty as the prime mover of popular politics" (Corner 2002a, 291). A noted Italian philosopher (and later Fascist official) was indifferent to whether Italy fought with or against Austria. A war—any war—was necessary to "cement the unity of the country in blood" (quoted in D. Smith 1989, 212).

These hopes that war would build the Italian nation were sensible. Much of what we know about the sources of nationalism support this expectation. Ever since Georg Simmel's classic study, scholars have seen war as an engine of nationalism. An external threat sharpens group boundaries and encourages society to close ranks around a common goal. The unity thus created remains after the war ends. "France owes the consciousness of its national unity only to its fight against the English," Simmel explains (1955, 100–101). War is sometimes seen as so critical that Jeffrey Herbst (1990) doubts whether African states—lacking severe external threats—will ever succeed in recasting societal beliefs into strong national identities. It is the wartime atmosphere of collective sacrifice and common struggle that constructs a distinct national identity.

Many of the specifics of Italy's war make it an easy case for the wartime creation of an "imagined community." Italy was not just at war; it was fighting a total war. World War I was the first collective endeavor in Italian history. It touched everyone. According to theories of nationalism, the war should have been a turning point. The greater the proportion of the population drawn into the war effort, the more likely war will create a national community. Anthony Smith (1981, 384–86) contends that the limited wars of the 1700s contributed to French nationalism, but it was the protracted wars following the French Revolution that cemented French unity. The total wars of the twentieth century furthered this process. The scale of modern warfare forced societies to work together and created emotional bonds with the state. Australia and New Zealand were "born as nations" during the Great War (Bryder 2008, 868). Out of shared sacrifice, strong national communities emerge. Without the enormous sacrifices and collective efforts required to wage an unlimited conflict, only weak ties remain. According to Miguel Centeno (2002), most South American states lack strong national identities because they have fought only limited wars.

Morris Janowitz is one of many scholars who see military service as a form of citizen education. A "nation in arms" connects individuals unlikely to otherwise meet, and the heat of battle forces them to recognize their commonalities. Service in state militias during the American Revolution shaped British subjects into Americans (Janowitz 1983, 26–32). French conscription strengthened bonds between state and society (E. Weber 1976, 298–302). The army becomes a "school of the nation" that reworks identities, remolding regional, religious, and class allegiances into a national whole.

This assimilation process should have been strong in Italy. Close to six million conscripts served in the army during the war. Millions of peasants who had never left their villages found themselves fighting next to strangers. Unlike the British and German armies (and with the exception of the elite Alpine units comprising middle-class men), the Italian army did not use a regimental system (Rochat 2010, 84; Wilcox 2011, 287). Italian soldiers served with men who came from different regions and spoke different dialects. They learned to communicate through intermediaries and with a new and original Italian (Graziano 2010, 61). Many learned to read and write for the first time (Wilcox 2012, 173). They also faced grueling conditions. The horrors of trench warfare along the western front are well known, but the Italian army also fought a horrific war. Conscripts endured eleven offensives against Austrian lines and never advanced more than eighteen miles and at a cost of almost one million casualties (Rochat 2010, 85; M. Thompson 2008, 5, 52, 67, 99). Never before had so many Italians from every region been involved in such a massive and punishing undertaking. Italy was, at least theoretically, "binding herself forever in sacrifice."[14]

Defensive wars are especially likely to diminish regional and class differences and to forge a national identity. The labor activist Pete Seeger's 1942 song "Deliver the Goods" captures this claim:

Now, me and my boss, we never did agree
If a thing helped him then it didn't help me
But when a burglar tries to bust into your house
You stop fighting with the landlord and throw him out

Finland's war of national survival against the Soviets (1939–40) helped heal the deep ideological divides its 1918 civil war had created. The war brought the Finnish working class and Social Democrats into the national fold, symbolized by the exhumation and official reburial of Socialists—those "treacherous Reds"—who were killed in 1918 (Kivimaki 2012, 486–87; see also Tepora 2007, 164–65). Moscow also profited from the national cohesion that invasion can produce. One reason Russian economic mobilization was more effective in World War II than in World War I was that so much of the fighting was on Russian soil (Gatrell and Harrison 1993, 449).

Italy was not initially fighting for its survival. World War I was not forced on it. But with Caporetto and the collapse of the eastern front, the war became a desperate struggle to halt invasion and avert total defeat. By the end of 1917, the Italian army had stabilized the front and the crisis had passed. But Italian forces had lost almost a hundred miles of territory and foreign armies occupied most of Italy's northeast provinces. Italy was fighting its first defensive war since unification in 1861, and it confronted the challenge of driving occupiers from thousands of square kilometers of territory. The second phase of Italy's war was one fought almost entirely on Italian soil.

World War I also provided a rich store of images that could have been woven into national myths. Anthony Smith (1981) stresses that wars, and especially total wars, provide a vast pool of experiences that can be molded into patriotic legends. Australian "diggers" suffered an astonishing casualty rate during the Gallipoli campaign (1915–16), and after weeks of horrific combat, a supposedly inferior enemy defeated Australia's best men. Yet this senseless battle gave birth to Australian nationalism (Hoffenberg 2001). It became synonymous with Australian honor, glory, and pride. The anniversary of the Gallipoli landing is the country's most important national holiday (Kelly 2012). The disaster at Caporetto might have been Italy's Gallipoli, but Italian nationalists also had a victorious battle to bind Italians together. The Battle of Vittorio Veneto was the final offensive on the Italian front. This victory finished off the Austro-Hungarian army and secured the dissolution of its empire. Vittorio Veneto could have become a symbol of Italian unity and pride, especially since Italians were not starting from scratch.

A sense of community is rarely created out of thin air. There are usually "markers" that provide the basis for transforming people into a community (Anthony Smith 1981, 379). Italy was rich with possible markers. A minority of the population spoke Italian, but the peninsula's geographic boundaries were more natural than those of most European states, and Rome had created a prefectural system across the provinces. Italians also shared a religion and a proud cultural heritage stretching back centuries to the Renaissance and ancient Rome. Even the divisions within Italy capture deeper commonalities. To speak of the "Roman question" or a "southern question" is to implicitly recognize a larger whole. Cultures are defined not only by consensus but also by the issues over which its members disagree (Swidler 1986).

The alienation of Italian labor was not an inevitable product of war. It was not bound to occur given Italy's social structure, the distribution of costs, or Italy's relative youth. Unlike the British, Italians had not had centuries to bind themselves to one another. But as the examples of New Zealand and Australia illustrate, war can forge a strong sense of national identity in relatively young states. World War I could have marked a great leap forward for Italian nationalism. Had officials been attentive to procedural justice, they, too, could have forged Italian nationalism through war. If Italy's leaders had included labor in decision making and treated it with respect, the war could have helped create an imagined community that bridged class and regional divides. But Rome squandered the opportunity. Preoccupied with disciplining labor and excluding it from governing, Italy's procedurally unjust mobilization turned the people against the state. It transformed what had been weak links between state and society into highly charged and negative ones. Salandra and his colleagues had failed to grasp that how they chose to fight the war would undermine an important reason for entering it. War can make the nation-state, but not when the state makes war as Italy did.

Conclusion: An "Electoral Caporetto" for the Liberal Elite

The first postwar national elections in Italy confirmed labor's transformation, but not as many scholars expect. Democratic theorists posit that access to the suffrage and participation in democratic elections forestalls the development of revolutionary socialist parties. Parliamentary representation is supposed to weaken the cohesion and radicalism of the labor movement and give the working class a stake in the system (Lipset 1985). Attempts to attract a simple majority will undermine the salience of class appeals (Przeworski and Sprague 1986). Yet Italy's parliamentary elections in November 1919 were both the freest in Italian history and a victory for a revolutionary socialist party.

More Italians could vote after the war than ever before, and with an electoral system that favored mass parties. Reforms in August 1919 had removed the few remaining restrictions on male suffrage and replaced the first-past-the-post, single-member constituencies with proportional representation. Yet political citizenship and electoral success could not tame revolutionary forces. The November 1919 elections were an "electoral Caporetto" for the liberal political class that lost the parliamentary hegemony it had enjoyed since unification. The Socialist victory was stunning. The PSI became the strongest party in Parliament just one month after the party declared its support for a dictatorship of the proletariat. The majority of PSI's support came from northern and central Italy. Socialists were especially strong in the industrial triangle that was the center of MI's disciplinary regime (D. Smith 1969, 326–28).

Italy's procedurally unjust policies do not alone explain labor's wartime development. The Russian Revolution also inspired the Italian working class. Some democratic theorists note the international sources of regime transitions. Events abroad can serve as demonstration effects for oppositional political movements, as the spread of political ideas contributes to a "contagion" or "snowballing" of regime change. Samuel Decalo (1992, 13–14) and Georg Sorenson (1993, 36) see a link between the collapse of communist regimes in Eastern Europe and the rise of protest movements in Africa. Samuel Huntington (1991b, 103) suggests that democratization in Spain and Portugal encouraged Latin American reformers to believe that they could do it, too.

Events in Russia did inspire hope for political renewal in Italy. News of the revolution spread rapidly and contributed to the belief that change was possible (Pernicone 1974, 207). The Socialist press and the Federterra often spoke about Russian developments, and members of the Soviet Petrograd toured Italy in the summer of 1917 (Snowden 1989, 32–39). More than forty thousand Turin workers greeted the visiting delegation with cries of "Long live the Russian Revolution, long live Lenin!" (Horne 2014, 232). However, that Russian events so captured the Italian imagination only makes sense against the backdrop of wartime mobilization and the domestic political change it induced. The prospects for regime change derive primarily from conditions at home (O'Donnell and Schmitter 1986, 18). A demonstration effect is unlikely to lead to regime change if the country lacks "favorable internal conditions" (Huntington 1991a, 13). News of the Russian Revolution also spread to British factories, and the Soviet Petrograd also visited the British Isles. The real-life example of the Russian Revolution resonated in Italy—but not in Britain—because Rome's unjust mobilization made workers and peasants receptive to these ideas. The next chapter explains why Britain's mobilization ensured that its labor movement was immune to the Russian example.

BRITISH LABOR'S MODERATE SOCIALISM

"Until August 1914," A. J. P. Taylor comments, "a sensible, law-abiding Englishman could pass through life and hardly notice the existence of the state, beyond the post office and the policeman" (1965, 1). Taylor understates the state's presence in British life, but he captures the dramatic change that mobilization for war introduced. During four years of war, state intervention exceeded anything imaginable in 1914. In the decades before the war, Parliament passed labor legislation, social service expenditures increased, and the government policed strikes and mediated some industrial disputes. But the British state played a minor role in industrial relations. Private enterprise dominated the economy, and employers were relatively free from state intervention. State officials preferred labor and management to settle their own disputes (August 2007, 120–21; Rubin 1987b, 7).

When war broke out, the official in charge of military procurement assumed that a market economy would suffice: "If only the government paid high enough prices and left private firms to their own devices, munitions would be forthcoming in abundance" (quoted in Tawney 1943, 5). But as trench warfare ground on, officials dropped their liberal principles and, in a piecemeal and ad hoc manner, assumed an active role in industrial relations. The state penetrated deep into working-class life. Whereas labor had previously conducted its affairs largely removed from the state, mobilization brought it into close contact with national and local officials. The government controlled the output and distribution of many products, and it regulated prices and food consumption. Officials exercised authority in state factories and thousands of controlled establishments producing for the war effort. For the first time, average workers were seeing ministry officials arbitrating wages and often settling on awards employers opposed (A. Reid 1985b, 161–62). Officials were also creating a seemingly endless list of regulations for factory life. In Taylor's view (1965, 2), "The history of the English state and of the English people merged for the first time."

As in Italy, British labor regularly interacted with officials and worked under the state's regulatory regime. And as in Italy, mobilization politicized British labor and transformed its interests and attitudes about the state. The parallels end there. The very different type of British mobilization led to very different results. Despite the difficulties the war entailed, and especially the government's failure to deliver on its promise to force employers to pay their fair share, the British working class remained reformist. The state's extensive use of procedural justice ensured that labor continued to see its future within Britain's parliamentary regime. But labor's interests evolved in important ways. Britain's procedurally just strategy diminished labor's traditional distrust of state power, and it eased the adoption of a policy agenda that included an important role for the state (moderate socialism). Reliance on procedural justice also helped to retain and probably increase labor's allegiance to the state. Officials rejected the type of unjust policies that encourage the working class to band together against authorities, and the inclusion of labor leaders in decision making created divisions between labor leaders and the rank and file.

These transformations are not as dramatic as in Italy, but the Labour Party's adoption of a moderate socialism was neither predictable nor inevitable before the war began (Horne 1991, 258–89, 292; Winter 1974, 271–72). These years marked a turning point in Labour's political development. As chapter 8 discusses, wartime changes in British labor were also crucial to understanding the failure of postwar democratic reform. But first, I test my hypotheses on the effect of British mobilization on labor's interests, identity, and attitudes about the state.

Labor's Prewar Moderation and Distrust of the State

Organized labor had carved out a place within the British economy in the decades before the war. Unionization initially expanded in the skilled workforce, and a new generation of "general" unions recruited unskilled and semiskilled workers. This "new unionism" meant that union density doubled in the decade before the war and reached a third of the eligible workforce (Gerber 2005, 14; S. Pollard 1983, 38). Many regional and sectional trade unions affiliated with the TUC, a voluntary federation that was the driving force behind the creation in 1900 of the Labour Representation Committee (the forerunner of the Labour Party). Unions and the

Labour Party had distinct identities, but they were linked to a degree that was unusual in Europe. Organized labor comprised almost all of Labour's members, it provided most of the party's funding, and it shaped its priorities (Worley 2005, 4).

Labourism

Labour was neither a revolutionary party nor an ideological one. Unlike in many European labor movements, radical ideas made little headway in Britain before the war. "Trade unions have little or none of the wild fancies and subversive schemes and idle rhetoric which are so commonly the stock in trade with their French and German fellows," a *Times* journalist remarked. "There is no trace now [1883] of a deep-rooted antagonism of the capitalist class as such, no belief whatever in a millennium to follow" (quoted in Phillips 1989, 11–12). The Labour Party also had no unifying political program, and it rarely engaged in principled debates (Harris 2000, 8–9). The notion of "labourism" probably best captures its approach. Labourism contained no fundamental critique of capitalism. It sought to improve living and working conditions and to guarantee union rights. Strong and independent working-class organizations were necessary to the gradual achievement of a just distribution of the nation's wealth; they were not the means to a new political or economic order. Labour "was not looking for a revolution, even a peaceful one, but merely a fair deal" (Thorpe 1997, 19). Organized labor was suspicious of the House of Lords, but it showed little interest in republicanism, proportional representation, or other political innovations. A leading Labour figure spoke for the vast majority in 1909 when he remarked, "They [constitutional reforms] will not bear examination. They may be but will-o'-the-wisps leading into bogs those who foolishly follow" (quoted in Evans 2003, 15).

There were British Marxists and there was a revival of interest in socialism in the 1880s. But the vast majority of trade unionists were not socialists before the war (Horne 1991, 23, 243; McKibbin 1990, 296). British labor developed few links with its European counterparts or with the Second International. "They did not as a rule like the degree to which continental unionists were tied up with Marxist politics" (Pelling 1963, 116). The socialists in the Labour Party were never more than a tiny minority of mostly middle-class adherents who tended to reject Marx's belief in the class struggle (Tanner 1997, 51). Trade unionists were suspicious of these intellectuals, whom they saw as naively caught up in a fairy-tale future. A prominent trade unionist dismissed them as "hare-brained chatters and magpies of Continental revolutionists" (quoted in Pelling 1963, 117; see also A. Reid 2000, 224). Socialists, in turn, opposed labor's narrow focus on economic goals (Thorpe 1997, 12).

The Labour Party was not on the verge of replacing the Liberals when war broke out.[1] Ideological affinities and organizational ties between them led to the formation of the Progressive Alliance in 1903, with Labour as the junior partner. Labour's gains, especially in the last general election before the war (1910), depended on agreement to run one candidate in each seat (Kirk 1998, 183, 194). Labour was unable to expand its appeal (Rubinstein 2003, 53, 64). Much of the working class, especially in unskilled and mostly white-collar unions, supported Liberal candidates. "The Liberals had become the party of the working class by 1910, leaving Labour on the sidelines" (Turner 1992, 24). Labour never polled more than 7 percent of the electorate before the war.

Labor's moderation does not mean that industrial relations were harmonious. The British working class expected conflict and struggle. It knew it had to fight to attain its fair share (Kirk 1998, 151). The strike had become the dominant form of labor activism by 1870. A wave of large, bitter, and often violent industrial disputes (and one of the most strike-prone periods in modern British history) occurred before the war. Known as the "Labour Unrest," it began in 1911 and eventually involved most sectors of the working class. Textile workers in the north walked out on the job. A nationwide coal-mining strike occurred in 1912. Two years later, railroad workers, miners, and dockers formed the Triple Alliance, which posed a serious challenge to the port of London. But the members of the Triple Alliance—like their counterparts across Britain—sought better wages and working conditions, not a new political or economic order (Cronin 1979, 47–51; Pelling 1963, 141; Rubinstein 2003, 54–55).

A Tradition of Self-Help and Distrust of the State

Skilled workers were more committed to self-help than the unskilled, but voluntarism was a powerful current in British working-class culture. Labor looked to itself and its voluntary organizations—unions, cooperatives, and friendly societies—to achieve its goals. Working-class life was "a life apart" before the war. Labor asked little of its government except to be left alone (Bourne 1989, 201). Distrust of the state was central to this approach. The working class was deeply suspicious of a state that taxed and recruited it and used its army to police strikes. The industrial areas in Scotland, Wales, and northern England were especially wary of state power. The Liberal Party had led prewar calls for social reform and many workers supported its candidates, but it was still the Liberal prime minister Herbert Asquith who cautioned labor in 1911 that he would use "all the forces of the Crown" against them in strikes (quoted in Sibley 2005, 2).

A separation of politics and economics was also central to labor's beliefs. The working class was "either intensely apathetic politically or prepared to let other classes represent their interests in local and national politics" (Winter 1985c, 366). The prewar Labour Party functioned largely as a trade union pressure group and adjunct of the Liberal Party (Thorpe 1997, 22). Many trade unionists, and especially the rank and file, reluctantly supported Labour's political activities. After the Trade Union Act of 1913 again allowed unions to collect levies for political activities, 40 percent of union members voted *against* their union having a political fund. A majority in some unions opted out of their contribution (Lawrence 2011, 254; Tanner 1990, 321).

Labor accepted some forms of state action, such as assistance to guarantee full employment and to enforce fair wages. But its distrust of the state meant that it did not promote ambitious social policies (Thorpe 1997, 19). It was "New Liberals" within Asquith's government who proposed schemes for an expanded state role to address problems afflicting the working class. Neither the Parliamentary Committee of the Labour Party nor the TUC was enthusiastic about prewar proposals for national health, unemployment insurance, housing programs, and compulsory education (Noel Whiteside 1987, 214). "All we want is liberty of action. We want no Parliamentary interference," the head of the boilermakers' union proclaimed. "We want the right to combine, and this we have; and the power that Union gives us will enable us to obtain all that we can reasonably expect" (quoted in Hinton 1995, 68–69). For the working class, "social reform mean[t] 'police,'" as a worker explained at the time (quoted in Cronin and Weiler 1991, 48; see also 47–49). The state was not to be trusted: it might intervene in the labor market and threaten long-fought-for labor rights. State-controlled systems might also threaten union benefit programs (and so their appeal to dues-paying members). It was better to rely on one's own associations than seek state solutions.[2]

British labor's prewar distrust of state authority also meant that it was skeptical about state "meddling" in negotiations with employers. Organized labor preferred voluntary collective bargaining. It did not seek state or third-party involvement in setting wages or working conditions, and it shared its employers' resentment of the modest role the state played in industrial relations.[3] Neither unions nor the Parliamentary Committee of the TUC supported an expansion of state arbitration. They did not trust the state to impose a fair deal (Pelling 1963, 128, 142). They wished to be left alone to negotiate on equal terms (Thorpe 1997, 5).

British labor did not want an activist state. Its key political objective was to check restrictions on union activities, which is why workers wanted a Labour Party in the first place (A. Reid 2000, 223). Working-class support for an independent political party in the early 1900s was a defensive move to regain organized labor's legal status. It was not a decisive break from the past. Parliament had secured the legal position of unions in the early 1870s, but a series of judicial decisions threatened labor's bargaining rights. These actions, and especially the 1901 *Taff Vale* decision (which held that unions could be liable for civil damages incurred during strikes), led union leaders to reconsider their lackluster support for the Labour

Representative Committee. After *Taff Vale*, a majority of unions affiliated with the Labour Party. They wanted a stronger voice in Parliament in order to reverse this decision (Pelling 1963, 107–15, 126; Tanner 2003, 41). Tellingly, once Parliament repealed *Taff Vale* in 1906, organized labor's support for political action again lapsed.

Trust and Moderation after a Procedurally Just Mobilization

The British state's wartime presence in working-class life politicized labor and challenged its traditional separation of politics and economics (A. Reid 1988a, 229). Writing in 1917, a boilermaker remarked on this change: "The prejudice of Trade Unionists against politics has hitherto held us back . . . but the events of the last three years have taken the scale from our eyes" (quoted in DeGroot 1996, 317). British labor broadened its focus beyond the narrow economic interests bound up in the job. The TUC committed to a new role for Labour after the war. It would become an independent party capable of shaping government policy (Horne 1991, 255). Many unionists who had reluctantly supported political levies before the war were now committed to greater Labour representation in Parliament. It was time to break out of the alliance with Liberals. Organized labor directly financed twice as many candidates in 1918 as it had before the war (Tanner 1990, 393–94). With the Labour Party's new role came a new conception of labor's interests that incorporated a crucial lesson from the war. Britain's reliance on procedural justice ensured that labor remained reformist, but it also "taught" labor that it could trust the state. Labor now saw the state as a potential ally.

Learning to Trust an Activist State

Extensive state intervention in the economy politicized British labor—as it had across Europe. But it was the type of mobilization that explains the content of that politicization and, in particular, labor's shift from its prewar labourism to a moderate (nonrevolutionary) socialism. Throughout the war, officials included labor in political and economic forums. They treated labor with respect and explained the reasons for decisions affecting it. By 1918, and as the third hypothesis expects, the state's extensive use of procedural justice had built labor's trust in the state. British labor had sufficient faith in the state's good intentions to support an activist state.

"THE BIRTH OF A SOCIALIST PARTY"

The appeal of statist policies developed during the war. In September 1916, the TUC adopted—without controversy—a resolution supporting nationalization of the railroad and mines, and extensive state control of shipping and the food industry. "The war has proved beyond all doubt the national weakness and danger of our prewar industrial system," the trade unionist who presented the resolution explained. "Our vital industries should no longer be left in the hands of capitalists whose first object is profits, and workers whose first object is wages. Such industries should be regulated by the State in the national interest" (quoted in A. Reid 2010, 281). Four months later and in response to strong local demand, the Labour Party adopted *Labour after the War*. This pamphlet was a composite statement culled from over a hundred resolutions from local organizations. It endorsed collectivist and interventionist reforms for the postwar era (Horne 1991, 225–33).

The Labour Party's 1918 constitution established its objectives for the postwar order. The centerpiece was Clause IV's commitment to socialism: "To secure for the workers by hand or by brain the full fruits of their industry and the most equitable distribution therefore that may be possible upon the basis of the common ownership of the means of production, distribution, and exchange, and the best obtainable system of popular administration and control of each industry or service." Clause IV signaled an important change. The *Manchester Guardian* featured the headline "The Birth of a Socialist Party" on February 27, 1918. "There is now for the first time embodied in the constitution of the party a declaration of political principles, and these principles are definitely Socialistic." Labour now accepted a large role for the state (Tanner 2003, 43–44). Sidney Webb drafted the original version of Clause IV, and it reflected Fabian views. Their socialism differed from that of guild Socialists and syndicalists who distrusted the state and who focused on the development of worker organizations. Fabians were statists. Their "administrative socialism" saw a democratic state as the trustee of the people and as the vehicle for achieving social justice (Winter 1974, 33, 36, 278). Socialist principles about collective rights over production and the state's responsibility to protect individuals from want would now guide Labour deliberations (Horne 1991, 251).

The Labour Party approved its platform for postwar reconstruction—outlined in *Labour and the New Social Order*—in June 1918. An enhanced role for the state was central to it. Largely authored by Sidney Webb, the first section, "The End of a Civilisation," proclaimed, "The individualistic system of capitalist production, based on the private ownership . . . may, we hope, indeed have received a death-blow" (Webb 1918, 3–4). The pamphlet sketched the "The Four Pillars of the House" that the party proposed to build. It committed Labour to the "immediate Nationalization" of key industries and economic regulation of the rest. It also called for "Common Ownership of the nation's land" and a capital levy (or graduated tax on personal capital or accumulated wealth) to pay off the war debt and fund social reform (Webb 1918, 4, 10, 15–18). Labour's turn was not to revolution but rather from distrust of state power to a belief that it could use the state to achieve its goals.

RANK-AND-FILE SUPPORT

The principles in Labour's postwar platform were not new to Britain. Fabians developed their statist approach before the war. But the widespread endorsement of these ideas within the labor movement was a significant departure.[4] Before the war, nationalization was "an aspiration rather than a program" that middle-class Socialists and intellectuals supported. Workers tended to ignore it (Morgan 2011, 242).[5] The war "transformed what had hitherto been the academic shibboleth of a minority into an immediate issue, and into a 'practical' demand of the organized workers as a whole" (Harrison 1971, 254; see also Worley 2005, 10). As with *Labour after the War*, Labour's 1918 platform reflected the concerns of the rank and file. Representatives of labor's principal institutions formed the War Emergency Workers' National Committee (WNC) in August 1914 to protect working-class interests. The WNC was attuned to local sentiments and worked closely with local Labour and trade union bodies in producing the platform (Harrison 1971, 214–29). *Labour and the New Social Order* was widely circulated and discussed in the press before its adoption (Horne 1991, 257). Given the structure of the party and its dependence on the unions, the platform articulated a socialism that conformed to union priorities (Worley 2005, 15). Clause IV was not controversial and it was accepted without comment (Thorpe 1997, 44).[6]

British labor's conversion to socialism was cautious. Some trade unionists remained ambivalent about an activist state, and Labour had yet to develop specific policies to address many labor problems, such as unemployment (Cronin and Weiler 1991, 51–56; Horne 1991, 255; Worley 2005, 13–17). But Britain's mobilization had changed labor's attitudes about the state: it no longer sought to keep the state (and middle-class Socialists) at arm's length. Webb and his colleagues had moved from the margins of labor politics to the center of it (Winter 1974, 6–7, 271–72). "For almost a century before 1914 Socialism had been written and talked about, but comparatively few had taken it seriously," one contemporary wrote (quoted in A. Reid 1985a, 70). Sidney and Beatrice Webb wrote a minority report on Poor Law reform in 1909. It was a powerful statement calling for a large state role in guaranteeing a minimum living standard, an early call for a welfare state.[7] But the TUC and Labour's Parliamentary Committee rejected the report (Pelling 1963, 127–28). Labor was too suspicious of state authority and too wedded to its tradition of self-help to accept Fabian ideas. Now, after years of a procedurally just mobilization, Sidney Webb wrote Labour's principal policy statements. State action would create the "new social order."

Historians stress that wartime state intervention weakened British labor's distrust of state power. They argue that state control of the coal mines illustrated the benefits of shifting away from private ownership (Horne 1991, 271; A. Reid 1988a, 229; Tanner 2003, 43; Wrigley 1987a, 34–37). They are correct up to a point. State intervention politicized labor and demonstrated the value of an activist state. As Ernest Bevin noted, the war taught him "that if an industry can be socialized for war, it can be socialized for peace" (quoted in Cronin and Weiler 1991, 52). But there is more to explaining this change than the degree of state intervention. The Italian state was also intensively involved in the wartime economy, but Italian labor reached the opposite conclusion. It rejected working with the liberal state. It was British labor's experience of a particular type of state intervention—one that embraced procedural justice—that explains labor's adoption of moderate socialism. Mobilization for war fostered working-class faith in the government as an alternative to private enterprise. Implicit in that vision was a newfound sense that labor could sufficiently trust the state to use it to realize working-class goals. Britain's procedurally just mobilization explains labor's shift from distrust to trust, as anticipated by the third hypothesis.

Unfair Outcomes Yet No Interest in Revolution

Labour's support for moderate socialism was a fundamental shift in labor's conception of its interests. But there was also continuity, especially in contrast to European counterparts. As hypothesis 1 expects, Britain's relatively just mobilization encouraged reformist demands. The government's inclusion of labor helps explain why, despite major grievances about pay and working conditions, and anger about the lack of comparative sacrifice, labor's wartime embrace of socialism never took a radical turn. The war demanded extraordinary sacrifices from the working class—and they grew tired of it. The number of strikes increased during the war despite the ban on strikes in the Munitions of War Act. Although there were fewer work stoppages during the war than before it, there were also many more strikes during World War I than during World War II (Thorpe 1997, 34). The government's failure to ensure that firms paid their fair share drove much of this industrial action.

Organized labor had made clear during its first wartime discussions with officials that its concessions came at a price. Employers must be forced to do their part. Officials promised in the Treasury Agreement to restrict profits in war industries, and they reiterated this pledge with the passage of the Munitions of War Act. Official wartime propaganda stressed shared sacrifice. Campaigns to encourage enlistment in the military and the purchase of war bonds asked, "Are you in this?" The government repeatedly called on *all* Britons to contribute. "You buy

War Bonds. We did our bit" declared a poster portraying a British soldier and sailor staring out at the viewer.

The message was clear and consistent, but so was the inequality. The word *profiteering* entered labor's lexicon during the war. Workers contrasted "the essential selfishness and unsatisfactoriness of capitalism" with "the patriotism and unselfishness of labour" (quoted in Tanner 1990, 368). The labor press depicted profiteers as "The Vampire on the Back of Tommy" and the "Brit Hun" (quoted in Simmonds 2012, 169). Yet the government proved unwilling to fulfil its pledges to provide fair outcomes, and officials admitted as much. An official report in 1917 noted that the excess profits tax "does not take the money out of the rich man's pocket in the same way that direct tax on his income would have done, and it has consequently failed in its moral effect on the working classes as a symbol of sacrifice" (quoted in DeGroot 1996, 72–73). The working class was angry that it was carrying an unfair burden, and it struck out in protest.

THE "CONSCRIPTION OF RICHES"

Knowledge of the mine owners' rising profits led to the first strikes under the Munitions of War Act (Brown 1983, 89). South Wales miners reasoned that their work stoppage was "just" (if illegal). The owners were making huge profits while using the "national crisis . . . to beat down the men's wages" (quoted in Tanner 1990, 368). The chair of the Arbitration Committee described the situation in 1915: "This question of profits assumed a dangerous aspect." If the government had done more to denounce "undue profitmaking, or profiteering . . . the trouble might have been lessened," the official explained. "When men saw that one class was gaining, and that they, as a whole, got no more pay in spite of increasing prices and cost of living, but were told it was unpatriotic to strike with a view to more pay, they objected" (Askwith 1920, 372–73). Anger over distributive injustice was also behind the engineering strikes in the Clydeside in February 1916. "The labour difficulty has been largely caused," an official concluded, "by the men being of the opinion that, while they were being called upon to be patriotic and refrain from using the strong economic position they occupied, employers, merchants, and traders were being allowed perfect freedom to exploit to the fullest the nation's needs" (quoted in Askwith 1920, 373).

The official report on a wave of industrial unrest in spring 1917 also attributed the action to the lack of shared sacrifice. "A strong feeling exists that the workers are not fairly treated in the apportionment of the results of the joint efforts of employer and employees" (Chance 1917, 8). It was distributive injustice, not real wages, that was the problem: "The actual increase in the cost of living does not appear to be so important a factor in the workers' minds as the belief that profiteering exists" (Chance 1917, 13). The report concluded that addressing the unrest required "secur[ing] to the working man a fair share of the product of his labor" (Chance 1917, 34). Eight individual reports from districts across England and Scotland were the basis for this report. Each reached the same conclusion: distributive injustice was the foremost source of unrest. Of the six causes noted in the summary report, three of the four most important stemmed from the inequality of sacrifice (Meeker 1917, 105). The report stressed that the workers were patriotic, "but since the beginning of the war there has gradually arisen a sense of injustice, and a feeling that there is a tendency to treat them as though they were rather the instruments of the community than members of it" (Meeker 1917, 107).

Workers were patriots, but not suckers—they were attuned to distributive justice and they demanded fair outcomes. Government rationing came too late and was too ineffective to calm anger over food shortages. A weekly newspaper from the East End of London described this sentiment in early 1918: "The unequal distribution of food has brought more discontent and dissatisfaction to the people of East London than anything we have known since the war started. Although less terrifying than the air-raids, the food scarcity has produced an amount of exasperation which German terrorism never did. At the back of it all is the feeling that there is plenty of food in the country but that the appropriation of it has been unequal and unjust" (quoted in Wilson 1986, 519). The working class was willing to endure hardship to defeat Germany, but they were incensed that others were not sacrificing as well.

The introduction of conscription in 1916 sharpened working-class concerns about distributive justice. Labor accepted the need for compulsory military service, but it believed that a capital levy should accompany the conscription of men. The WNC popularized the "conscription of riches" slogan in its call for progressive taxation. Its pamphlet on military service raised the essential question, "How could the government pretend that this compulsory service was necessary when it was not 'seizing the wealth of the nation'; when it was only the lives, not the property of men, which the government was proposing to commandeer" (quoted in Harrison 1971, 240). The pamphlet stressed that the rich—many of whom did not even work—should be forced to contribute through taxation on their incomes.

The "conscription of riches" became an official aim of the trade union movement by the summer of 1916. The campaign spoke to common concerns among workers and united disparate elements of the Labour Party. Ramsay MacDonald, who had resigned as party leader because of his opposition to the war, declared, "The treatment of the two essentials to national success in the War—life and wealth—is flagrantly unequal" (Horne 1991, 235). The traditional and prowar elements of the labor movement also supported the campaign. The Triple Alliance of railroad workers, miners, and dockers endorsed the conscription of wealth in June 1917 (Horne 1991, 238). Leaders of the most important labor organizations—including the WNC, the TUC, the Labour Party Executive, and the Miners' Federation of Great Britain—met with Andrew Bonar Law, the chancellor of the Exchequer, in November 1917. Sidney Webb spoke for the group, and he lobbied hard for a capital levy. Webb feared that repaying the war debt would absorb public revenue that could otherwise be spent on postwar reform (Harrison 1971, 251; Horne 1991, 234). A capital levy was only fair. It would serve as a quid pro quo for military service during the war and as a vehicle to reduce the national debt after the war.

A MODERATE SOCIALISM

The demand for equality of sacrifice was not a veiled attack on the war. To the contrary, the "conscription of riches" campaign was so effective because labor could express its patriotism *and* its discontent. The working class was proud of its support for the war, but the lack of reciprocity was unacceptable (DeGroot 1996, 295–96). It was angry that the government reneged on its promises to extract a proportionate sacrifice from the upper classes. But that anger did not translate into radical politics or a rejection of the state. Whereas Italy's procedurally unjust strategy radicalized Italian labor and alienated it from the state, British labor continued to believe in Britain and its parliamentary regime. This contrast highlights the relative importance of procedural justice. Distributive justice matters: the lack of comparative sacrifice was a major source of British labor's dissatisfaction, and it drove much of the industrial unrest. But the inequity did not weaken labor's support for the war or shake its confidence in Britain. It is perceptions of *procedural* justice that influence assessments of the authority (or the state) as a whole.

Labour's platform for reconstruction, *Labour and the New Social Order*, contained an indictment of capitalism that was new to Labour, and that other major British parties did not share. But it was not a call for capitalism's destruction (MacIntyre 1975, 100–110; Winter 1974, 273–74). Labor wanted a new *social* order (not a new political or economic one). Fabians wanted a more advanced and regulated form of capitalism, and labor was committed to an evolutionary and constitutional path to this new order (Horne 1991, 243; Wrigley 1987c, 85). No one sought to destroy the political system or contemplated violence. This shift in labor's interests was not the first salvo in a class war.

The Fabians derived their name from a Roman general whose patient avoidance of pitched battles secured his ultimate victory over stronger forces. Webb and his colleagues saw the advent of socialism as a part of a distant future, one arrived at by peaceful means (Winter 1974, 38–38, 278). The British Left initially welcomed the Kerensky regime as a more palatable ally than czarist Russia in the fight against autocratic Germany, but the October Revolution frightened most

Labour leaders. It convinced them of the pressing need for a nonviolent and democratic alternative to Vladimir Lenin's revolutionaries (Pelling 1963, 156–57; Winter 1974, 276). "If you want me to lead the Labour Movement as a Bolshevist," Arthur Henderson declared, "I give you notice that I am done with the job" (quoted in Pugh 2010, 130). The Independent Labour Party (ILP) and the smaller Marxist British Socialist Party convened a conference at Leeds in June 1917 to honor the Russian Revolution. Delegates proposed establishing "Workers' and Soldiers' Councils" across Britain based on the Russian model. The Labour Party opposed the convention, and the rank and file showed no interest in the councils. Several months after the conference, an official report noted, "The Councils are attracting little attention and show little sign of becoming important" (quoted in Wilson 1986, 523). None were created. "Almost unnoticed, [the proposal] withered away" (Stephen White 1974, 166).

British industrial conflict never assumed radical undertones (A. Reid 1985a, 66–68). An official report on labor unrest in 1917 dismissed "feelings of a revolutionary nature" as a cause of industrial action across Britain. The report's only mention of "revolutionary" or "radical" was to note its irrelevance (Barnes 1917, 5). Even the most militant unrest—the series of unofficial work stoppages that shop stewards led—was temporary and its militancy exaggerated.[8] The shop stewards were radicals who distrusted state authority and sought worker control. Their followers were not. "This was a classic case of militant desperadoes out of touch with their supposed followers," a historian observes (DeGroot 1996, 115). The rank and file sought to *defend* their privileged position within the *existing* system (Hyman 1987, 135; Searle 2004, 711). They sought higher and fairer wages, not the overthrow of the wage system.

Labor's new interest in nationalization also reflected traditional trade union grievances. Common ownership of the means of production was a vehicle to attain national wage standards, minimum wages, and better working conditions. It was not about creating a new socioeconomic order (Currie 1979, 101; Tanner 1990, 360, 372). The same could be said of *Labour and the New Social Order*. Labour's 1918 platform was novel in its support for an activist state, but it was also a defensive and conservative program. It sought to retain the wartime state and labor's wartime gains—such as rent control and regulation of unskilled labor.

British politicians were apprehensive about the wartime rise of industrial unrest (and especially the shop stewards), but they soon understood that labor posed no revolutionary threat. Neither minutes from cabinet meetings nor the papers of wartime leaders reveal anxiety about domestic Bolshevism (Schuker 1981, 356). Even those in Scotland Yard most obsessed with "socialist agitators" acknowledged there was little to fear (Bourne 1989, 210; Searle 2004, 767). Mobilization had politicized British labor, and its newfound trust in the state eased adoption of a moderate socialism, but the war years had not moved it closer to revolution or radical demands. To the contrary, war had brought Labour closer to the political establishment. The party's new approach attracted members of the Liberal Party, and Labour and trade union leaders welcomed these former Liberals to the party. But they opposed any links with Communists. Labour rejected the British Communist Party's attempts to affiliate with it, and the party forbade Communists from attending Labour meetings (Mowat 1955, 20; Tanner 2003, 43-44). As the first hypothesis anticipates, Britain's procedurally just mobilization encouraged reformist demands.

Procedural Justice and Labor's Allegiance to the State

Historians debate the strength of British working-class nationalism before the war. Some stress labor's attachment to the empire, the monarchy, and other symbols of British power. According to this view, the working class identified with its class and community, but it also saw itself as part of a larger whole (Kirk 1998, 146; Pugh 2002, 14; Sibley 2005, 68). At an English Socialist camp in 1914, a speaker explained that "there will be no need to change the existing form of government" when establishing socialism. "Are we going to keep the King?" someone in the audience called out. "Of course, we are," the speaker replied. "In England the King does what the people want. He will be a socialist King" (quoted in J. A. Thompson 1971, 341). Workers might be denied their fair share of the nation's wealth, but they celebrated the empire's success (August 2007, 150). They knew "they were superior to any workers elsewhere in the world" (DeGroot 1996, 10).

Others historians are skeptical of working-class enthusiasm for empire. They argue that imperialism was a middle-class project, and that too much attention has been paid to labor leaders and parliamentarians and not the workers themselves. According to this view, the working class was apathetic about British imperialism. Jingoistic support of the Boer War was mostly a middle-class phenomenon, and unemployment—not patriotism or the "needs of the country"—explains working-class enlistment in the army (Cunningham 1981; Price 1972). Only one of the dozen trade union leaders in the House of Commons supported the Boer War at its outbreak, and this parliamentarian lost his seat in the subsequent election (Pelling 1968, 82–100).

Regardless of the extent of nationalism within the working class during the Edwardian era, it is important to distinguish between nationalism on the one hand, and trust in and identification with the governing regime on the other. Historians who argue that British workers felt part of a "concrete community" acknowledge the limits of this sentiment. The working classes "believed in a Britain that was not necessarily the state. It was a Britain in which they had a stake. It was a Britain worth defending, whatever the sins of the government" (Sibley 2005, 68; see also Berger 1994, 20–21). The working class may have believed in Britain, the monarchy, and the empire, but these beliefs went hand in hand with suspicion of the state and fear of its coercive power.

Historians have revised the popular image of unbridled enthusiasm at the outbreak of war. The crowds that filled Trafalgar Square in August 1914 were not representative of the country as a whole. Politicians had incentives to exaggerate popular sentiment for war (Simmonds 2012, 35). Nevertheless, the British people—including the working class—supported the war, and they continued to believe it was just even when there appeared to be no end in sight. Britain's wartime reliance on procedural justice had not only taught labor that the state might be *trusted*. It also helped the state maintain, and probably increase, labor's *allegiance* to Britain, which supports the third hypothesis. Unlike the Boer War and other previous conflicts, there is no debate about British labor's unceasing support for World War I. British labor was resolved to win the war, and its support never wavered.

Patriotic Defense of Britain

It took the German violation of Belgian neutrality (one month after the war began) to persuade some Labour leaders and Liberal newspapers, such as the *Manchester Guardian*, that the war should be fought (Bourne 1989, 210; Thorpe 1997, 32). There was also a pacifist and anti-imperialist faction in the Labour Party, a small but significant section of Labour MPs opposed the war, and the Labour-affiliated ILP was the main antiwar organization. But antiwar attitudes were a minority position within the labor movement. Ramsay MacDonald resigned as chair of the Parliamentary Labour Party in August 1914 rather than support war appropriations. The prowar parliamentarian Arthur Henderson, who replaced him, represented the majority of working-class opinion that opposed MacDonald's "woolly middle-class radicalism" (Tanner 1990, 365). The vast majority of trade unionists and most Labour MPs supported the war (Tanner 2003, 42; Turner 1992, 192). The Parliamentary Labour Party voted for special war expenditures in August, and Labour's Joint Board (comprising representatives from the Labour Party, the TUC Parliamentary Committee, and the General Federation of Trade Unions) called for an industrial truce later that month (Rubinstein 2003, 73; Wilson 1986, 221). The level of industrial unrest sharply declined for the next six months. The TUC joined with the Labour Party to support the national recruiting campaign (Pelling 1963, 150).

The flood of enlistments in the military was unprecedented and contrary to British traditions. Unlike the Germans and French, the British did not see military service as an inescapable and legitimate responsibility of citizenship or as a rite of passage and proof of masculinity. The British army had been the last resort for the unemployed. However, by December 1914 over one million men had signed up (Sibley 2005, 1, 16). They joined for many reasons, and they expected a short war. But financial hardship did not drive the vast majority of working-class men into the army. Enlisting imposed financial costs on all but the lowest paid, and urban workers from occupations with full employment enlisted at rates outpacing their rural counterparts (Dewey 1984, 206–9; Winter 1985a, 25–64). Working-class volunteers from even the more militant unions rushed to enlist. Nearly a quarter of the munitions, metals, and shipbuilding workers had joined up by summer 1915 (Searle 2004, 800). Officials had to limit the number of volunteers from "essential" industries to keep munitions plants running (Tanner 1990, 362). This voluntary expansion of the armed forces was "one of the greatest mass movements of modern British history" (Sibley 2005, 3).

Government officials and labor leaders had feared working-class opposition to military conscription when it was introduced in January 2016, and the "combing out" of industrial workers sometimes prompted labor unrest (Sibley 2005, 34). But the labor movement accepted compulsory military service as necessary for military victory. The war must be won, for "95 percent of soldiers are working class," a leading trade unionist explained (quoted in Bush 1992, 130). The boilermakers' union agreed to act "with loyalty and unselfishness. . . . We are going to continue doing our best for comrades in the fight and for our country which we love" (quoted in Tanner 1990, 361).

Despite mounting casualties, housing and food shortages, inflation, and restraints on labor mobility, labor's support for the war was never in doubt (Horne 1991, 55). At its first wartime congress in September 1915, the TUC confirmed its determination to "prosecute the cause of the Allies to a final and complete victory" (quoted in Horne 1991, 220). Delegates at a TUC meeting in September 1918 welcomed Samuel Gompers, the famously prowar and anticommunist American labor leader. TUC delegates even sent congratulatory telegrams to Douglas Haig, the commander in chief of the British army, who was later popularly branded "the Butcher of the Somme" (Wilson 1986, 658). Members of the labor movement—including well-known individuals in the Labour Party—formed their own virulently nationalist organization, the Socialist National Defense Committee, in 1915. The committee sought to combat "the pernicious and pestilential piffle of the Pacifist cranks," its secretary declared (quoted in J. L. Thompson 2007, 320).[9] It established branches throughout Scotland and England, published the chauvinist *British Citizen and Empire Worker*, and organized prowar demonstrations that attacked conscientious objectors and "shirkers" (Douglas 1972, 534).

Individuals who opposed the war lost working-class support. Keir Hardie, the first Labour Party leader, spoke out against the war in August 1914: it would only enrich arms dealers and further impoverish the poor. The reaction was swift. A working-class audience in his constituency booed him off the stage with cries of "Rule Britannia." Later that evening, crowds assembled around the home where Hardie was staying, and shouted "Turn the German out" (quoted in Hochschild 2011, 95). After Hardie died in September 1915, his constituency rejected Labour's candidate (who supported the ILP's antiwar stance) and elected someone from the fiercely nationalist British Workers League (Douglas 1972, 533). MacDonald was isolated for most of the war after he resigned as party leader, and Philip Snowden, who would become chancellor of the Exchequer in 1924, lost his seat in the 1918 general election because of his antiwar stance (Bourne 1989, 106–7). There was little room in the labor movement for antiwar activity. The Labour Party marginalized ILP members at its 1917 conference and ILP's membership rolls fell dramatically during the war (DeGroot 1996, 120; Searle 2004, 763).

Disillusion did slowly set in. Anticonscription and antiwar groups grew as the war dragged on. There was also some working-class support for a negotiated peace after Russia's exit from the war (Johansen 2013, 63). But mass opposition never arose. The middle class and political intelligentsia dominated the anticonscription and antiwar groups, and these groups always remained small (Powell 2004, 83). Working-class support for a negotiated peace was limited and did not translate into a rejection of the war (Horne 1991, 47; Turner 1992, 197–98). Large working-class crowds attended the National War Aims Committee's meetings designed to combat calls for a negotiated peace (Horne 1997, 209). Labour Party delegates overwhelmingly supported a resolution in favor of a "fight to the finish" against Germany in January 1917 (Bourne 1989, 210). Later that summer, Henderson endorsed a proposal to send delegates to an international Socialist meeting in Stockholm to discuss proposals to end the war. German and Austrian delegates would be attending. But this Labour leader had misread working-class sentiments. Many local mining branches called for the resignation of any delegate who attended, and merchant seamen refused passage to delegates headed to the meeting (Rubinstein 2003, 92–93; Wilson 1986, 523–26).

Industrial (Not Antiwar) Unrest

The frequency and nature of wartime unrest also illustrate labor's allegiance to the state and its support for the war. The industrial truce negotiated when the war began was generally respected despite inflation and restrictions on labor mobility.

Industrial action did increase during the last two years of the war, but even in the worst year—1918—the number of work stoppages was a fraction of that in the calmest prewar year. Britain lost about six million days to strikes in 1918 as compared with around forty million days in 1912, and the vast majority of strikes in 1918 occurred *after* victory was clearly on the horizon (DeGroot 1996, 81, 110; Gregory 2008, 204; Wilson 1986, 520, 656).

Italian protests often escalated into violent attacks on symbols of the state. British strikes rarely assumed a political or, especially, an antiwar tenor. The first important challenges to the industrial truce occurred in South Wales and the Clydeside in early 1915. Both focused on local issues, such as wage rates and access to decent housing (DeGroot 1996, 12–13; Gregory 2008, 187–96, 288; Wilson 1986, 222–24). Discontent continued to build as the months passed, especially as only rural wages kept pace with inflation. A wave of engineering strikes erupted in early 1917 and spread to over forty-five towns (Bourne 1989, 209). Shop stewards led these unofficial strikes, but this action did not evolve into antiwar protests. They fit into the typical wartime unrest about relative wage rates and living and working standards (S. Pollard 1983, 46). When violent working-class action occurred, it was directed at symbols of Germany (and not one's own state as in Italy). Anti-German riots caused hundreds of thousands of pounds of damage during the war. The most severe began in Liverpool in 1915 and spread across England and Wales, leading to the looting of German shops, the destruction of their interiors, and more than 866 arrests (Panayi 1989).

British labor fought to protect its privileges and to maintain its standard of living, but not at all costs. In early 1916 and following a strike on the Clydeside, the secretary of the ASE explained that his members stood with Britain: "If arbitration has not worked out to the satisfaction of many members, that is no argument, under present national conditions, for stoppages of work. . . . We have given our pledge, not to the Government as a Government, but to the nation through the Government. . . . We are dealing with the nation's requirements while in a state of war" (quoted in Horne 1991, 79). Similar sentiments were on display during a wave of engineering strikes in spring 1917. Men producing antisubmarine devices refused to interfere with the war effort and continued production (Waites 1987, 208). An official inquiry concluded that this reaction was common: workers were determined "to help the State in its present crisis" (Barnes 1917, 5).

This resolve to defeat Germany existed even in regions where industrial unrest was widespread and labor was less integrated into the national effort. An official report on South Wales in October 1917 found "there can be no question that, as a whole, the mining population is sound and solid in its determination that Germany shall be defeated" (quoted in Wilson 1986, 653). Attempts to organize opposition went nowhere, while official efforts to rally support for the war were a resounding success. Crowds poured into the streets to attend the South African general Jan Smuts's prowar address. Four months later, and following a winter of food shortages, a government report reached the same conclusion about labor in general. The Labour Party conference had been "a victory for the orthodox and loyal" sector. The "overwhelming bulk" of organized labor was "loyal and temperamentally conservative." Even on the "Red Clydeside," officials reported that "the national loyalty of the majority of workers" was not in doubt (quoted in Wilson 1986, 654).

Rising industrial unrest, including an upsurge of discontent in the summer of 1918, revealed a range of working-class discontent. But labor's frustrations with the wartime economy never diminished its commitment to military victory or its willingness to serve. Working-class communities would not have welcomed deserters, as did Italian peasants. British labor did not tolerate conscientious objectors or other "shirkers." Workers threatened to strike in 1917 when management in a bullet factory promoted a conscientious objector to the rank of foreman (Wilson 1986, 522). A firm producing ordnance provided its employees with military service badges in September 1914 as visible symbols of their role in the war effort, and to protect them from social pressure to enlist (Bourne 1989, 184). The Admiralty quickly adopted this scheme for its contracts, and the cabinet quickly endorsed the "badging" system (Simmonds 2012, 84). Men preferred to work in firms where they could be "badged" because it indicated participation in war work (even though this brought Ministry of Munitions restrictions on strikes and labor mobility). So strong was this sentiment that it complicated the production of the first British tanks. Officials did not designate the company producing tanks a "controlled" firm because it wanted to keep their development secret. But the company had difficulty retaining skilled workers, as many preferred jobs in firms that were publicly recognized as vital to the war effort (Wilson 1986, 520). Employers would request that the government designate their firm "controlled" because they correctly believed that workers would be reluctant to strike if they thought their actions might undermine the war effort.

Britain was forced to introduce military conscription, but the rate of voluntary enlistment is remarkable. Half of the British soldiers were volunteers even though conscription lasted twice as long (Sibley 2005, 22). This voluntary spirit continued despite months of bloodletting with little progress. It reappeared when British forces faced severe challenges, as the reaction to the March 1918 offensive illustrates.[10] Whereas Italian labor cheered the German and Austrian victory at Caporetto, the German assault on British lines prompted new waves of voluntary enlistment and industrial restraint. British workers continued to support the war and to volunteer for life (and often death) in the trenches. They were angry about the lack of shared sacrifice and they wanted the war to end (on British terms), but as hypothesis 3 expects, the perception of procedural justice helped to maintain, and probably increase, labor's allegiance to the state (Pugh 2002, 171, 526).

Labor's Collective Identity

The Italian and British labor movements were fragmented before the war. But unlike in Italy, where the state's procedurally unjust strategy led to an unprecedented level of solidarity, in Britain mobilization kept labor apart. The influx of war workers did more to intensify intraclass rivalry than to create a shared sense of purpose distinct from the state. Britain's inclusion of labor officials in government bodies also separated union leaders from the rank and file. In one sense, this lack of working-class solidarity is nothing to explain. Divisions and conflicts of interest, rooted in different cultures, income levels, skills, and occupations, are normal features of working-class life. But the contrast between Britain and Italy is notable and, as the second hypothesis expects, underscores the difference the type of mobilization makes in labor's fragmented or united identity.

Intraclass Rivalry

Economic mobilization drew unskilled and semiskilled labor into the factories and transformed the demographics of the British workforce. At the same time, government policy increased homogeneity among this diverse workforce. The gap between skilled and unskilled wages lessened by the war's end (Cronin 1989, 465–66). In some cases, the difference was cut in half (Simmonds 2012, 172–73). Officials encouraged national wage bargaining, arbitrated industrial disputes, introduced war bonuses, and required the recognition of unions in controlled establishments. These policies all disproportionately benefited unskilled and semiskilled workers. The promotion of dilution also helped level hierarchies within the labor movement. Replacing manual tasks with machine work narrowed distinctions between skilled and semiskilled or unskilled labor (A. Reid 1988a, 221).

This increased homogeneity did not generate working-class solidarity. To the contrary, the erosion of wage differentials was a major grievance among skilled workers during the war. They fought to preserve their preferential wages—a far cry from Italy's egalitarian demands during the last two years of war (Searle 2004, 824; Wrigley 1987a, 28). Anger over preferential wages sparked one of the first major wartime strikes in February 1915 (Corfield 1993). This pattern continued throughout the war. Reliance on piece rates advantaged unskilled workers, which generated resentment among skilled workers and demands for compensation (DeGroot 1996). The desire to reestablish wage disparities often drove strikes among iron and textile workers (Tanner 1990, 363–64; Wilson 1986, 526). A major inquiry into labor conditions in June 1917 reported that the narrowing of wage differentials was an important cause of unrest among skilled workers (Corfield 1993). They were unhappy that "learners and women are able to earn higher wages at piece work" (quoted in Wilson 1986, 522). Even the shop stewards' movement, which is often heralded as the vanguard of worker protest, reflected intraclass tensions—such as the desire to retain craft differentials—not class solidarity (Bourne 1989, 210).

Throughout the war, skilled unions, such as the main engineering group (the ASE), resisted closer ties with general unions even though these broad-based unions were rapidly growing. The ASE's members displayed "a contemptuous superiority toward the less skilled" (Tanner 1990, 363). There were similar tensions between skilled and unskilled unions in other sectors. The Associated Society of Locomotive Engineers and Firemen charged the National Union of Railwaymen with "Prussianism," and the union sued the society in return (Tanner 1990, 364). Even the extension of unemployment insurance in 1916 created intraclass conflict. Skilled workers often had workshare systems to cope with unemployment, and they resented the "unfair tax" on their earnings to subsidize semiskilled and unskilled laborers (Noelle Whiteside 1980, 864–74).

While skilled workers feared that "diluted" workers would undermine their status, unskilled workers had their own grievances about their skilled counterparts. They resented that engineers could avoid military service, especially since the unskilled often did similar work (Horne 1991, 80). One of the general unions protested the "secret diplomacy on the ManPower question" that led to the "trade card scheme" that gave skilled unions control over military exceptions (quoted in Tanner 1990, 363). Unskilled workers were also angry when the ASE negotiated the replacement of the trade card scheme with an official agreement to first "comb out" all dilutees before conscripting skilled workers (French 1995, 86).

Despite war weariness and increased industrial unrest, wartime mobilization created new sources of intraclass tension—not solidarity. There was also intraclass conflict within the skilled workforce, within the unskilled workforce, and across the gender divide (Tanner 1990, 363). Grievances continued to be directed almost as much against other workers as against employers and the state. In 1918, the head of the federation of general unions lamented "the old evil of differentiation between workers" (quoted in Tanner 1990, 364). The head of another general union grumbled that he "didn't want any more humbug about this solidarity of labour" (quoted in Lawrence 2011, 243). After the war, Henderson commented on this disunity: "No one man, however, could bestride so fragmented a movement as the British labour movement" (quoted in Lowe 1978b, 665).

Co-optation of Labor Leaders

Bringing labor officials into government and including them in decision making helped bridge state and society. But procedural justice also created fissures within the working class, especially between its leaders and the rank and file. It was a win-win strategy for the government.

Shop stewards were not new to factories, but the war transformed them from being union spokesmen to being leaders of unofficial labor unrest. The skilled workforce in engineering (where the shop stewards were strongest) resented dilution, the lack of job mobility, and the "combing out" of workers. They also resented their leaders' involvement in these policies. Labor officials had agreed to dilution in the Treasury Agreement and they managed its implementation. David Lloyd George appointed Henderson to chair the committee responsible for organizing dilution (Wrigley 1987a, 55). Whether Lloyd George aimed to divide the labor movement or simply sought its compliance, the effect was the same.[11] The government's co-optation of union representatives created a vacuum that unofficial workshop committees filled. A major government commission on the sources of industrial unrest in 1917 concluded that many workers had lost confidence in their official leaders (Barnes 1917, 7). Notably, where labor leaders were not involved in the design or implementation of government policy (such as in mining), no split between the leadership and the rank and file occurred (Wrigley 1976, 23). As hypothesis 2 expects, Britain's relatively just mobilization foreclosed the development of labor solidarity.

Conclusion: A Khaki Election for Conservatives

British labor's wartime transformation seems unspectacular when compared with Italy. Despite an unprecedented economic mobilization requiring massive state intervention into working-class lives, the labor movement remained fragmented, reformist, and committed to the state and the war. It could have been otherwise. Contrary to arguments that take labor's interests, identity, and political attitudes for granted, this (and the preceding) chapter demonstrates the impact of mobilization strategies on how labor understood what it wanted and who it was. British labor rejected calls to do "as in Russia," but its political attitudes had significantly evolved. The war years saw the development of a distinctive new approach (a moderate socialism) that helped sharpen the Liberal-Labour divide and contribute to Labour's becoming one of the two major parties.

But Labour's displacement of the Liberal Party would have to wait. The first general elections after the war confirmed British labor's reenergized nationalism. Held a month after the Armistice, this khaki election was the first British election with universal male suffrage. It was also a triumph for the Conservatives and a major defeat for Labour.[12] This may seem puzzling, but the Tories were also the party most identified with British victory. After four years of war (and official support for procedural justice), much of British labor identified more with its nation than with working-class interests. The contrast with Italian labor could not be sharper. The first postwar Italian elections were a referendum against those who supported the war. The triumph of the popular parties in Italy "was the revenge of those who had not wanted the war over those who had made it" (Maier 1975, 128).

Italian and British labor did share an important political attitude. Both movements had high hopes for the future. They had fought and labored during the war, and they expected to be rewarded when the Armistice came. There would be "land for the peasants" in Italy and "homes for the heroes" in Britain. Yet both movements ultimately got little of what they thought was their due or what they were promised. The next two chapters explain these foiled expectations. They show how British and Italian mobilization strategies decisively influenced the collapse of Italy's weak democracy and the failure of British postwar reform.

COMPLIANCE, REVENGE, AND THE RISE OF ITALIAN FASCISM

British and Italian labor appear to have been in similar positions immediately after the war. Huge strike waves swept both countries, and expectations for reform were high. Both movements seemed poised to capitalize on their growing strength and their contributions to the wartime emergency. But a curious contrast developed between the two cases. Whereas British labor's ambitious program for democratic reform amounted to little, Italian labor won major concessions from the state and employers. The postwar reform legislation was a "watershed" in Italian history (Quine 2002, 296). Here the contrast becomes surprising. As disappointing as the postwar period was to British labor, the state's failure to deliver on its promises did not spark a dangerous escalation of industrial unrest. British labor had worked hard for the war effort; it had agreed to limits on industrial action; and it expected to be repaid for its vital role in British victory. Yet it was clear within a few years of the Armistice that the government's plans for reconstruction would be "dropped into the dustbin" (Tawney 1943, 15). The failure of British reform angered the labor movement, but the working class continued to comply with government authority.

Italian labor went a decidedly different direction. The government enacted "far-reaching and pioneering social legislation" in the immediate postwar years, and the PSI, and its affiliated urban and rural unions, gained powerful footholds in the liberal regime (Quine 2002, 296). Yet labor refused to settle into routine politics. Italy's procedurally unjust mobilization had alienated it from the state and radicalized its demands. The labor movement seemed more intent on taking revenge on authorities than in exploiting its newfound strength to enact further reform. Urban and rural protest continued to escalate and to challenge basic property rights. Within a few years, Fascism triumphed, and labor's postwar gains were gone. It was not the war itself or inherent weaknesses in the liberal regime that destroyed Italy's fledgling democracy. The strategies Rome chose to gain labor's wartime compliance transformed the labor movement into a united revolutionary force that provoked the violent reaction that carried Fascism to power.

This chapter explains the contrast between the Italian and British labor movements' reactions to their wartime experience of procedural justice. I explain why British labor complied with a government that reneged on its promises for reform. I also discuss why Italian labor sought revenge on a state that was providing so many material rewards. Explaining the choice for compliance or revenge requires understanding how each state's mobilization shaped labor's political beliefs. In combination, and as summarized in table 1, they explain British and Italian labor activism. I then draw on the work of democratic theorists to discuss the implications of these war-induced changes in the labor movement for the fate of each democracy. Chapter 8 examines how British labor's wartime development helps explain the failure of Labour's ambitious agenda for postwar reform. But I first turn to describing the extent of democratic reform in both cases. I then explain the contrasting trajectories of the British and Italian labor movements, and why the nature of Italian protest precipitated the Fascist seizure of power.

British Labor's Compliance

The Labour Party did not wait for the Armistice to articulate its vision for reconstruction.[1] It developed a distinctive program during the war that was central to its December 1918 electoral campaign. "The Labour Party protests against any patching up of the old economic order," the platform declared. "It stands for such a systematic reconstruction of industrial and social relations as will give to the workers by hand or by grain the full fruits of their labour" (quoted in Kellogg and Gleason 1919, 413). The enactment of Labour's program would have marked a revolution in British social policy. It would have meant the creation of a welfare state and the provision of social rights.

The government seemed prepared to support Labour's proposals. On becoming prime minister in 1916, David Lloyd George created the Committee (and later Ministry) of Reconstruction to lay the "foundation of a new order" (quoted in Wilson 1986, 817). To run the committee, Lloyd George appointed Christopher Addison, whose commitment to social reform had led him to politics. Prominent trade unionists served on the ministry's committees that produced reports on housing, education, and any number of policies designed to build this new order

(Searle 2004, 817; Tawney 1943, 9). Wartime pledges to repay labor's sacrifices continued in peacetime. Lloyd George vowed during the election that "our task" is "to make Britain a fit country for heroes to live in."[2] His initial efforts following the coalition's December 1918 victory seemed promising. Hundreds of labor officials participated in the National Industrial Conference in early 1919, which produced (and gained official support for) ambitious plans that would translate the coalition's electoral pledges into concrete reforms. On hearing of these plans, the Belgium foreign minister noted that there were "two methods of making the revolution . . . the Russian and the British method" (quoted in Lowe 1978b, 650). The Fabian Beatrice Webb was similarly impressed: "Soviet Government peacefully incorporated in the British Constitution; a revolution in a fit of absentmindedness, without machine guns or barricades—without even waving a red flag" (quoted in Lowe 1978b, 650).

The new Parliament passed reform legislation, and there was discussion of further reform. But the government failed to deliver on most of labor's demands, and it limited the effect of legislation it did enact. "The Government appeared determined to prove that postwar reconstruction is a contradiction in terms" (Tawney 1943, 16). Whether it was on housing, a capital levy, nationalization, education and health care, or a national minimum wage, labor received little of what it had been promised, and what it thought it was due.

Britain: "A World Not Renewed"

The provision of "homes fit for heroes" was the most important reconstruction issue.[3] "Nowhere were war-time pledges more vehement and far-reaching" (Abrams 1963, 43–44). Officials knew the situation was dire. Most working-class dwellings were miserable before the war, and rent control and shortages of construction materials worsened the crisis during the war (Searle 2004, 805). Officials also acknowledged that the government had to play a central role in the provision of housing. Several official commissions in 1917 concluded that private enterprise could not carry the load. "There is only one alternative: the state itself . . . is alone in a position to assume responsibility" (quoted in Ravetz 2001, 75; see also Abrams 1963, 53). Lloyd George pledged that his government would address the shortfall. Providing working-class housing was one of the coalition's "first tasks," the 1918 electoral manifesto declared (quoted in Cook and Stevenson 2014, 119). A Conservative MP and the president of the Local Government Board also spoke of the party's commitment to housing: "To let them come home from horrible, waterlogged trenches to something little better than a pigsty here would, indeed, be criminal . . . and a negation of all we have said during the war, that we can never repay those men for what they have done for us" (quoted in

DeGroot 1996, 200). The Conservative leader Austen Chamberlain agreed that it was imperative that the government create a housing program: "We must push on with it immediately at whatever cost to the state" (quoted in Pope 1991, 65).

The Housing and Town Planning Act of 1919 (the Addison Act) was a watershed in British social policy. The government would provide generous subsidies to local authorities to construct half a million homes of relatively high standards within three years (Wilson 1986, 805–10). Yet "nowhere was the failure to provide relief more clear and calamitous by the end of 1920" (Abrams 1963, 43–44). Lloyd George abruptly reversed course in 1921 and appointed Sir Alfred Mond to replace Addison as the minister of public health. Mond terminated state support of housing. It was time, the millionaire chemical manufacturer announced, "to get the country back to the old economic system" (quoted in C. Addison 1922, 16). As official commissions had foretold, Mond's reliance on private enterprise meant that the number of homes fell far short of the demand. Millions continued to live in squalid conditions. Less than half of the planned homes were constructed, and by 1921 close to a million new homes were needed to cover basic needs (Simmonds 2012, 181). Even the standards of those built declined. By 1923, officials no longer required that "homes fit for heroes" contain bathrooms (Deacon 1982, 130–31). The government had abandoned its promise to secure decent housing for all. "The newly married should be so happy that they can enjoy living in one room," Mond remarked (quoted in Kinnear 1973, 11). The embittered Addison later joined the Labour Party and entitled his book on the housing program *The Betrayal of the Slums*.

A capital levy was also central to Labour's plans for reconstruction. Calls for the "conscription of riches" were a potent slogan during the war and the 1918 electoral campaign. The Labour Party repeated its demand for a tax on all war wealth in 1919 and 1920, downsizing its proposal in hopes of gaining support. A capital levy was again central to Labour's 1922 election manifesto and its 1923 party conference (Comstock 1920, 400; Eichengreen 1990, 210–13).

A tax on wealth had a socialist pedigree. It would redistribute wealth and ensure sufficient revenue for social reform. Yet labor could be cautiously optimistic that it would be enacted. Individuals across the political spectrum worried about the cost of servicing a wartime debt that was enormous by historical and contemporary standards. For many economists, a levy would allow a reduction in income tax rates and help lower the debt and debt service charges. For their liberal colleagues, a levy could create a more equitable division of wealth. Labor's proposal even garnered support in normally unsympathetic quarters. Some Treasury officials initially supported a capital levy. The government's chief economic adviser and a permanent undersecretary to the Treasury promised in November 1917 that the privileged would do their bit: "The masses may be trusted to see that the rich man's burden remains on his back" (quoted in Daunton 2002, 69; see also 66–68; Cronin 1991, 56, 73–76). The same month, a delegation of labor leaders met with Andrew Bonar Law, the chancellor of the Exchequer and a Conservative uninterested in social reform. The chancellor was "significantly sympathetic" to their proposal, stating, "My own feeling is that it would be better both for the wealthy classes and the country, to have this levy of capital and reduce the burden of the National Debt."[4]

Law's remarks "brought this proposal within the realm of practical politics."[5] Parliament reviewed plans for a capital levy in spring 1918, and leading politicians seemed to support it (Wrigley 1992, 103). "Well informed gossip states that the Prime Minister [Lloyd George] is warmly enamoured of it," the *Economist* exclaimed.[6] But in the face of fierce opposition from the Conservative Party and commercial and financial quarters, Labour's determined efforts to shift some of the burden to the upper classes failed (Cronin 1991, 73–74). The rich were not forced to pay their fair share. Servicing the war debt consumed about a third of government expenditures throughout the 1920s, helping to edge out spending on social programs (Daunton 1996, 884, 893; Wrigley 1992, 103).

Nationalization was an additional item on Labour's postwar agenda that seemed imminent in 1918 but that also failed to materialize. The government had assumed control of some of Britain's largest sectors during the war, and voices across the political spectrum supported nationalization after the war. A conservative editor noted that nationalization of transport, electricity, and coal was inevitable (Mowat 1955, 16–18, 28–30). Winston Churchill championed state control of the railroads (Jenkins 2001, 339). Facing the prospect of a miners' strike in early 1919, Lloyd George appointed a commission composed of businessmen, trade unionists, and academics to consider the industry's future. A majority favored some form of public ownership. Nothing came of this discussion. It appears that Lloyd George was just playing for time. He announced in August 1919 that the government had decided against nationalizing the mines. All wartime economic controls disappeared by 1922 (Pelling 1963, 162; Pugh 2002, 175–76).

The war also raised hopes of expanded working-class access to education and health care. All major political parties had endorsed education reform by 1917, and Lloyd George's appointment of a liberal reformer to head the Board of Education signaled the War Cabinet's recognition of its importance. German schools were "the most formidable institution Britain had to fight," Lloyd George had earlier remarked (quoted in Pope 1991, 60). The first steps seemed promising. The Education Act of 1918 "was one of the more significant pieces of social legislation to be passed during the war" (Turner 1992, 363). It raised the school leaving age to fourteen and made provisions for compulsory part-time education of children aged fourteen to eighteen. Both reforms had been the focus of the TUC's education campaign (Crosby 2014, 261). The act also called for nursery schools and the provision of medical inspections, baths, and recreational facilities in schools. Yet just as with the housing program, progress in education was "decidedly limited" (Wilson 1986, 814). Most of its provisions were implemented partially or not at all. The continuing education programs were never established, and the modest expansion of secondary school enrollment primarily benefited the middle class (Wilson 1986, 814–19). There would be "No New Heaven on Earth" for the education of working-class children.[7] Only a small minority of British children would continue beyond elementary school. The promise of better health care for all was equally disappointing, despite the creation of the first Ministry of Health in 1919 (Pope 1991, 61–64).

The government's response to labor's demand for unemployment insurance and a national minimum wage was mixed. The government provided "out-of-work donations" to demobilized soldiers and munitions workers in 1918. These were noncontributory payments (recipients had not paid into an insurance fund). The Unemployment Insurance Act of 1920 extended these benefits to most workers. This program was initially contributory, but amendments provided noncontributory payouts and support for dependents (DeGroot 1996, 96–100, 301; Mowat 1955, 45–46, 127–28). The Labour Party criticized the payouts as mocking the poor—they were short term and too small to support a family—and some Labour MPs walked out of the Commons in protest. But a precedent was set. The nation appeared to accept its responsibility to provide a minimum standard outside the humiliations of the Poor Laws (Wilson 1986, 822–25).[8]

The government also seemed responsive to labor's demand for a national minimum wage. It extended one to munitions and agricultural workers during the war; it accepted the National Industrial Conference's recommendations for a national minimum wage after the war; and Parliament considered a minimum wage bill. Yet these efforts were "virtually barren of positive results" (Lowe 1978b, 650). The Trade Boards Act of 1918 authorized public boards to set minimum wages for nonunionized occupations, but the enthusiasm (and budgetary support) did not endure. The idea of a national minimum wage was dead by 1921 (Horne 1991, 362).

Some sectors of organized labor achieved substantial wage increases from their employers, as well as reductions in working hours in the years immediately after the war. The main engineering union dubbed the latter "one of the greatest triumphs of British trade unionism" (quoted in Wrigley 1987c, 76). Railroad workers attained their best settlement ever, and miners successfully pressed for reforms (Cronin 1992, 97; Wrigley 1987c, 77). However, the vast majority of strikes in the immediate postwar period led to compromises. In no year did workers win more strike actions than their employers. Indeed, employer victories outpaced those of workers in 1919 and 1921 (Cronin 1979, 222–23). Regardless, what labor did achieve either was short-lived or came at no direct cost to the government. Most of the progress in wages and working conditions disappeared when the postwar boom ended (Horne 1991, 362; Wrigley 1982b, 94). Labor had lost three-quarters of its wage increases by 1922 (Mowat 1955, 125).

Procedural Justice Explains Compliance

British labor fought to ensure that the government fulfilled its promises. It expected and demanded payback for its wartime service, and it was angry that the state did not force employers and the propertied classes to pay their fair share. Labor watched as one after the other of the government's plans for reconstruction amounted to little, if anything at all. Yet despite the failure to build this "new social order" and the unprecedented mobilization of organized labor, British industrial action remained peaceful and legal. Officials were anxious about the level of strike activity, and they worried about unauthorized strikes and calls for "direct action." But the British government was not facing a labor movement that fundamentally challenged state authority. The findings from social justice research explain labor's reaction.

The three years after the Armistice saw some of the most intense industrial strife in British history. Collective bargaining had spread across diverse sectors of the economy during the war, including low-paid clerical and unskilled workers. Union density among male workers rose from 32 percent in 1914 to 45 percent in 1918. Female union density shot up even more, from 9 to 23 percent (Wrigley 2018, 70–71). Overall, union membership almost doubled between 1914 and 1919 (Cronin 1979, 236). This growth in unionization (and low wartime unemployment) improved trade union finances. The political funds used to sponsor candidates for Parliament nearly quadrupled by the war's end. Labour Party membership also increased, rising from about four million in 1914 to six and a half million in 1918 (Shepherd and Laybourn 2006, 25).

Organized labor tried to wield its newfound power to extract concessions from the state and employers. A massive strike broke out in the Clydeside in January 1919 at the same time that Belfast was experiencing the largest and longest industrial dispute in its history. Across Britain, miners and metalworkers organized large strikes, a railroad strike crippled British transport, and large-scale unrest hit the shipyards and textile industry. Over one million workers participated in one mining strike (of several serious ones) that alone led to the loss of seventy-two million working days (Rubinstein 2003, 112–13). Never before or since had Britain experienced such an explosion of industrial unrest (Cronin 1992, 93). The number of working days lost to strikes swelled from around ten million in 1913 to close to ten times that amount in 1921 (Cronin 1984, 241). The level of unrest even outpaced that of Italy. Yet despite this unprecedented mobilization, the labor movement received little more than a string of broken promises.

Social justice research finds that how people respond to outcomes depends on more than the outcome itself. It is the interaction between process and outcome that shapes subsequent action. Individuals are more likely to comply with undesirable directives, such as job assignments and pay systems, if they see the decision-making process as fair (Brockner 2010; Cropanzano and Greenberg 1997; Skarlicki and Folger 1997). They are also reluctant to sue someone who treats them with respect, regardless of the case's legal merit. Two studies found that individuals in federal tort and contract actions who accepted mediation (instead of going on to formal trials) felt they had been fairly treated. The favorability of the mediator's decision (or the outcome) had little direct effect on their willingness to accept the decision, even though the awards involved large sums of money (Lind et al. 1993; see also Tyler and Huo 2002). As several theorists put it, procedural justice "serves to 'cushion' the blow of negative outcomes" (Tyler, Casper, and Fisher 1989, 639).

The British government benefited from this fair-process effect. The inclusion of labor in economic and political forums helped make otherwise undesirable outcomes tolerable. British labor's experience of procedural justice discouraged vengeful reactions to failed promises for the future. The fair processes inclined labor to accept bad outcomes. But London also benefited from a virtuous circle: fair processes ensured that British labor identified with the state (hypothesis 3), and this sense of shared identity further contained negative reactions to unrealized expectations. Research on retributive justice—or the restoration of a sense of justice through the imposition of a punishment—finds that individuals tend to be forgiving of authorities with whom they identify.[9] Even when workers view authorities as responsible for a bad outcome, they are likely to explain away the bad outcome as unintentional or understandable given the situation. They may seek compensation, but they do not experience moral outrage or seek to retaliate for the wrongdoing. They continue to comply with the authority's directives. This is what occurred in Britain. Labor identified with Britain. It did not blame the government for the war. Prussian militarism was responsible for the hardships it endured (Pugh 2002, 171). British labor accepted "even disagreeable measures" if necessary to defeat Germany. "Even at the severest period of discontent," one historian noted, "there was no widespread tendency to describe the war as something created by, and in the interest of, the ruling class" (Wilson 1986, 653).

The British government's widespread use of procedural justice allowed it to maintain labor's allegiance and compliance while imposing high costs. The Italian government's different choices led to different results. Italian popular protest intensified despite the enactment of significant reform.

Italian Labor's Revenge

The immediate postwar years in Italy—the "Red Biennium"—were also a period of intense popular unrest. But unlike in Britain, this protest appeared to pay off. Left-liberal governments endorsed political and economic reforms that benefited the popular classes. Giovanni Giolitti often spoke during the war of the inevitability of reform: "How many millions of workers of the cities and fields will return to their humble houses, will return with the consciousness of their rights and demand a new order marked by great social justice that a grateful Fatherland will not be able to deny them" (quoted in De Grand 2001b, 210). Italy's last wartime prime minister, Vittorio Orlando, agreed in November 1918 that peace would bring a new world: "The war is at the same time the greatest political and social revolution history records, exceeding even the French Revolution" (quoted in Maier 1975, 52). Not everyone was on board. Right-wing liberals and nationalists quickly shed their wartime promises to labor. They derided those calling for postwar reform as being part of a "Bolshevik-Giolitti bloc" (Maier 1975, 124). They did not, however, control Italy's postwar governments.

Prime ministers Francesco Nitti (June 1919–June 1920) and Giolitti (June 1920–July 1921) were responsive to the interests of the working class. Both sought to create broad coalitions that included members of the new Catholic Party, former syndicalists, and reformist Socialists (though the last always demurred). Nitti believed in an activist state that would rebuild the economy and promote social, economic, and political reform. He sought to construct a "broader democracy" founded on "social principles" (Pironti 2016; see also D. Smith 1989, 238, 243). Giolitti also made key concessions in hopes of buying off discontent, satisfying what he saw as legitimate aspirations, and domesticating the radical Left. "In 1919 the Italian state entered a new stage," explains one historian. "The central government became directly and financially involved in the delivery of statutory entitlements based on a democratic conception of social rights and citizenship" (Quine 2002, 108).

"A Bold Program of Reconstruction"

Large-scale wars always generate calls for capital levies, but few of these campaigns succeed.[10] World War I was no exception. British labor failed in its determined efforts to impose a one-time wealth tax. The policy was also controversial in Italy: "The usual storm of abuse and panic immediately arose" (Eichengreen 1990, 203; see also 191–202). Yet Giolitti enacted a capital levy. The effect was less than it might appear—payments could be made over a twenty-year period. Nonetheless, Italy stood alone in Europe in imposing a capital levy after the war. And this policy was not a one-off. Immediately after the war, Giolitti spoke forcefully about the need for broader tax reform. "This will be the era of liberty, of social justice, of fruitful labor, of progress, of prosperity ... if the wealthy classes will accept with patriotic fervor the financial sacrifices that will be necessary ... to maintain the commitments made to the popular classes" (quoted in De Grand 2001b, 201). Nitti and Giolitti developed policies to shift the tax burden away from the working class, including increases in inheritance and vehicle taxes, progressive income taxes, and a confiscation duty on war profits (Elazar 2001, 78–79; Peck 1942, 130–33; Zamagni 1993). Giolitti also sought to limit tax evasion by creating a public registry of shareholdings to track wealth in stocks and bonds. Opposition to the registry was fierce—Giolitti depicted the bankers and industrialists as "billionaire sharks"—and the government postponed its implementation until 1921 (quoted in De Grand 2001b, 233).

Within a few months of the Armistice, Italian officials created a state-run pension scheme for manual and nonmanual workers. The government extended the system to sharecroppers and tenant farmers in January 1920, which meant that the system insured a third of the Italian workforce. This was a significant departure from the prewar system of voluntary occupational pension plans that covered 2 percent of Italian labor (Quine 2002, 3, 107). The legislation included the idea of extending the pension scheme to self-employed workers, and it held out the possibility of providing a basic universal benefit to every citizen without exception (Ferrera 2018, 107). The government also granted unemployment insurance to full-time industrial and agricultural workers in October 1919. The inclusion of rural labor in a state-run system was groundbreaking (though the payments guaranteed only a minimum income). No other country provided unemployment benefits to its rural workforce (Quine 2002, 104–7). Giolitti also extended the state-instituted compulsory accident insurance—funded by a surcharge on employers—to agricultural workers (Elazar 2001, 79; Snowden 1989, 53).

The redistribution of land to southern peasants was the most significant agricultural reform in the postwar era. The government had established a veterans' association in 1917—the Opera Nazionale Combattenti—to assist the reintegration of ex-combatants. The association provided access to credit and job training, but its most important role was distributing small plots of uncultivated land (C. Schmidt 1938, 30; Snowden 1989, 40–42). The program's slow implementation—the association was poorly run and had too little land—angered veterans, who led a wave of land occupations in 1919. The official response to these illegal land seizures was *not* to call in the troops, as Rome had done in the past. Nitti's ministers of agriculture were sympathetic to their demands. The Visocchi and Falcioni decrees first temporarily (September 1919) and then permanently (April 1920)

sanctioned land occupations. Prefects now had the authority to retroactively legal-
ize the seizure of lands that peasants had begun to cultivate (F. Adler 1995, 169).
Thousands of acres passed from private hands to peasant cooperatives; the estimates range from one hundred thousand to five hundred thousand acres (Elazar
2001, 80). Some of the southern "great estates" disappeared (Clark 2014, 251).
Nitti's and Giolitti's governments also promoted agricultural cooperatives in
northern Italy. With access to easy credit and official support, their numbers doubled in the immediate postwar years, thus increasing worker control and anger-
ing landowners (C. Schmidt 1938, 22–29; Squeri 1983, 331–32).

Employers conceded to many of labor's demands during the Red Biennium.
Two-thirds of the strikes in 1919 and just over half in 1920 led to "complete or
substantial" concessions to labor, a rate that outpaced both the prewar period and
the British experience (Elazar 2001, 53; Maier 1975, 175). The metalworkers'
union won two long-sought goals in early 1919: an eight-hour day without a reduction in wages and the recognition of shop floor committees in factories. Both
concessions soon spread to most of Italian industry (Horowitz 1963, 137–43;
Seton-Watson 1967, 521). Federterra also won an eight-hour day (a shift from the
prewar "from sunrise to sunset"), and paid vacations for some agricultural workers (C. Schmidt 1938, 22, 29). Soaring wartime inflation had cut into labor's wages,
but 1919 saw real wages recover almost all the ground lost during the war.[11] Labor
made further gains beyond inflation in 1920. Based on an index of 100 in 1913,
real wages of agricultural and industrial workers rose to 123 and 134, respectively,
by 1922 (Maylander 1922, 1263; Zamagni 1993, 239). Federterra also won major
concessions from landowners that gave sharecroppers better terms (De Grand
1989, 42; C. Schmidt 1938, 29; Snowden 1986, 167–69). These workplace victories
improved working-class lives. Based on an index of 100 in 1913, food consumption rose to 109 in 1919 and climbed to 117 by 1922 (Zamagni 1991, 148).

A slight redistribution of wealth had occurred. Italian labor was now better
off than it had been in the past. And it was improving its position relative to the
middle class, and especially state employees (Zamagni 1993, 238). The government played the prominent role in most of these advances. It also legislated a
shortened workday in February 1919 and fixed a minimum wage the following
fall (Zamagni 1991, 150). The government appropriated large sums to public
works programs and mediated labor disputes, often to the benefit of labor, as in
the Paglia-Caldo contract in October 1920 that gave Federterra full control over
labor recruitment. Giolitti's mediation during the occupation of the factories also
led to large and retroactive wage increases (Maylander 1922, 1263–65). Italy's
postwar governments were responsive to working-class interests, and they were
creating a welfare state.

Economic and Political Power

Italian labor emerged from the war more powerful than ever before. Unions enrolled a broader category of workers, and their membership rolls skyrocketed (Tasca 1938, 66). Membership in the CGL had slightly increased during the war. It then shot up, growing fivefold to more than a million members in 1919 and then doubling to over two million by the end of 1920 (Horowitz 1963, 141). This increase in union density was greater than what occurred in Germany, France, and Britain (F. Adler 1995, 154). There was also a flood of new recruits into agricultural unions. Federterra membership swelled from one hundred thousand in 1918 to over eight hundred thousand in 1921 (F. Adler 1995, 171–72; Cardoza 1982, 274, 290). The Catholic rural unions experienced a similarly spectacular growth, rising from about 63,000 members in 1914 to 162,000 at the Armistice, and then jumping again to over 1 million by 1920 (C. Schmidt 1938, 28; Seton-Watson 1967, 520). The PSI also became more powerful after the war. The removal of the few remaining restrictions on male suffrage in 1918 increased the size of the working-class electorate (De Grand 2001b, 215). Less than a year later, and despite conservative opposition, Nitti introduced a proportional representation system that would undermine the power of the old liberal parties. The future now belonged to mass parties, such as the PSI and the PPI. As a member of the liberal elite ruefully predicted, the new electoral system meant "the abdication of the Liberal Party" (quoted in Clark 2014, 255).

The November 1919 parliamentary elections proved him correct. The popular classes triumphed. Support for the two mass parties reached 80 percent in several of Italy's most important regions. The PSI dramatically improved its position, doubling its votes and tripling its representation from 1913 (Cardoza 1982, 272–73; Knox 2007, 270; D. Smith 1969, 326). The PSI was now the largest party in Parliament—it won about a third of the seats—and its institutional strength had grown. The PSI's membership quadrupled from 1914 to 1920, and its revenue was four times greater in 1919 than in 1918 (De Grand 1989, 35; Peck 1942, 188). The 1919 elections also confirmed the strength of the PPI, which became the second-largest party. It increased its number of seats to one hundred from twenty-nine vaguely designated as clerical in 1913, and its membership almost doubled in the second half of 1919 (Maier 1975, 128). The Liberal Party was bitterly divided between interventionists and neutralists, and between liberal democrats and conservatives. It fought separate campaigns and was now a minority party (F. Adler 1995, 175). Giolitti's Liberal Union had only forty-one seats (a decline of 229) and Nitti's Radical Party just twelve (a decline of fifty). Only in the south did the liberal establishment win over half the votes.

The popular mass parties repeated their success in municipal elections the following year (1920). Socialists swept to power in more than a quarter of local governments and almost a third of the provincial councils. The PSI did especially well in the rural provinces of northern and central Italy, winning more than 65 percent of the communes in Emilia-Romagna and over 50 percent in Tuscany (Squeri 1983, 328). This was again a substantial advance. Out of 8,059 communes, Socialist control jumped from 300 in 1914 to 2,162 in 1920 (Snowden 1989, 53). The PPI did almost as well. Italian communes had little independence, but these results were important. They gave the Catholic and Socialist peasant leagues control of local patronage, welfare services, and public works contracts. The localities that mass parties dominated tended to provide better welfare benefits, pay higher wages, and introduce progressive taxation (Clark 2014, 253; Forsythe 1993, 276).

Procedural Injustice Explains Revenge

The Italian labor movement had not reached some working-class nirvana. But it did well during the Red Biennium. Labor's achievements were significant whether compared with its prewar position or with British labor's postwar gains. A US government report (Maylander 1922, 1274) noted the "enormous financial burdens" of Italy's postwar policies. "It must be readily conceded that the Italian Government has gone very far in trying to humor the working classes and keep them contented." Nitti's and Giolitti's governments had granted labor many long-sought goals, and electoral reforms and the growth of rural and urban unions had strengthened the PSI's political power. One could reasonably expect Italian labor to play an increasingly influential role in parliamentary politics to the benefit of the popular classes.

Reformist Socialists believed that the postwar period was an auspicious time to pursue far-reaching reforms. At the 1919 party congress, Filippo Turati stressed the implications of universal male suffrage for the PSI: "Eight to nine tenths of voters are authentically proletarian," he explained. His colleagues should capitalize on this envious position as it "puts in your hands the conquest of the state and, in fact, all of the conquest that you wish to achieve by insurrection" (quoted in McNally 2017, 322). The PSI's resounding success in general elections the following month confirmed Turati's assessment, especially as the PSI had ready partners in Nitti's and Giolitti's governments. Historians concur that the PSI could have achieved most of its May 1917 program if it had worked with bourgeois parties within the liberal order (De Grand 1989, 34; Horowitz 1963, 131). But that was not the direction that the majority wished to go. Turati declined Giolitti's offer of a cabinet post in 1920 because he feared his Socialist colleagues would denounce his decision and expel him from the party (Maier 1975, 183; D. Smith

1989, 244). Turati wrote to a colleague about the options before him: "You say that it is our moment. It would be if we had, or could have, the masses and the party with us. But you know perfectly well that the reality is different" (quoted in De Grand 2001b, 231). Italy's procedurally unjust mobilization had ensured that Turati's moderate socialism had neither popular nor party support.

As in Britain, popular unrest exploded across Italy in the immediate postwar years. *Scioperomania* (strike mania) took hold of Italian politics. Massive industrial strikes occurred across the north. Bitter agrarian disputes engulfed commercial farms in northern and central Italy, with the largest and longest joining share-croppers and day laborers for a six-month strike in 1920 (Elazar 2001, 54). Agricultural workers belonging to Catholic unions acted against landowners in the north. Key categories of public-sector workers went out in droves for the first time (F. Adler 1995, 170). Even the south saw an outbreak of popular protest. Never before had Italian labor engaged in so many work stoppages. Five to six times more industrial workers struck during the Red Biennium than during the decade before the war. The number of agricultural strikers shot up by an even larger proportion. Almost ten times more rural workers struck in 1920 than the annual average before the war. The number in 1920 was double the prewar peak in 1905 (Seton-Watson 1967, 521; Snowden 1972, 273; Zamagni 1991, 152).

Much of this protest was legal and nonviolent, but unlike in Britain, much of it was not. The state's wartime exclusion of labor from political and economic forums had been doubly dangerous for the liberal order. The same processes that led to a virtuous circle in Britain led to a vicious circle in Italy. Individuals have a heightened sense of injustice when procedures are unfair. They show a marked disinclination to comply with authorities who treat them with disrespect (Huo et al. 1996; Lind et al. 1993). Their resentment and anger also make them more likely to retaliate against the authority, and to take revenge on it (Aquino, Tripp, and Bies 2006; Bobocel 2013; Goldman 2003). This retaliation can take many forms, including theft, sabotage, and violence (D. Shapiro, Trevino, and Victor 1995). In one example, researchers tracked how variations in procedural justice affected reactions to a pay cut. All of the employees subsequently stole from their employer, but those who perceived procedural injustice not only stole more but also stole objects that were of *no value to them* (Greenberg 1990).

This desire for revenge is especially likely in situations, such as in Italy, where labor is alienated from the state. When an out-group is the source of injustice, victims are especially likely to attribute blame to that authority, and to see damages as intentionally inflicted. They are also likely to experience the moral outrage that motivates a desire for "just deserts." This is what occurred in Italy. Years of a procedurally unjust mobilization had transformed labor's indifference toward the state into a rejection of it. The urban and rural workforce did not give the government (with whom they did not identify) the benefit of the doubt. Labor held the government responsible for the hardship the war imposed (Seton-Watson 1967, 449). The war had not been fought for them or for a state with which they identified. The war had been "for the *signori* [the gentlemen]".

Depictions of Italy in the immediate postwar period are filled with references to "revolts," "insurrections," and "civil war" (Knox 2007, 250; Snowden 1986, 163). Historians speak of the "bitterness," "the fierce thirst for vengeance," and the "strong desire to punish" that drove the rural and urban masses (Foot 2009, 34; Knox 2007, 220, 231; Salvemini 1973, 140). Violent demonstrations against the cost of living broke out in villages and towns across Italy in summer 1919. Shops and warehouses were sacked and "citizen committees" took control of distribution (Clough 1968, 353–56; Seton-Watson 1967, 520). "Everywhere the liberal press reported violence, lawlessness, and apparent social dissolution" (Maier 1975, 177). Violent clashes with the police were frequent, and rural strikes often erupted into violence and arson (Squeri 1983, 330). Landowners who attempted to bypass peasant leagues might have their barns burned and livestock killed (Absalom 1995, 107).

The farm and factory occupations are the best-known examples of this escalation of protest. Thousands of peasants forcibly occupied uncultivated land (Seton-Watson 1967, 521). These actions began around Rome and quickly spread south through Calabria and Sicily. Peasants seized almost all the large Sicilian estates in one month alone (Maylander 1922, 1273). The government later gave the occupations official sanction, but this direct (and illegal) action led to the redistribution of almost eighty thousand acres without the owners' consent and almost twice that amount after "friendly agreements" between peasants and landowners (Cardoza 1982, 247). Land seizures were not new to Italy, but the scale and nature of the postwar occupations were unprecedented (Snowden 1986, 164–65). Rural workers belonging to Catholic leagues in the north also crossed the legal and nonviolent divide. They disrupted farm production with tactics similar to those Socialists used in Turin. Catholic leagues in a province south of Milan wrested control of large dairy farms from their owners with the slogan, "The peasant [to be] no longer a worker, the landowner no longer the master" (quoted in Foot 1997, 419). Peasants in a northern province took a landowner's sons hostage until he unconditionally agreed to their demands (Salvemini 1973, 137).

The factory occupations began in September 1920. Factory councils elected by workers had spread through most metalworking factories in Turin after the war. The shop stewards aggressively campaigned for worker control in spring 1920, and the conflict simmered during the summer. Then a lockout sparked a general confrontation in August. Within days, half a million workers occupied factories and shipyards across northern Italy. Almost two hundred factories passed over to worker control in Turin alone. For almost a month, half a million workers managed the factories and organized production. Many raised red or black (anarchist) flags and organized "communist kitchens" in factories. Some produced barbed wire and munitions for self-defense and posted "Red Guards" at factory gates (Clark 2014, 249–50). The shop stewards sought more than better wages and improved working conditions. They also wanted to force the socialization of production and a radical reorganization of the economy. Their 1919 program declared that they would "set in train in Italy a practical exercise in the realization of communist society" (quoted in Williams 1975, 122–23).

Nitti's and Giolitti's concessions in the immediate postwar period could not placate Italian labor or quell the unrest. Procedural injustice during the war meant that an alienated labor movement doubted anything beneficial the state might do. Rome was responsible for its suffering and labor would get its revenge. As a prominent economic historian notes, strikes increased in 1920 "not as a result of frustration of workers' economic demands" (Zamagni 1991, 150). Labor's demands became more radical and strikes more frequent from one year to the next (Zamagni 1993, 241). In the industrial sector, the number of strikers rose 20 percent from 1919 to 1920. A more dramatic jump occurred in the agricultural sector, where the number of strikers doubled from 1919 to 1920 (Elazar 2001, 52). Overall, the number of strikers increased from the already high number of 1.5 million in 1919 (a tenfold increase from 1918) to 2.3 million in 1920 (Neufeld 1961, 547). This intensification of radical protest would become the death knell of Italy's liberal regime. Italy's wartime mobilization had opened a path to the Fascist seizure of power.

Wartime Mobilization and the Triumph of Italian Fascism

My hypotheses do not anticipate the rise of Fascism. They predict how mobilization strategies shape labor's interests, identity, and attitudes about the state, not regime transitions or the strength of a democracy. However, my hypotheses do explain a necessary condition for Benito Mussolini's success: the rise of a labor movement intent on destroying the economic status quo. World War I devastated economies across Europe. Governments faced the loss of overseas markets, demographic challenges, and unprecedented rates of indebtedness and inflation. Governments across Europe also faced an explosive growth of labor militancy. Unions grew in strength, the shop stewards' movement came into its own, and workers made new demands on states and employers. This labor unrest occurred in victorious and defeated nations alike. And it occurred in the democracies that survived the postwar period and those that did not. Where Italy stood apart was the ascendance of a radical labor movement challenging property rights. Italy's procedurally unjust mobilization created the conditions that provoked a countermobilization that destroyed the liberal order.

Challenges to Property Rights

Many democratic theorists stress the importance of moderation during transitions to democracy. Adam Przeworski argues that democratization is likely to fail if popular movements do not limit their demands. The working class must understand that challenging the economic order risks short-circuiting the path to democracy. "A striking feature of the Spanish transition to democracy," Przeworski stresses (1986, 63), "is that the political system had been transformed without affecting economic relations in any discernible manner." According to this reasoning, only some types of working-class mobilization are good for democracy. Labor movements that threaten property rights are likely to provoke antidemocratic reactions (Valenzuela 1989, 449). Even scholars who see the working class as consistently the most prodemocratic class driving democratization fear that radical mass movements will lead to a breakdown in democracy (Rueschemeyer, Stephens, and Stephens 1992, 98, 141–43). Much of the Italian case confirms this argument. Labor's radical demands ignited the backlash that crushed Italy's weak democracy.

Italian labor did not moderate its demands even as it gained material rewards and increased its economic and political power. Unrest escalated as labor agitated for, and often received, concessions that threatened the economic status quo. After adopting a radical program in summer 1919, Federterra led a series of powerful strikes that forced large landowners to agree to the *imponibile di mano d'opera* and the *collocamento di classe*. These provisions undercut landowners' profits but their effect went much further. The Socialist leagues sought to make agricultural contracts so onerous that peasant collectives would ultimately take over the land. These agreements "created an effective monopoly of the labor market, and threatened to render much of the title to property nugatory" (Snowden 1972, 274). In the red provinces of Ferrara and Bologna, no farm laborer could get a job except through Socialist labor exchanges; no employer could hire nonunion labor (Clark 2014, 241).

Labor's demands across Italy challenged the economic order. The agreements Federterra reached with sharecroppers in 1920 threatened the institution of sharecropping itself (Snowden 1989). Southern peasants seized private property and immediately began to farm it. Urban workers occupied factories and took charge of production. Even the Catholic rural unions in the north sometimes took control of large agricultural enterprises (Foot 1997, 423). In the eyes of the rural elite, labor's objectives were placing the "rights and prerogatives of property in jeopardy" (Snowden 1972, 273; 1989, 29–51). If these developments continued, property and labor relations would be permanently transformed.

There appeared to be no relief in sight for Italy's propertied classes. The Socialists' success in the 1920 municipal elections marked a fundamental shift in the rural balance of power. Ruling elites lost control of an unprecedented number of local and provincial bodies in central and northern Italy to radical Socialist councils. The League of Socialist Communes declared that its members would use their power to further the class struggle: they "intend[ed] to represent the working class exclusively" in accordance with "the new communist law" that placed the needs of the community "absolutely above that of the rights of private property" (quoted in Snowden 1989, 170). Landowners who for generations had been "cock of the walk" (Tasca 1938, 94) were now marginalized from local power structures (Snowden 1989, 53–55). The conservative press issued dire warnings that revolutionary policies were now front and center on the local (Socialist) agenda. The imposition of confiscatory taxation, the municipalization of gas and electricity, and the strengthening of local cooperatives would all undermine the economic status quo. Socialists in Bologna proposed forcing "gifts" from local banks to address the city's budget deficit; those in the city of Ferrara called for the creation of "proletarian militia" to provide public order (Squeri 1983, 330–33).

Rome appeared unable or unwilling to combat labor's challenge to hierarchies of wealth and power. Nitti's government endorsed drastic reductions in the cost of essential foodstuffs following widespread looting against the cost of living. It "rewarded" telegraph and telephone employees with pay for the days they were on strike (Clark 2014, 249; Maier 1975, 175). Officials repeatedly failed to reassure the propertied classes that their interests were secure. Rome sanctioned illegal land seizures in the south, leading to accusations that officials were collaborating with "rural Bolshevism" (quoted in F. Adler 1995, 169). Officials observed strict neutrality in most labor disputes. The government stood aside as peasant leagues imposed compulsory systems of manpower obligations on landowners. Giolitti and the PPI ministers seemed "bent on destroying the position of landowners throughout the country" (Clark 2014, 253). Giolitti's maneuvering resolved the factory occupations, but his refusal to send soldiers to remove the workers enraged industrial elites and produced a lasting breach between them and the liberal state (Zamagni 1993, 241).

Fascism Is the Answer

Infuriated at the "absentee state" and facing radical demands, rural elites came to believe in the necessity of Fascism's violent solution. Fascists were all that "stood between them . . . and the creation of a new social order in which their privileges and positions would be swept aside" (Snowden 1989, 193; see also Elazar 2001, 69, 85). The official voice of the PSI was using blood-curdling language to describe the upcoming collapse of capitalism, yet Rome seemed more willing to concede to labor's demands than uphold law and order. With big electoral gains for a PSI preaching the need for a violent seizure of power, traditional parliamentary politics lost its appeal. Regardless of the reality of the coming revolution—the PSI had no plan for its launch—the fear of insurrection was real (Absalom 1995, 102–3 109; Salvemini 1928, 55). A sense of despair and betrayal seized the propertied classes. Something had to be done to halt the growing assault on private property, to wrest local government out of Socialist hands, and to return "normality" to the countryside.

The propertied classes would take matters into their own hands if the liberal state would not guarantee property rights against labor's onslaught. Fascism promised decisive action, and by the end of 1920, the reaction had begun. Landowners and commercial farmers allied with local Fascist squads conducted a terrorist offensive to destroy the rural Socialist and Catholic infrastructure (Cardoza 1982, 294–352). This brutal campaign began in the Po Valley, and it rapidly spread to rural areas in central and northern Italy. Fascist squads traveled the countryside systematically attacking peasant leagues, PSI headquarters, cooperatives, social clubs, and newspapers (Absalom 1995, 106, 114–15). They ejected Socialists from local government, ordered labor leaders to move to different regions, and humiliated some by forcing them to drink large amounts of castor oil. In spring 1921, the squads destroyed the Socialist infrastructure in the province of Bologna, often burning down local trade union headquarters and attacking, and sometimes killing, local officials (Cardoza 1982, 338–52).

By 1922, Fascist squads controlled much of northern Italy (Corner 1997, 269–70; C. Schmidt 1938, 36). They and their allies then created alternate labor organizations that annulled the Federterra contracts and returned control of the labor market to landowners. Private property rights were once again guaranteed, and the threat of confiscatory taxation gone. Left-wing labor organizations were no longer free to develop their own independent organizations or even hold public meetings (Maylander 1922, 1275).

It was this explosion of Fascism in agricultural regions that transformed Fascism into a mass movement.[12] Rural Fascist squads saved Italian Fascism from extinction. Mussolini's electoral strategy had failed: Fascists did not gain one seat in the November 1919 parliamentary elections. Fascism also made little headway (or was seen as unnecessary) in those regions of Italy, such as most of the south (except Apulia), where the landlord's economic and political power was secure (Franzosi 1999, 144). Instead, Fascism swept through those areas where PSI had triumphed in the elections and where the Federterra and militant Catholic leagues had asserted control over farms and the rural labor market (Misner 2015, 189). Fascist reaction gained momentum in those regions where labor's radicalism challenged basic property rights.

Wartime Mobilization Is Key

Many factors contributed to Fascism's conquest of the countryside. Police and military collusion, and the army's provision of weapons, transport, and personnel, were critical to Fascists' ability to break Socialists' and militant Catholics' hold on local government and labor organizations.[13] Fascism's mass base among small peasant landowners was also important. Wartime inflation had increased the number of small landowners, and they too feared Socialist plans for collectivization (Cardoza 1982, 321–23; Snowden 1972, 276–81). Other aspects of the war aided Fascism's success. Middle-class veterans inured to combat and bitter about Italy's "mutilated victory" joined squads whose "novel barbarism" fueled this explosion of political violence (Lyttelton 1982, 265; 1996, 17–18).

These factors are important, but explaining Fascism's appeal depends on the *content* of labor's postwar demands, which Italy's unjust mobilization produced. Rural elites would not have needed the support of small landholders, the army's manpower and material, or the armed squads' systematic brutality if there were no radical labor organizations threatening the established order. Britain also experienced an explosion of labor unrest in the immediate postwar years. Indeed, British strike action *outpaced* Italy's along many dimensions. About two and a half times more British than Italian workers struck in 1919. The difference decreased to about one and half times more British strikers in 1920, but it widened to almost three times more in 1921. The number of days lost to strikes was also much larger in Britain: it was nearly double that in Italy in 1919, again slightly dipping in 1920, but then shooting up to eleven times more in 1921. The number of days lost to strikes per worker was greater in Italy in 1919 (eighteen versus around thirteen), but that was for the last time. Slightly more days were lost per worker in Britain than Italy in 1920 before sharply rising to almost four times more in Britain in 1921 (Zamagni 1991, 151–52).

This comparison of the frequency of work stoppages in Italy and Britain is important. The size of the postwar strike wave was unprecedented for Italy, but it is the *content* of labor's demands—not the *frequency* of unrest—that is central to explaining the Fascist reaction. "Industrialists and landowners were alarmed less by the size and violence of strikes than by the radical demands of the strikers" (Cardoza 1982, 291). This conclusion confirms democratic theorists' expectations about the danger that *radical* labor activism (not activism per se) poses to democracy. British labor struck often and for long periods, but its demands remained moderate throughout this tumultuous period. And unlike in Italy, British democracy emerged unscathed. The comparison of British and Italian strike rates is also important because it illustrates that it is not the fact of war but the *type of mobilization* that explains the fate of Italian democracy. Britain fought in the war for longer than did Italy, and it lost proportionally more men. Italy's unjust mobilization—not the war itself—radicalized the labor movement, alienated it from the state, and created unprecedented labor solidarity. Italy's wartime mobilization had turned discrete economic protests with pockets of radical demands into a united revolutionary struggle.

Conclusion: Wartime Choices and Democracy's Demise

The collapse of Italian democracy was not an inevitable consequence of structural features of the Italian economy or the decision for war. The Italian government chose a procedurally unjust mobilization that transformed Italian labor and the terms of political debate. Italy's wartime leaders could have adopted a different strategy to gain labor's compliance that would have led to different results. They could have followed Giolitti's precedents and reached out to labor and included it in economic and political forums. They could have used the wartime mobilization to bridge class divides, to build Italian nationalism, and to join Italians who had long lived apart. But after forty-one months of a procedurally unjust mobilization, the die was cast. The political machinations that had sustained the liberal order could not weather labor's wartime transformation. Giolitti's old political remedies could not rescue the liberal state from the repercussions of radical mass protest.

Developments in Britain were not as dramatic, but they are also important to understanding democracy's fate. As discussed in the next chapter, they illustrate the weakness of conventional arguments linking war to democracy. They also explain how Britain's wartime mobilization helped undermine labor's ambitious plans for democratic reform.

REVISITING COMPETING ACCOUNTS, AND THE FAILURE OF BRITISH REFORM

Britain and Italy are easy cases for conventional arguments suggesting that large-scale wars advance democracy. The war's enormous scale should have generated social solidarity, an enlightened and empowered state, and the bargaining leverage to ensure paybacks for wartime support. World War I was the first total war in European history, and neither Britain nor Italy could have fought the war without labor's support. Yet in neither case did the war lead to significant and robust democratic reform. Within four years of the Armistice, Italian labor's dreams of a just society disappeared into a Fascist nightmare. British democracy fared relatively well, but the promise of further democratization was betrayed: the government reneged on its promises to enact postwar reforms.

Arguments that link war to democracy assume that societal actors—including labor—value democracy and that they seek to profit from the crisis to further political, civil, and social rights. But by the time the Armistice came, Italian labor wanted revolution, not democratic reform. In other words, Italian labor's mobilization-induced transformation undermines conventional accounts. One cannot assess labor's ability to use war to advance democracy if labor does not support democracy itself. Unlike its counterpart in Germany, the PSI no longer put the defense of democratic institutions before the socialist revolution. The Catholic peasant leagues and the PPI did hope to achieve their goals in Parliament, as did moderate Socialists. But Italy's unjust mobilization had reduced reformists in the PSI to a small minority.

The PSI was uninterested in using its sizable parliamentary delegation to pursue democratic reform. Those dominating the party after 1918 wanted no part of "parliamentary cretinism," in the words of Antonio Gramsci (borrowed from Karl Marx). "The parliament of deputies elected by universal suffrage," Gramsci explained, is "not democracy" but "the mask of bourgeois dictatorship" (quoted in McNally 2017, 323–24). The PSI dismissed parliamentary politics as a bourgeois game to deceive workers. Reformist Socialists criticized this attitude and their colleagues' parliamentary inaction. In 1920, Claudio Treves accused the PSI of remaining "in the Chamber like a stranger making some noise every now and again to mark his presence and importance, inconveniencing all others a little, but taking no part in the real decision-making" (quoted in McNally 2017, 322). But Treves's reproach fell on deaf ears. If Socialist deputies had a role to play, it was in making the liberal state ungovernable—the old "worse is better" ploy. Turmoil would strengthen the hand of those awaiting revolution (De Grand 1989, 43). Italian labor—an apparent beneficiary of the link between war and democracy—no longer sought to strengthen Italy's democracy. Most PSI deputies had set their sights on revolution, not the pursuit of concrete and attainable goals. Conventional understandings cannot account for this situation. They fail before they even get off the ground.

The British case is different. There is every reason to think that popular classes could capitalize on an increase in social solidarity, an empowered state, or wartime bargaining power to further their rights. British labor believed in democracy, and it emerged from the war committed to a specific set of democratic reforms that the government appeared to accept. Yet the history of postwar British reform is a history of disappointment and broken promises.[1] Britain fought and won a war of enormous dimensions, but labor received little in return. Public housing, a capital levy, nationalization, improved access to education and health care, and a national minimum wage all disappeared from the government's agenda. The thwarting of British labor's expectations demonstrates the limits of conventional arguments linking war to democracy detailed in chapter 1. It also illustrates how wartime mobilization influences the nature of postwar politics and so the likelihood of democratic reform.

A Consensus on Egalitarian Norms Inspires Democratic Reform?

Scholars who focus on changes in values and beliefs argue that wars, and especially large-scale wars, create a spirit of national reconciliation. Participation in a collective endeavor bridges class and regional divides. It forges a new political consensus that embraces egalitarian goals. "The common sacrifices, sufferings and services in which all sections of our people have taken part," a Scottish trade unionist and Labour politician remarked just after the war ended, "is bound to produce a different atmosphere and an entirely different relationship amongst all sections of our people" (quoted in Abrams 1963, 49). War creates an "increased feeling of social solidarity," said the president of the Board of Education in the House of Commons in 1917: "Every just mind begins to realize that the boundaries of citizenship are not determined by wealth, and that the same logic which leads us to desire an extension of the franchise points also to an extension of education. There is a growing sense . . . that the industrial workers of the country are entitled to be considered primarily as citizens and as fit subjects for any form of education from which they are capable of profiteering [sic]" (quoted in Maclure 2005, 173). According to this argument, everyone comes together to defend the nation and everyone comes to believe that all should share in the country's wealth once the danger has passed. A caring state should replace the uncaring one.

The rhetoric was uplifting but the reality was not. There is little evidence of social solidarity in Britain during the war. Middle-class groups organized assistance for POWs, servicemen's families, and Belgian refugees (Gregory 2008, 98). A dentist offered to extract teeth free of charge for any man who enlisted (DeGroot 1996, 64). But these were acts of charity, not evidence of newfound egalitarian norms and a desire to rethink the distribution of resources. British labor was volunteering for military service at surprising rates, and organized labor agreed to a no-strike pledge for the war's duration. But the middle classes accused workers of profiting from the war emergency while they—the middle class— unfairly assumed most of the war's burdens. Trade unions were "holding the country to ransom," members of more privileged classes complained (quoted in Wilson 1986, 780). Fur coats became "munitions overalls," as resentment about industrial workers' apparent prosperity grew (Simmonds 2012, 175). Women filling vital and dangerous jobs in munitions factories were criticized for lavish spending and promiscuity (Bourne 1989, 190). Even the continuation of professional soccer elicited criticism of the working class, those "loafing lads." One observer noted disparagingly that "among the poor and ignorant, the uprising of the proper spirit is slow work" (both quoted in DeGroot 1996, 227).

There is even less evidence of solidarity once the war ended, especially after unwarranted fears of radical unrest had passed. The middle and upper classes sought a return to the "normalcy of 1914," and as soon as possible. Few conservatives were any more interested in democratic reform after the war than they had been before it. The middle class became increasingly concerned about postwar inflation, high taxes, and what it saw as excessive industrial wages and overgenerous social reforms (Wrigley 1992, 112–13). "Almost overnight, reconstruction moved from being a social imperative to an unaffordable extravagance" (Simmonds 2012, 296). Two leading press barons launched a virulent attack on government spending in 1919. The "antiwaste campaign" called for abandoning wartime planning controls and slashing social spending. The *Times* and the *Daily Mail* attacked Christopher Addison—the minister leading the housing program—as the exemplar of "squandermania" (Simmonds 2012, 296). The extension of paltry sums for the unemployed was decried as a "symbol of national demoralization" (Mowat 1955, 127–28).

Labor unions denounced the antiwaste campaign as an attack on the working class but the movement resonated with a middle class who resented high taxes and state benefits to the unemployed. A member of Parliament noted in 1920 that his constituency "hate[d] and despise[d] the working classes," which it saw as "great masses of humanity which accept[ed] none of its standards, and maintain[ed] life on a totally different plane" (quoted in McKibbin 2010, 47). Popular novels depicted the working class as "non-washing," as lacking honor, and as pursuing its sectional interests at Britain's expense. Any professed sympathy with those who had labored for British victory was gone. Members of the Anti-waste League won three by-elections against coalition Conservatives in 1921. The abrupt end to the housing program "revealed a latent hatred among the propertied classes for any bold scheme of betterment for the underprivileged" (Wilson 1986, 813).

The problem with accounts positing a rise in egalitarian norms is not their focus on ideational change but the location of it. Expectations for a better future spread like wildfire among popular classes, but despite the war's immense scale, it did not generate a willingness to build a new society within privileged classes. These solidarity arguments say more about how countries would like to be remembered than who they actually are. British middle and upper classes did not envision the construction of a new social order. The financial and industrial sectors were determined to roll back labor's wartime gains and to prevent the acquisition of new ones.[2] These elites expected "to skip happily back into their prewar world" (Tawney 1943, 14). "Education is an excellent thing in its way, but there are limitations to its economic usefulness," explained a prominent businessman critical of Labour's education reform. "The whole nation can't become Bachelor of Arts and I am perfectly certain they would be no happier if they were" (quoted in Grieves 1989, 104). Letters to the editor urged officials to teach the miners a lesson. Their call for nationalization revealed the miners' inability to put the national interest above sectoral ones (Lawrence 2011, 239). The chair of Midland Bank spoke for London's financial interests when he called for "ruthless, relentless, and remorseless" budget cuts (quoted in Mowat 1955, 130). The spokesman for the engineering and manufacturing association referred to workers as "the enemy" (Waites 1976, 44). Indeed, war had perhaps done more to aggravate class tensions than to bridge them (McKibbin 1974, 236–47; Searle 2004, 824). The postwar years saw a "growing abhorrence of policies which smacked of egalitarianism" (DeGroot 1996, 302). "I am afraid of the class hatred which is the quiet volcano over which the English life is built," noted D. H. Lawrence (quoted in J. Lawrence 2011, 239).

Research on distributive justice helps explain why large-scale wars fail to generate societal support for postwar reform. Individuals' assessments of how they are doing relative to others are invariably skewed. People exaggerate their personal contributions to collective efforts compared with others, leading to inevitable conflict (Tyler and Smith 1998, 600). The British middle class thought that munitions workers were shirking military service; the upper classes believed they unfairly bore the war's financial costs; and the working class was convinced that profiteering was rampant. Even the "aristocracy of labor" resented the wartime advances of its unskilled colleagues. If different social groups all believe that it is they who disproportionately shoulder wartime sacrifices, it is not surprising that each would resist rewarding others once the war ends.

Ironically, the *belief* that wartime solidarity would lead to postwar reform may have frustrated British labor's aspirations. Many politicians and civil servants who supported reform believed a version of this wartime solidarity argument. They assumed a basic harmony of interests, and they were persuaded that war brought the country together. Confident that the experience would generate support for reform, they failed to do the necessary groundwork to overcome resistance to their policy objectives (Abrams 1963, 57–61). The proposals for reform were likely to have faltered regardless—there was powerful resistance to them—but reform efforts could have proceeded with a more realistic appraisal of the difficulties ahead if supporters had understood that this was a political issue, not an administrative one. The public rhetoric of social solidarity kept many reformers from seeing that there was no natural link from apparent wartime cohesion to postwar democratic reform.

An Empowered and Enlightened State Leads to a Deepening of Democracy?

According to some scholars, the more that war increases state capacity, the greater the likelihood for postwar reform. Four years of war did empower the British state. It put in place many of the ingredients necessary for Labour's ambitious program of postwar reform. "There had been nothing like it before. Departments, bureaux, committees, controllers were created and piled on top of each other" (Mowat 1955, 13; also see 28). The government established ten new ministries and 160 new boards and commissions, and it nearly tripled the number of civil servants (Cronin 1991, 58–63). New agencies had vast authority in areas where the state had played little to no role (Tawney 1943, 1–3). The Ministry of Munitions' more than fifty departments oversaw almost the entire process of munitions production (R. Adams 1978, 45–52; Wilson 1986, 232-34). Officials controlled much of British trade, directed agricultural production, fixed prices, and rationed food.

The British state had become the "new Leviathan" (Mowat 1955, 13). It was no longer a liberal state with a limited role in the economy. And this new state had newfound fiscal power. British tax revenues increased nearly sixfold during the war (Lawrence 1993, 995). The war also seemed to have enlightened the state, or had its purported "inspection effect." Mobilization shined a spotlight on chronic problems, and politicians appeared committed to addressing them. David Lloyd George eloquently spoke of this apparent link from war to reform: "Those of you who have been at the front have seen the star shells, how they light up the darkness and illuminate all the obscure places. The Great War has been like a gigantic star shell, flashing all over the land, illuminating the country and showing up the dark, deep places. We have seen places that we have never noticed before, and we mean to put these things right."[3] The number of men who failed the army medical exam exposed the miserable state of working-class housing and the inadequate medical care. Doctors classified half of the recruits as either "unlikely to be used for combat" or "unfit for any form of military service" (Pope 1991, 4). The war was especially revealing of "the defects and shortcoming of [Britain's educational] system," a government report noted in 1918 (quoted in Wilson 1986, 815). British military technology lagged behind that of other belligerents, and especially states that financed scientific research and education, such as Germany.

Britain had reformed its civil service in the 1870s, but the war created a novel situation. It provided the institutional and intellectual legacy to ease the adoption of progressive reform. Politicians and administrators now had the bureaucratic and regulatory structure to promote social rights. They had gained detailed knowledge about the nation's industrial capacity and experience directing most aspects of the economy (Abrams 1963, 48; R. Adams 1978, 94). They also had newfound expertise in areas that were central to labor's reform agenda, such as the provision of housing. Never before had British officials known as much about the economy, been as intensely engaged in the implementation of social and economic policy, or had the opportunity to demonstrate that they could effectively control the economy and manage production.

The government could have capitalized on this increase in state capacity to deliver on its promises for social reform. It rejected this opportunity. There was no government commitment to maintain state agencies necessary to fulfill electoral promises (Pugh 2002, 167). To the contrary, there was a "headlong rush to decontrol" (Simmonds 2012, 298). Much of the wartime state was dismantled even faster than it had been built. "The work of demolition was done thoroughly, as well as in haste," the classic study of British wartime control concludes. Within three years, "the whole structure had vanished" (Tawney 1943, 7). More than half of the wartime ministries did not survive demobilization (Mowat 1955, 28). Officials privatized munitions factories and returned mines to their owners (Wrigley 1982a, 46). The wartime state was stripped away until "the old departments emerged in their prewar innocence" (Taylor 1965, 76). State control was a short-term expediency to address the national emergency. There had been no ideological conversion to state intervention within much of the ruling elite.

The government reduced some tax rates after the war, but the fiscal power of the wartime state remained. The estate tax rate tripled during the war, and it continued to rise after the war. Income tax rates increased fourfold (S. Pollard 1983, 32; Runciman 1993, 56). Repaying war debts and other associated costs absorbed much of the increase, but the ratchet effect was real. Tax revenues never declined to their prewar level. The government had access to more of the nation's wealth than ever before, and this made possible a doubling in spending in real terms on social services from 1913 to 1921 (Lawrence 1993, 995). For the first time in British history, the working class received more in social services than it paid in taxes (Runciman 1993, 57). The wartime elimination of primary poverty (or the provision of the minimum required for physical health) continued after the war (Winter 1985c, 366). This change is partly attributed to higher wages, but it is also due to official policies, and especially the Unemployment Insurance Act. Five times more people had access to unemployment relief after the war than before it (DeGroot 1996, 301–2, 330).

This increase in social spending should be put in perspective. The war broke down some resistance to tax increases, but Labour failed in its determined efforts to enact a capital levy that could have paid the war debt and freed spending for social programs. A doubling of spending sounds impressive—but a doubling of little is not very much, especially compared with what labor wanted, and what it had been promised. The "progress" in education, medical care, and housing did not begin to meet the need. It is also misleading to suggest the war had an "inspection effect," or that it revealed chronic social problems that the government then addressed. World War I did not expose the poor health of army recruits, the deficiencies in British education, or the shocking state of working-class housing. It simply reminded the middle and upper classes of what they already knew. The British army had rejected unhealthy recruits for prior wars, and there had been endless discussions about the need for education reform before the war (Sherington 1976, 67–74). Publications that exposed the scale of poverty had been widely discussed. Books such as Henry George's *Progress and Poverty* (1881) and Mrs. Humphrey Ward's *Robert Elsemer* (1888) were best sellers (S. Reid 1955, 10). Charles Booth's detailed studies of the wretched conditions of London's poor generated intense media interest in the 1880s and 1890s. Booth became a household name, and his findings were widely known in official circles (Bales 1999). As a Liberal reformer, Lloyd George referenced Booth in his prewar speeches (Wrigley 1992, 40).

The bureaucratic, regulatory, and fiscal structures built in Britain during the war were essential for an activist state. They could have served as the foundation for Labour's new social order. In fact, officials had anticipated retaining this empowered state. The cabinet planned to extend economic control into peacetime to ensure a robust reconstruction. Officials assumed that Britain would face a powerful Germany after the war, and they assumed that balancing Germany would require an activist state. Industrialists and many politicians were unhappy about continuing state control of the economy, but they accepted its necessity for national security. Germany's decisive defeat removed this imperative. The immediate threat of an economically strong Germany was gone. Germany's collapse cleared the path for the reassertion of orthodox economic ideas and the return to a limited state ill equipped for social democratic reform (Cline 1982, 158; Searle 2004, 817).

Lloyd George's coalition government had been prepared to sacrifice economic doctrine for national security. But once the fear of a resurgent Germany had passed, so did any commitment to retaining the wartime state necessary to realize Labour's reform agenda. The government was unwilling to maintain economic controls for the benefit of the working class. The defeat of reconstruction was due to a lack of political will, not state capacity. Many civil servants were eager to use Britain's empowered state and their wartime expertise for peacetime reconstruction, but the government (and its constituents) were not on board (Pugh 2002, 175). The capacity to institute reform is meaningless without the desire to do so. Paradoxically, the decisiveness of victory over Germany guaranteed the meagerness of the "reward."

The state capacity argument linking war to democratic reform captures an empirical reality: war builds the state. But this argument is as apolitical as those focusing on the generation of egalitarian norms. These arguments assume that collective struggles or greater state capacity lead to the "granting" of political, civil, and social rights. Previously marginalized groups "earn" their rights by demonstrating good behavior and contributing to the war effort, and not—as is almost always the case—by engaging in hard-fought battles to wrest rights from entrenched elites. Rhetoric to the contrary, economic and political elites rarely become benevolent and enlightened during wartime emergencies.

There is an additional problem with arguments focusing on wartime increases in state capacity. These accounts assume that state building serves the interests of the disenfranchised, and the pursuit of additional rights. They rarely recognize that the opposite is often the case. The Italian case illustrates the risks of wartime state building for postwar democracy. As in Britain, mobilization for war strengthened the Italian state. Wartime spending was double that spent in the preceding fifty years altogether (Bosworth 2005, 69). The number of ministries and public servants nearly doubled, and Italian civil servants gained confidence in their ability to manage the economy (De Cecco 2002, 73; Gibelli 2010, 469; Tomassini 1996, 578). As in Britain, much of this Italian wartime state was dismantled after the war (Tomassini 1991, 86). Unlike in Britain, its effect lingered, but its legacy benefited neither labor nor democracy. Italy's wartime state inspired the Fascist one (F. Adler 1995, 95). The state's wartime repression of labor taught industrialists and other economic and political elites "useful" lessons about the value of a strong state disciplining the working class. Mussolini created the Board of Civil Mobilization soon after coming to power, and he appointed General Alfredo Dallolio—the general who directed MI during the war—to run it (Tomassini 1990, 203). The Fascist government also revived wartime labor legislation (Corner 2002b, 35; Corner and Procacci 1997, 236). The wartime precedent appealed to those disillusioned with the liberal order. Italy's wartime state became an instrument of repression.

Wartime Leverage Allows Labor to Extract Concessions and Rights?

The last set of arguments linking war to democracy focus on bargaining between state and societal actors. As with the preceding accounts, the scale of the war is crucial. But here the focus is not on the transformation of values and beliefs or an increase in state capacity but on society's ability to extract concessions from the state. These payback arguments *are* political: nothing is attained without a struggle. Elites do not reward the less privileged for their wartime service. Instead, societal actors seize on the war emergency and use their wartime leverage to force the leveling of inequalities and the enactment of greater rights. But these arguments neither consider the full range of societal interests, nor the variety of resources available to governments. They also fail to carry their political logic into the postwar period to explain why states often renege on bargains struck in wartime.

The scale of World War I was unprecedented. Almost 14 percent of the British population and half of the men between the ages of fifteen and forty-nine served in the armed forces. More British soldiers were killed on the first day of the Battle of the Somme than any other day in British military history. Overall, more than seven hundred thousand (or 13 percent of those mobilized) made the ultimate sacrifice (Gatrell and Harrison 1993, 430). The demands at home were also immense. Unemployment virtually disappeared, plunging from an average prewar rate of 4.5 percent to under 1 percent during the war (Pigou 1941, 31; Searle 2004,

801). Skilled workers were in especially short supply. Officials were forever de-
vising some new plan to resolve labor scarcity. They never succeeded: there was
an acute shortage of manpower during the final year of the war (Wrigley 1976).

British officials understood the leverage that total war gave labor. "A great
[coalminers'] strike would be equivalent to a military defeat," a War Cabinet document exclaimed (quoted in Tanner 1990, 357–58). Yet despite unprecedented
bargaining power, British labor received little payback in return for its wartime
service. Almost across the board, labor's wartime leverage did not pay off. Attending to all sources of state power—and especially patriotism's appeal—explains
this result. Payback arguments are correct that total wars reconfigure power relations and vastly increase the power of key sectors of the industrial workforce.
But these arguments emphasize material power at the expense of a vital source of
state strength in wartime: patriotism. British labor willingly, and sometimes enthusiastically, contributed to the war effort. It expected its efforts to be rewarded,
but it did not exploit its wartime leverage to maximize its advantage. Its interests
were not just material. Labor believed in Britain, and it supported what it saw as
a just war against German aggression.

The British government negotiated agreements with organized labor in spring
1915 to ensure productivity. Labor agreed to renounce the right to strike and to
suspend trade union customs for the war's duration. It also accepted restrictions
on labor mobility. These were significant concessions. Labor would be unable to
exploit labor scarcity to bid up wages. Simplifying production processes was a direct threat to the status, income, and security of skilled workers. "The prerogatives
of the trade unions—those concessions in shop practices wrung so slowly from
their employers over years of struggle—were swept away" (R. Adams 1978, 84).
Trade union practices were "labour's Magna Carta," yet organized labor agreed to
suspend them during the war—and perhaps for longer (Commons 1922, 717). It
was reasonable to doubt whether firms that restructured work processes to accom-
modate unskilled (and cheaper) labor would ever return to prewar practices.

What did British labor get in return for these concessions? Not much. Officials pledged to restore trade union practices after the war and agreed to limit
profits in war industries. That was it. A small group of militant trade unionists
fiercely condemned the Munitions of War Act as selling out labor's fundamental
rights. The agreement was a "highly dangerous measure" that posed the "greatest threat to organized labor," one militant declared at the time. But what was
especially galling was that union officials and the rank and file had endorsed the
act! The government had not forced these provisions down labor's throats: the
labor movement had been "pathetically willing" to give up its rights for "nothing
in return" (quoted in Rubin 1987a, 255, 261). Historians concur with the mili-
tants' critique: "Trade union leaders gained little and conceded a lot," one noted

(Horne 1991, 219, 80). Another concluded that "the government made some hardly burdensome concessions" (DeGroot 1996, 113). Officials promised that peace would bring a *restoration* of labor's prewar position, and even then, that promise was nonbinding. Labor had not extracted any quid pro quos during the war that would *advance* its social, political, or civil rights. Organized labor had agreed that it would leave the war with no greater rights than when it entered it.

British labor had also consented to an industrial truce in August 1914 without extracting meaningful concessions. At that time, labor leaders may have believed they had little bargaining power since most participants thought the war would be short. But the spring 1915 negotiations (referenced earlier) occurred when everyone knew that labor was an appreciating asset. It had become clear that military victory depended on the production of an unparalleled quantity of munitions. Lloyd George may have depicted the Munitions of War Act as "an honorable bargain and a patriotic bargain," but that was true for only one side (quoted in Horne 1991, 79). Despite its strong bargaining position, organized labor agreed to terms that favored the state and employers (and that infuriated those on the far left).

British labor generally lived up to its wartime obligations. Industrial unrest increased as the war continued and as inflation outstripped earnings (Gregory 2008, 192). But there were fewer days lost to strikes during the entire war than in any single year since 1909 (Tanner 1990, 361). This wartime quiescence was unusual: British labor was strike prone, well organized, and cognizant of its industrial strength. The relative absence of strikes was also unexpected given trends in labor activism before the war. A large strike wave (the Labour Unrest) swept Britain from 1911 to 1914 as thousands struck and millions of working days were lost. In fact, industrial-labor relations were at a boiling point in summer 1914, and everyone expected the intensification of labor activism in the fall. It was only cut short by the outbreak of war.

The war had created the ideal conditions for industrial action, but British labor rallied to the flag and agreed to an industrial truce. As labor's reaction to the German offensive in spring 1918 illustrates, the British working class "was prepared to forgo making full use of its strength" (Wrigley 1982b, 94).[4] Despite a list of grievances, labor refused to strike during Britain's "hours of greatest need." It did not seize on the state's vulnerability to drive the best bargain. Or any bargain at all. To the contrary, labor threw itself into the war effort without demanding much in return. The leadership of the Labour Party was also willing to put aside working-class interests for the war's duration. In internal discussions about whether to accept Lloyd George's invitation to join the wartime government, Arthur Henderson encouraged colleagues to "concern themselves more with what they were to give to the national effort than with what they were likely to receive in concrete benefits" (F. Leventhal 1989, 61). Just like the rank and file, Henderson was set on "cooperat[ing] with the Government even if it meant temporarily sacrificing political or economic objectives" (F. Leventhal 1989, 54).

British labor's patriotism (and passivity) dismayed militant trade unionists, and some assumed that labor would wake up from its slumber and use its wartime leverage to bargain for better rights. "Daily I see signs amongst the working class of a mighty awakening," Arthur Cook, a prominent member of the miners' union, wrote in April 1916. "The chloroforming pill of patriotism is failing in its power to drug the mind and consciousness of the worker. He is beginning to shudder at his stupidity in allowing himself to become a party to such a catastrophe as we see today" (quoted in DeGroot 1996, 125). Beatrice Webb shared Cook's concern that labor's patriotism kept it from getting a good deal. But she did not believe these sentiments would pass. Webb remarked that British labor viewed assertive wartime industrial action as "sordid and unpatriotic," and she noted that labor leaders too easily succumbed to patriotic blackmail. She thought that the British working class displayed a "curious self-complacency" and trust in the government (quoted in Tanner 1990, 361; see also Searle 2004, 802).

Organized labor must often strike a delicate balance in wartime. It risks provoking repression or being labeled disloyal if it bargains hard for compensation. But neither dynamic occurred in Britain. To the contrary, just weeks after the Munitions of War Act outlawed strikes, Lloyd George conceded to almost all of the illegally striking South Wales miners' demands (Wrigley 1992, 72). Nor did British labor refrain from strike action because it feared work stoppages might harm its legitimacy with the wider public. British labor did not seek to *demonstrate* its patriotism. It *was* patriotic. It believed the war was just and that it merited its support.

Wartime Mobilization and the Failure of Postwar Reform

Britain's mobilization strategy helped safeguard these patriotic sentiments. The extensive use of procedural justice meant that labor continued to identify with the state through four long years of war. Indeed, the war years may have strengthened labor's attachment to the nation-state. Seeking to exploit this patriotic fervor, Lloyd George called a snap election just three days after the Armistice. He joined forces with the Conservative Party to continue the wartime coalition under his leadership. Coalition Liberals and Conservatives divided up seats to campaign against Labour and the Asquithian Liberal rump (Simmonds 2012, 118). Lloyd George's calculations paid off: the party most able to appeal to labor's nationalist and jingoistic sentiments—the Conservative Party—triumphed at the polls. These electoral results illustrate British labor's patriotism and its support for the war.

They are also key to explaining the failure of postwar reform. Ironically, the first British election with universal male suffrage brought to power the party most opposed to Labour's ambitious program for social reform.

The power resources (or social democratic) model is one of the most influential explanations for the development of the welfare state. It contends that the strength, *especially in government*, of social democratic labor movements explains the variation in public policies for furthering social justice and equality between classes. The welfare state is a class issue, and relative power among classes is crucial. Those classes who stand to benefit most from welfare policies, such as wage workers, drive the formation and growth of welfare states. It is not, however, representative institutions and electoral processes alone that lead to redistributive policies. It is the organizational strength of social democratic labor movements—reflected in the structure and size of trade unions and the strength of left-wing parties in government—that translates electoral strength into policies favoring the working class. According to this model, the growing power of reformist labor parties in government led to the expansion of the social democratic welfare state (A. Hicks 1999), while the weakening of labor unions in the 1980s and 1990s has meant the contraction of social rights.[5]

Much about the British case confirms the power resources model. The Conservative Party's electoral success in December 1918 (and the exclusion of Labour from government) all but guaranteed the defeat of labor's reform agenda. Conservatives received twice as many seats as their coalition partners, Lloyd George Liberals, and almost six times more than the Labour Party. This Tory victory occurred even though electoral reform earlier that year (February 1918) had tripled the size of the electorate and doubled the size of the working-class vote (Matthew, McKibbin, and Kay 1976).[6] All men could now vote, regardless of property or class, and plural voting (where one person can vote in more than one constituency) was drastically curtailed. The Representation of the People Act was the most significant expansion—both proportionally and absolutely—of the British electorate, yet the chief beneficiary of the introduction of mass democracy was the party most identified with the capitalist class. A historian and Labour MP noted the irony: "Karl Marx had declared that, in Britain, universal suffrage would have as its 'inevitable result . . . the political supremacy of the working class.'" When this prediction was put to the test in the 1918 general election, "the outcome was two generations of Conservative hegemony" (quoted in McCrillis 1998, 2).

Homes for Heroes? "Hang the Kaiser!"

As the leader of the Conservative-Liberal coalition, Lloyd George initially campaigned on reconstruction. "The principal concern of every Government is and must be the condition of the great mass of the people who live by manual toil," the manifesto declared (F. Craig 1970, 29). Lloyd George also affirmed that a desire for revenge would not dominate the peace settlement. But he quickly understood that what the public wanted most was to punish Germany. At a campaign stop, Lloyd George spoke of the coalition's pledge to build "habitations fit for the heroes who won the war." The crowd responded with cries of "Hang the Kaiser!" (quoted in Simmonds 2012, 286). Lloyd George increasingly "succumbed to the nationalist popular mood of the moment" (Wrigley 1992, 92, 96). Other candidates followed suit. After being criticized for not reflecting the popular nationalist mood, a Conservative candidate famously called for "squeezing Germany like a lemon until the pips squeak" (quoted in Grieves 1989, 72). A coalition candidate campaigning in the Manchester slums said it was the "trial and execution of the Kaiser" that animated the electorate (Wilson 1964, 39).

Coalition candidates increasingly campaigned on avenging German aggression, not reconstruction at home. The Conservative Party's canvassing of the national electorate had found that the top three issues were indemnities from Germany, punishment of the kaiser, and repatriation of enemy aliens. Housing reform polled a distant fifth (N. Keohane 2010, 164). A Conservative candidate's poem captures this national mood:

> The German Fleet, as you all know,
> Is safely moored at Scapa Flow;
> The crafty Huns will have to pay
> And your friend BULL will show the way.
>
> Vote for BULL should be your cry
> As you'll discover bye and bye,
> He'll do his best to get the fruits
> Of Victory over German Brutes. (Quoted in McCrillis 1998, 41,
>   38–42)

Coalition candidates depicted Labour as pacifist and pro-German to attract working-class support (Mowat 1995, 2–5; Turner 1992, 317–18). A conservative newspaper declared that the election was "a straight fight" between the coalition, which sought "to exact stern justice from the guilty Teutons," and the Labour Party, which wanted to befriend "the unrepentant butchers of Europe," (quoted in N. Keohane 2010, 119).

The Labour Party also accurately gauged the electorate's mood. Labour candidates publicly distanced themselves from party members who had opposed the war. Many adopted the Conservative Party's anti-German rhetoric (Pugh 2002, 532–33). But the Labour Party could not match the Torys' nationalist appeal.

Labour had yet to articulate a left-wing patriotism that could appeal to the popular mood (DeGroot 1996, 300; Wilson 1986, 665).[7] It was the Tories who exploited patriotism as "a pathway into popular opinion which reinforced old electoral loyalties and won new support" (Tanner 1990, 381). In fact, many Conservatives saw defeat of Germany as central to the party's postwar resurgence. "They wanted the war to go on until victory was achieved in order that the great narcotic of national glory could be shoved down the throat of social revolution" (D. Newton 2002, 36). Some leading Conservatives supported broadening the franchise in 1918 in part because they recognized the depth of working-class patriotism (Pugh 2002, 172).

Additional factors influenced working-class Toryism in 1918, and Conservatives continued to secure large numbers of working-class votes between the wars (McKibbin 1990, 287–88). But the khaki election results are striking. In 1924, there were 5.5 million union members and 5.5 million Labour votes; in 1929, there were 4.9 million union members and 8.4 million Labour votes. But in 1918, union membership was 6.5 million yet Labour received 2.4 million votes (Dunbabin 1980, 242).[8] Turnout was low and skilled workers who could vote before the war tended to support Labour (Turner 1992, 137). But many newly enfranchised members of the working class—the workers least likely to benefit from union welfare schemes and so with the most to gain from Labour's reform agenda—leaned Conservative in 1918. National pride had trumped economic self-interest. Tories may have represented the interests of the privileged classes, but Conservatives were "the party of nationalism and conscription, of unstinted support for the generals, of empire and British naval supremacy" (Wrigley 2003, 512). Labour's association with antiwar elements "fatally hampered" its electoral prospects (Wilson 1966, 177). This broadened electorate had pushed the campaign onto grounds that played to Conservative strengths. And it doing so, it ensured that there would be no "payback" for labor's unwavering support for the war effort. The labor movement would not have the necessary "power resources" in the postwar period to enforce bargains struck during war mobilization.

A Chamber of "Hard-Faced Men"

The 1918 general election was a landslide for the Conservative-Liberal coalition. It was returned with an enormous majority, the largest since 1832. Lloyd George led the coalition, but it was the Conservative Party that came out ahead. It was the largest party in the governing majority (with 382 seats compared with the coalition Liberals' 127). This was a dramatic reversal of the Conservative Party's parliamentary fortunes. The party made a net gain of 108 seats compared with the last general election in 1910. The Conservatives' determined support for the war helped them recover from years of general election failures and remove the divided Liberal Party from its preeminent position. Herbert Asquith's Liberal faction now had just thirty-six seats. The Labour Party did increase its vote share, but the results were disappointing. The 1918 election was the first time Labour ran enough candidates to be a contender for power, but it won only fifty-seven seats, just fifteen more than in 1910 (Kinnear 1981, 38–40). Prominent Labour leaders who had opposed the war, such as Ramsay MacDonald, Philip Snowden, and George Lansbury, lost their seats during this jingoistic campaign.

The Conservative Party's triumph did more than anything to frustrate Labour's plans for a new social order (Abrams 1963, 44–47; Horne 1991, 351–52; Mowat 1955, 2–10). Conservatives governed in coalition with Lloyd George Liberals until 1922. Conservatives dominated the cabinet and enjoyed a large numerical superiority in the Commons. The newly elected Conservative MPs included a record number of corporate directors, bankers, and businessmen. As future British prime minister Stanley Baldwin famously observed, "a lot of hard-faced men who look as if they had done very well out of the war" now sat in Parliament (quoted in DeGroot 1996, 312). These men, drawn from commerce and finance, opposed new expenditures on education and housing. They wanted no part of a capital levy, nationalization, or greater state intervention in the economy (Grieves 1989, 100–102; Wilson 1986, 814). They wanted to roll back the higher taxation and state control that the war had demanded, and they aggressively attacked Lloyd George's progressive social policies (Pugh 2002, 177–78). They did not want to reward labor for its wartime sacrifices.

The coalition government was the government of the "Geddes Axe," which has become shorthand for callous meanness. In August 1921, Lloyd George appointed Sir Edward Geddes to chair a committee of wealthy businessmen to provide advice on how to roll back public expenditures. The committee recommended in early 1922 the elimination of some government departments, and drastic cuts in spending for housing, public health, and education. Lloyd George accepted the assessment and "effectively ended the era of reconstruction" (Cronin 1991, 80).[9] The Geddes Axe was a dramatic signal of the government's intent, but it was not the first. Lloyd George had dispensed with Addison—the liberal reformer—in March 1921, and he had increasingly appeased coalition Conservative backbenchers. Conservatives had never supported Lloyd George's reform agenda, and they became increasingly uneasy about it after the postwar boom ended. Dominating the government, and with the "antiwaste" wind in their sails, they succeeded in their determination to block social reform (Turner 1992, 318). And they had been voted into office with the help of the working class.

The power resources approach recognizes that conservative governments sometimes adopt welfare policies as a strategic response to a strongly mobilized

Left (Korpi 1989). German chancellor Otto von Bismarck offered health, accident, disability, and unemployment insurance to the working class in the 1880s in a failed attempt to halt the rise of the Social Democratic Party. During World War I, the British government responded similarly to the potential for widespread civil unrest. An outbreak of rent strikes in 1915 across industrial centers, and especially in the "Red Clydeside," aroused fears within the governing elite. Officials worried that the protests would spark a walkout in the shipyards and possibly a general strike. This apprehension precipitated the passage of the Rent Restrictions Act of 1915, which guaranteed security of tenure and froze rents at their August 1914 level. A Conservative member introduced this "outrageous interference in property owners' time honored rights," and the legislation gained all party support as it sailed through Parliament (Ravetz 2001, 72).

Anticipation of masses of British soldiers returning home looking for work also sparked fears of radical unrest, and again the government made housing a priority (Ravetz 2001, 71–80). In 1919, a junior minister explained the connection: "The money we are going to spend on housing is an insurance against Bolshevism and Revolution." King George V agreed: "If unrest is to be converted into contentment, the provision of good houses may prove one of the most potent agents in that conversion" (both quoted in Towers 1995, 23). But once these fears receded, so did the government's "commitment" to homes for returning "heroes." The coalition's diminishing support for a capital levy also followed declining apprehension about social unrest (Cronin 1991, 75).

The Labour leader Arthur Henderson had cautioned against supporting the coalition. In his first major statement during the 1918 electoral campaign, he asked whether "anyone seriously believe[s] that a Coalition Government in which the Unionist [Conservative] Party is the dominant partner will undertake to carry out a drastic programme of reconstruction." The coalition was not the "all-party, all-class arrangement" it purported to be. It was "the response of the 'possessing classes' to Labour's bid for political power and its program of economic and social reform." A coalition victory, Henderson correctly predicted, would foreclose the adoption of policies to further social rights.[10] The Labour Party's interests had evolved during the war—it now endorsed a moderate socialism that called for the provision of education, health care, housing, and social security. But the British working class would have to wait almost three decades, until Labour's landside electoral victory in 1945, before it could realize these goals. These results confirm the power resources model: without access to the levers of executive power, and posing little threat to Lloyd George's coalition government, the labor movement was unable to force the government to uphold its promises for a better future.

Conclusion: How the Politics of War Affects the Politics of Peace

Conventional arguments that link war to democracy are correct in their assertion that large-scale wars transform values and beliefs and increase state capacity. But they wrongly claim that the politics of war differs from the politics of peace. These arguments naively assume that a war emergency suspends the rough and tumble of routine politics. This is especially true for arguments that expect the wartime development of egalitarian norms, but the state capacity accounts are also apolitical. It is as if the provision of tools means that the work will be done. Payback arguments do not make this mistake. They recognize that rights are extracted (not "granted") and that the redistribution of resources is fiercely fought (and not "earned"). But payback arguments err in recognizing only a narrow set of material interests that leaves no room for patriotism's powerful pull on societal actors. They also fail to extend their focus on wartime bargaining power into the postwar period. Whether wartime leverage translates into democratic reform depends not on the scale of the war but on what political actors want and their relative ability to pursue these policy agendas once the war ends.

Understanding how the politics of war affects the politics of peace requires recognizing that a war emergency does more than provide societal actors with an opportunity to bargain for a better deal. Mobilization for war has the potential to transform the nature of the societal actors themselves, influencing their political objectives and how they seek to achieve them. Wartime mobilization shaped the development of British and Italian labor in ways that profoundly influenced the prospects for democratic reform. These mobilization strategies help explain why British labor's hopes for postwar reconstruction led to little positive change. And they explain Italian labor's wartime transformation and the escalation of popular protest that provoked the Fascist destruction of the liberal regime.

The concluding chapter suggests how mobilization strategies influence other societal factors critical to democratic governance. It also warns against the popular belief that war advances democracy, and sets out a number of additional lessons about the causes and consequences of war.

CONCLUSION: BRINGING THE POLITICS OF WAR INTO THE POLITICS OF PEACE

Many studies treat war as an interruption, not a transformation. The war years may suspend political developments, but politics ultimately returns to its normal—that is, prewar—course. Book chapters entitled "Postwar Politics" immediately follow chapters entitled "Prewar Politics," with at best a nod to the wartime period. It is as if the experience of war does not affect the identities, interests, and political attitudes of societal actors that define postwar politics. Even studies acknowledging the novelty of postwar conditions rarely provide theoretical explanations for wartime change. Dylan Riley traces the prewar development of Italian civil society and notes that World War I "set off a wave of associationalism that continued into the postwar period" (2005, 298–99; 2010, 41). But he does not document or explain the wartime development.

Most political science research on the consequences of war focuses on scale or outcome. Scholars argue, for example, that large-scale wars encourage the development of civil society (Kage 2010), or that states emulate the regime type of victorious states (Gunitsky 2017). This scholarship enriches our understanding of war's effects, but variations in scale and outcome are neither the only nor necessarily the most important ways that wars differ. Even states that confront similar wartime challenges and emerge victorious do not respond to these challenges in the same way. Britain and Italy chose radically different strategies to gain labor's compliance. Documenting this variation is more difficult than assessing a war's scale or outcome—it requires a detailed reconstruction of the historical record—but this variation is no less important because it is time consuming to assess. Understanding postwar politics in Britain and Italy requires explaining how mobilization for war altered what labor felt about the state, what it wanted, and what it imagined was now possible. Wartime mobilization and postwar politics were inextricably linked—a return to prewar politics was impossible.

Sometimes war is nothing more than an interruption, putting on hold routine politics. Sometimes war influences the timing of political developments, thus accelerating or delaying long-term historical processes. But sometimes war's role is fundamental. War can dislodge established ways of thinking and open alternate paths of political development. These periods are infrequent, but they can be critical junctures that transform the political order. We cannot know the conditions under which war is a catalyst, transformative, or merely an interruption if we neglect the variety of ways states fight wars at home and abroad.

This book illustrates the importance of bringing the politics of war into the politics of peace. State strategies to gain labor's compliance with the war effort transformed British and Italian labor in ways that were crucial to postwar political settlements and the possibility for democratic reform. Attending to how labor movements react to variations in procedural justice underlines the importance of process (and not just outcomes) and the role of affect (and not just institutions). Procedural justice shapes labor's wartime development, as well as other factors important to democracy's fate, including nationalism, political trust, and civil society. That war transforms society does not mean, however, that war is good for democracy. Wars rarely have the democratizing effect that scholars expect and activists hope. Yet the belief that war encourages democratic reform may be beneficial. This misperception may decrease the likelihood and duration of wars.

Wartime Politics and Its Consequences for Peace

Social science helps us understand what relationships are causal and what is generalizable, and to create hypotheses to explain important political outcomes. There is no direct link between mobilization strategies and the strength or success of democracy. The routes to democracy are many, and they depend on multiple factors. However, mobilization strategies have predictable consequences for organized labor, which is often a crucial actor in transitions to, and the strengthening of, democracy. The research on social justice was especially useful in explaining one of the most important yet least tractable transformations that war can induce: ideational change. Mobilization for the Great War transformed British and Italian labor in ways that were fundamental to the fate of each democracy.

Had Italy not participated in World War I or had it adopted a less punitive strategy, its nascent democracy might have survived. But Antonio Salandra and his colleagues chose war and an unjust mobilization that sealed Italy's fate. The unified, radicalized, and alienated labor movement that emerged from war undermined Italy's parliamentary regime. As democratic theorists expect, large-scale unrest targeting property rights provoked an antidemocratic reaction that destroyed the liberal regime. The political maneuvering that had sustained Italian liberalism before the war could not absorb radical challenges to it. Mobilization for war also transformed British labor. The government's procedurally just policies dislodged labor's traditional approach to economics and politics. It eroded labor's distrust of state power, and it created space for socialist principles that were previously minority ones within the labor movement. The war ushered in a new chapter in Labour history, but it did not lead to social rights. As theorists of the welfare state anticipate, the Conservative Party's postwar control of executive power foreclosed that possibility.

Mobilization for war is not the only factor that influences the labor movement. Long-term processes and large-scale structures can matter more. But if "war makes the state," it is not surprising that war also makes societal actors. Just as Charles Tilly's (1975, 633–35) wartime leaders did not anticipate that their extractive activities would create states, British and Italian policy makers did not anticipate the long-term consequences of wartime policies to address immediate needs. The war-induced changes in labor's beliefs were often unintended and undesired. Italian officials chose war partly because they hoped a short, victorious war would build a national consensus around the nation-state. But urban and rural labor emerged from the protracted war alienated from the state and primed for revolution.

The Importance of Justice

The experience of justice and injustice influences the thoughts, feelings, and behavior of societal actors in peacetime and in war. This is a central lesson in this book. Labor cares what it gets, but its interests cannot be reduced to the material well-being of workers. Multiple motivations, some narrowly egoistic and others not, drive political action. E. P. Thompson long ago taught us about the "moral economy" of collective protest. Hunger and high food prices often triggered English riots, "but these grievances operated within a popular consensus as to what were legitimate and what were illegitimate practices" (1971, 79). James Scott (1976) found that violations of customary entitlements—not deprivation or exploitation—enraged Burmese and Vietnamese peasants and created conditions ripe for rebellion. Thompson's and Scott's findings are not an artifact of the eighteenth century or subsistence farming. Economic practices are always embedded in social norms about justice, and these moral economies shape reactions to life experiences. Attending to the role of justice in political behavior is crucial, and it highlights two additional theoretical points about the importance of process and the role of affect.

PROCESS AND NOT JUST OUTCOMES

A concern about process is not a roundabout way to be concerned about outcomes. Individuals care about procedural justice because participating in decision making allows them to maximize their rewards. But individuals also care about the treatment itself. Individuals assess procedures based on whether they influence the outcome *and* whether authorities treat them with dignity and respect. The consequences of procedural justice occur regardless of whether individuals influence outcomes. People care about justice as an end in itself.

Appreciating how much people care about process helps correct the field's narrow focus on war outcomes. The conventional wisdom suggests that military victory legitimizes the regime in power, while defeat undermines it. Losing a war weakens ruling elites, sparks popular mobilization, and sometimes clears the path to democracy. For Charles Tilly (1993) and Theda Skocpol (1979), war does not generate the social problems underlying revolution, but defeat in war often becomes a prerequisite for action. Jack Goldstone (1991) argues that democratization is more likely following a military defeat than a victorious revolution. Samuel Huntington (1991b) and Dietrich Rueschemeyer, Evelyne Huber Stephens, and John Stephens (1992) see defeat in war as contributing to the downfall of authoritarian regimes. Military defeat may also affect the durability of democracies. John Higley and Michael Burton (1989) argue that defeat and occupation is one of the few conditions that can create a stable democracy.

The Italian and British cases remind us that process is also important. It is not just *whether* a state wins or loses, but *how* the war is fought. The process (or conduct during the war) can have effects that are independent of, and more important than, the war's outcome. Italy was a victor of World War I. Its monarchy and liberal institutions withstood the test of war, and its army helped destroy its historical rival, Austria-Hungary. Yet the regime lost the battle for popular support.[1] Italy's unjust mobilization delegitimized the political order, and Italy's victory in 1918 could not resurrect the regime in labor's eyes. The majority of Italians greeted news of the Armistice with denunciations of the war and the sacrifices it entailed. The freest elections in Italian history in the wake of a victorious war led to the decisive defeat of the governing class that had prosecuted the war. It was the parties that were "untainted by the responsibility for the [victorious] war" that triumphed at the polls (Webster 1960, 58). In contrast, the commitment to, and trust in, the state that the British use of procedural justice engendered encouraged the working class to see British victory as its triumph. Britain's mobilization created bridges between state and society, and labor entered the postwar period believing in Britain and committed to the political and economic order. The freest elections in British history in the wake of a victorious war led to the electoral success of the Conservative Party, which was the party *most* identified with British nationalism but also the party *least* committed to Labour's postwar agenda for democratic reform. War outcomes are important, but so is the process of getting there.

Policy makers should be especially interested in understanding the psychology of procedural justice when wartime demands make the provision of favorable outcomes difficult. States can grant cost-of-living adjustments and housing supplements to munition workers, but these are expensive propositions, especially when revenue is stretched thin. In contrast, officials can provide labor with adequate explanations for policies that affect it, and they can involve labor in decision making for little additional cost. Officials may resist this outreach as they fear setting precedents or find labor's inclusion unpalatable. But furthering procedural justice can be a cost-effective way to maintain support while imposing high costs. The more that a state recognizes the right to collective bargaining and brings labor's representatives into the political forum, the more it can ask from labor without igniting unrest. In contrast, states that deliver bad outcomes through unjust procedures are likely to pay a steep price. This coupling will lead labor (or other societal actors) to focus on what it is *not* getting. Labor will also be more likely to seek revenge, especially if it is alienated from the state. States with little procedural justice that do not moderate their demands are likely to break under the strain. People become angry and vindictive when outcomes are unfavorable and procedures are unjust.

Attention to process can also help manage controversies facing local communities in peacetime. After suffering catastrophic flash floods, residents in Ellicott City, Maryland, had to decide how to save the rest of the town. Many citizens supported tearing down parts of the historic sector, but many others ardently opposed the proposal. The hydrologist advising the county explained what he had learned about these situations: "You need to come up with an answer that satisfies the engineering specs and also the human needs. And the way to do that is for officials to make room for people to make suggestions, to not feel rushed or condescended to. Otherwise, distrust will flourish and your town could die a social death even before the next storm wipes it out." Ellicott City officials did not impose the "best" or most "rational" outcome on residents. They proposed alternatives and held meetings where individuals could be heard. Not everyone agreed with the final decision, and there was conflict along the way, but most of the town accepted the plan.[2] A study of contentious land-use issues reached a similar conclusion: fair processes increase trust in government and the public's willingness to accept decisions. And this occurs regardless of whether individuals can affect the result (Grimes 2006; see also Magalhaes and Aguiar-Conraria 2019).

AFFECT AND NOT JUST FORMAL INSTITUTIONS

The scholarship on democratic victory examines why democracies tend to defeat authoritarian states. Dan Reiter and Allan Stam (2002) contend that soldiers in democracies fight harder because they are confident their governments will keep their wartime promises or risk being voted out of office. David Lake (1992) argues that regimes based on popular consent are more likely to win because the public can punish a regime's rent-seeking behavior. But in stressing the role of electoral incentives, this literature neglects the emotional power of nationalism and trust, especially in a wartime environment.

Neuroscientist Antonio Damasio (1994) brought to popular attention emotion's central role in rationality and beliefs. Psychologists now view basic psychological distinctions—such as between feeling and thinking, or between cognition and emotion—as misleading (Barrett et al. 2007). Feelings are not simply motivations for being rational or acting on a belief. Emotion constitutes and strengthens beliefs (Markwica 2018; Mercer 2010). Trust, for example, is more than a reflection of institutional incentives: it depends on a feeling of optimism in another's goodwill (Mercer 2005). Trust involves not knowing whether another will keep a commitment but trusting that they will (or won't). The emotion in trust allows for certainty beyond evidence. Incentives matter too, of course. But people do not merely respond to incentives; they are also changed by their experience of them. Obtaining or being denied material rewards or being treated with dignity and respect affects how people feel, which influences what they think, what they want, and how they behave.

Institutions provide important links between states and society. But the affective ties binding labor to the state are also important. Mobilization strategies influence these emotional bonds—positive or negative, strong or weak—and these feelings of trust and identification in turn influence politics. While Italy's 1912 electoral law established near-universal manhood suffrage, 40 percent of British males were disenfranchised in 1914. Yet it was the British (and not the Italian) working class that rallied to the flag. Assuming that the links between state and society are institutional obscures the emotional power of nationalism in generating consent (Feinstein 2020). It also neglects the extent that affective ties can trump concerns about material gains. British labor tried to use its wartime leverage to improve its standard of living, but its motives were not only instrumental. Labor conceded much more than it gained in negotiations with the government, and it volunteered for military service when the demand arose. In the first postwar elections (and in the flush of military victory), working-class voters contributed to the Conservative Party's electoral triumph. The Tories opposed Labour's program for reconstruction, but Conservatives presented an image that appealed to working-class patriotism and that overrode its material self-interest.

A focus on institutional incentives also obscures the factors that encourage trust in a state's promises for the future. Whereas skilled labor in Britain accepted David Lloyd George's assurances that officials would help restore trade union practices once the crisis passed, Italian labor distrusted its government's intentions and dismissed its claims for the future. For the Italians, only a new political order would realize their aspirations. Both Italian and British labor had access to the voting booth—both could punish the regime for reneging on promises—but only the British identified with the state and trusted its assurances for the future.

International relations scholars sometimes draw such sharp distinctions between democratic and authoritarian regimes that commonalities between them escape consideration. Democratic institutions are important, and electoral incentives can be powerful. But nationalism and the emotional bonds between citizens and their nations can also influence political action. What distinguished Britain and Italy was not so much their electoral systems but British labor's affective ties to the state. British labor continued to support the war despite the sacrifices it entailed. Even citizens of the most odious authoritarian states sacrifice for the homeland. Ordinary Germans, and ordinary German workers, supported the Nazi regime despite increasing hardships at home (Gellately 2001; Ludtke 1994). Hitler's regime generated acclaim from broad sectors of society (Gregor 2006). That German working-class consent was based in part on its allegiance to a racist ideology makes that consent no less consequential. Conscripts fought with enthusiasm and commitment, and willingly died for Hitler's regime until the last months of the war (Gurfein and Janowitz 1946).

Governance in democratic and authoritarian regimes is not based on sanctions and rewards alone. Democracies are more likely to generate consent, but the feeling of participating, of being part of a larger and meaningful community, is often independent of the structure of domestic political institutions. The manipulation of fear and greed is important, but those are not the only—or even the most important—emotions for successful governance.

Procedural Justice and Democracy

Political scientists debate the importance of nationalism, political trust, and civil society to democracy. Some scholars see them as integral and others downplay their role. There is also disagreement about the origins of each. Examining how mobilization for war influences labor's development contributes to these debates.

It demonstrates the crucial role of procedural justice in the production of nationalism and political trust, attitudes that can be as critical to postwar politics—and to democracy—as they are to the war itself. It also highlights how fair processes can affect the nature of civil society's engagement in politics.

NATIONALISM

Democratic theorists have long discussed the importance of nationalism to democratic politics. Fifty years ago, Dankwart Rustow (1970, 351) claimed that national unity is the indispensable ingredient for democratization: "The people cannot decide until somebody decides who are the people." Juan Linz and Alfred Stepan's (1996, 16–35) distinction between state building and nation building echoes this belief. Miguel Centeno (2010, 262–63) stresses that war can create the "imagined community" that functioning democracies require. Indeed, the more protracted a war and the greater its demands, the more likely that the experience will strengthen bonds of patriotism and give birth to a nation (Centeno 2002). Many scholars agree. They see wars, and especially large-scale ones, as contributing to nation building.

The importance of nationalism to democracy remains an open question, but this book offers a new understanding of the conditions under which war strengthens the national community. Larger wars may be more likely to build solidarity than limited conflicts (as many scholars argue), but *how* states mobilize their societies for war—and especially the extent of procedural justice—can be decisive. The British case follows the familiar script of a large-scale war intensifying national bonds. The British rallied around the flag and directed their suspicions at "foreigners." During the war, rumors spread across Britain that grocers of German descent were poisoning foodstuffs. Allegations that German invaders would kill every British boy and send thousands of girls to stud farms gained traction (Simmonds 2012, 168; Wilson 1986, 740). After the war, many newly enfranchised members of the working class voted against their material interests. They were more interested in hanging the kaiser than building homes for heroes.

The contrast with Italy underscores that there is more to the relationship between war and nationalism than the war's scale. Italy also fought a war of unprecedented dimensions, but Rome chose a procedurally unjust mobilization that aggravated the divide between labor and the nation-state. The injustice of wartime mobilization transformed the urban and rural workforce's indifference toward the state into a profound alienation from it. Just as in Britain, unsubstantiated rumors spread widely, but in Italy their target was not an external enemy. Near the end of the war, rumors circulated that Rome was eliminating unproductive members of society. The state was using Italian babies to make salami to ensure adequate supplies for the front (Giovanna Procacci 1992). This alienation was not preordained. If Giovanni Giolitti had been in power, Rome would likely have chosen procedurally just policies that would have helped bring labor into a national community that went beyond the boundaries of the narrow elite that had been Italy.

The British and Italian examples show how the experience of justice shapes identification with the state. Policy makers in peacetime and war can capitalize on the power of fair processes to strengthen the national community and to encourage the allegiance of new groups to the nation-state.

POLITICAL TRUST

Scholars continue to debate the importance of trust to democracy. Some see it as essential (Putnam 1993), while others see trust's role as overrated. Indeed, some theorists contend that some degree of distrust of political leaders is good for democracy (Norris 1999). Scholars also disagree about the origins of trust. Rationalists assume that the incentives and knowledge from a history of interaction produce trust (R. Keohane 1984). Neo-Tocquevilleans see participation in voluntary associations as crucial (Putnam 2000). Social psychologists view social identification (or a sense of "groupness") as facilitating the belief that others have one's best interests at heart (R. Kramer, Brewer, and Hanna 1996).

This book stresses how justice produces trust. I argue that it is not what actors receive, or their ability to punish cheaters, that explains this belief in others' good intentions. It is the perception of procedural justice that leads to trust, and this occurs—according to social justice research—regardless of whether individuals influence outcomes. Being treated with dignity and respect and receiving explanations for decisions are sufficient to generate trust in the authority. The British state's extensive use of procedural justice overcame labor's distrust of state power. Wartime mobilization "taught" labor that it could trust the state to play a positive role in achieving labor objectives. It helped move British labor toward moderate socialism.

This understanding of the origins of trust has policy implications, especially to pundits and politicians anxious about the decline of trust in government. Some scholars stress the importance of reinvigorating civil society on the assumption that social trust between citizens translates into political trust between citizens and their governments. However, social trust and political trust are different concepts with different origins (K. Newton 2001).

Interaction within voluntary associations can produce *social* trust. Face-to-face contact in union activities can generate a cooperative spirit between union members that facilitates collective action. This social trust is unlikely, however, to extend to government institutions (or spread beyond the boundaries of the group). That Italian workers trusted each other did not mean that they also had faith in the state's good intentions. Indeed, a strong sense of in-group cohesion heightens negative reactions to outside authority. In Italy, increased labor solidarity coincided with growing distrust of the state. In contrast, Britain's promotion of procedural justice produced *political* trust between citizens and their governments: fair processes encouraged labor to trust in the state's good intentions. The implication is clear. A key to cultivating trust in government lies in the promotion of procedural justice, not the promotion of civil society. It is the political trust that procedural justice generates that can positively affect democracy.

Of course, states should do more than encourage an illusion of participation. The human relations approach to industrial psychology that Elton Mayo (1933) pioneered called on managers to foster a sense of involvement in order to increase worker morale, satisfaction, and thus productivity. Critics charge that this approach validates the manipulation of the workers, denies inevitable conflicts of interest, and is just another way to control workers, though in a subtler way than Taylorism. Historians also deride aspects of British wartime policy as providing labor with lots of access but little power. These criticisms are important. Individuals should be treated with respect, and they should understand the reasons for decisions that affect them. But they should also have influence over decisions. Individuals should *have* power and autonomy and not just *feel* as if they do.

CIVIL SOCIETY

Ever since Alexis de Tocqueville remarked on American civic-mindedness, scholars have touted civil society as vital to healthy democracies. Private voluntary associations that serve as intermediate institutions between the family and the state encourage political participation and check state power (Putnam 1993). Scholars have also noted that mobilization for war fosters associational life. But whether this war-induced growth in civil society is good for democracy depends on the character of that civil society—not just its density (Bermeo 2003, 162–68). And this once again returns us to the strategies states use to gain labor's compliance with the war effort. The extent of procedural justice in mobilization strategies has the power to transform civil society—to make it revolutionary or reformist, trustful or distrustful—and so influence its impact on democracy.

Theda Skocpol et al. (2002) argue that large-scale wars build civil society. Total wars sweep up much of society and reshape associational life as the state enlists—voluntarily or not—most citizens in the war emergency. The joint action required to harness the nation's resources for industrial warfare creates new forums for community involvement and augments the membership rolls of existing groups. This war-induced associationalism occurs broadly. Rieko Kage (2010) found that civic engagement increased in thirteen industrialized countries after World War II. Like much of the scholarship on war and democracy, this research stresses the war's scale. The larger and more protracted the struggle, the greater the growth in civil society. One of the greatest surges in American associational life occurred after the Civil War, the most total of America's wars (Skocpol et al. 2002, 136). Even in authoritarian states, and regardless of whether the state wins or loses, large-scale mobilization fosters civic engagement (Kage 2010).[3]

The scale of a war is important. Major wars build civil society, as does war in general. Michael Bauer et al. (2016) review a large literature that suggests that exposure to war-related violence increases civic engagement and prosocial behavior. But this war-induced expansion of civil society is not necessarily good for democracy. Critics of the neo-Tocquevillean approach have shown that a vigorous associational life sometimes endangers democracy. The "frenzy of associational life" in Weimar Germany eased Hitler's path to power. "Had German civil society been weaker," Sheri Berman (1997, 402) explains, "the Nazis would never have been able to capture so many citizens for their cause or eviscerate their opponents so swiftly." Dylan Riley (2010) shows that vibrant civil societies do not insulate individuals from authoritarian mass appeals. Italian, Spanish, and Romanian Fascism prospered in areas thick with voluntary associations.

Berman's and Riley's works are important correctives to neo-Tocquevillean romanticism: civil society and authoritarianism can go hand in hand. But the *nature* of associational life (not just its density or strength) is also important to democracy's fate. Riley (2005) provides a remarkable accounting of the number of cooperatives and leagues across sixteen Italian regions. But he examines the strength of the associational sphere, not these organizations' beliefs, or their links to the state. He does not discuss their political attitudes and objectives, or how they intend to achieve them. Yet whether civil society is good for democracy depends on the character of that society. Robert Putnam (2000, 22) distinguishes between "bonding" and "bridging" forms of social capital, with the latter contributing to democracy because it crosses societal groups. But there is more to it than that. What these actors want, and their relationship to the state, is central to whether their war-induced growth strengthens democracy. And the character of postwar civil society depends on the *type* of mobilization—not the *scale* of the war. The strategies that Britain and Italy used to gain labor's compliance shaped labor's wartime development and its contribution to postwar democracy.

World War I affected British and Italian civil society as Skocpol and her colleagues expect. Large-scale mobilization created new forums for citizen involvement and connected previously scattered individuals and groups. This newly formed associationalism in Britain furthered civic participation. Hundreds of new voluntary service organizations joined forces. They aided soldiers and their families and worked with state agencies to support the war effort. One organizer complained of a surfeit of volunteers. "It is most perplexing to know how to fit in all these amateurs" (quoted in Gregory 2008, 98). War mobilization also empowered British labor, increasing its density, its ties to the state, and its understanding of its role in advancing the democratic project. London's relatively just policies ensured that labor emerged from the war committed to the state and to reformist goals.

However, the Italian case shows that mobilization for war can generate a robust and vibrant civil society that *undermines* democracy. Trade union density also increased in Italy during the war, but the unjust mobilization transformed the labor movement in ways that threatened the stability of its weak liberal regime. Riley (2005, 299) finds that Fascism first took root in the regions of Italy that Putnam heralded for their civic-mindedness. This rich associational life eased recruitment and provided necessary organizational tools. But that alone does not explain Fascism's success in those regions. The prior associational life had been of a particular sort. Fascism initially succeeded where rural Socialist leagues (the Federterra) posed the greatest threat to property rights and the economic status quo. It is what these groups wanted (not their density or strength) that explains elite support for Fascist squads.

A vibrant civil society will not enhance democracy if it is contemptuous of it. "Civil society must be autonomous from the state, but not alienated from it," a democratic theorist explains (Diamond 1996, 238). "It must be watchful but respectful of state authority." The PSI was the largest party in Parliament after the first postwar elections, but it refused to work with the bourgeois liberal order. Socialist deputies stormed out of the opening of the new session yelling "Down with parliament" (quoted in J. Pollard 1998, 27). Mobilization for war created a robust civil society that helped undermine Italian democracy. Italy's weak state and weak party system were ill equipped for this new era of *radical* mass politics. Lacking strong political institutions, and facing labor challenges to property rights and the liberal order, the wave of associationalism doomed Italian democracy.

The Italian case demonstrates that a powerful and active labor movement is not an unalloyed good. Organized labor can be vital to democratization. Pressure from below can push negotiations forward even when elite bargaining dominates the process. Mass protest can also advance civil and social rights once democracy has been achieved. After World War II, the strength of organized labor and the British Labour Party's control of government led to the broad extension of social rights. But there is no simple relationship between the strength of organized labor and democracy. Italy's well-organized and politically engaged labor movement pushed politics in the opposite direction.

Democratic theorists often assume that organized labor is a consistent champion of democracy. "Those who have the most to gain from democracy will be its most reliable promoters and defenders," Rueschemeyer, Stephens, and Stephens (1992, 57) explain in their classic study extolling labor's role in democratization.

Recent accounts concur. Charles Boix (2003) and Daren Acemoglu and James Robinson (2005) assume that the lower and working classes support democracy while the rich oppose it. Labor does often advocate for, and profit from, democracy. But this support is not automatic. Organized labor also backs nondemocratic regimes and coups against elected governments. "Latin American labor movements were contingent democrats," Steve Levitsky and Scott Mainwaring (2006, 21) explain. Berman (2006) also cautions against seeing labor and left-wing parties as a "unified whole" supporting democracy. Some orthodox Marxists and other radicals may see democracy as useful in the struggle for socialism, but they do not value democracy as an end in itself. When that is the case, social solidarity can undermine the national cooperation necessary for democracy, and especially for its consolidation.

It bears repeating that the danger labor activism posed to Italy's weak democracy is not inherent in strikes and other contentious action. It was the strength of Italian labor's *radical* demands that triggered the Fascist reaction. Popular mobilization itself is not a risk to democracy, though some democratic theorists suggest otherwise. The "transitology" literature sees democracy as the outcome of strategic interaction between regime hard-liners and soft-liners (O'Donnell and Schmitter 1986). Organized labor and popular mobilization are peripheral to this process, *except as potential spoilers that must be restrained*. According to these scholars, mass politics can derail the entire process by increasing the potential costs of democracy to those benefiting from the authoritarian regime (Di Palma 1990). It is better to channel mass protest through institutionalized politics to avoid overloading the regime and creating a backlash within it (Huntington 1991b). Some democratic theorists couch these arguments in disclaimers: it is "unlimited," "excessive," or "unrestrained" grassroots mobilization that leads to the renewal of repression. But there is a danger that these qualifiers get lost in the noise.

Persistent and large-scale mobilization is not something democratizers should fear. Nancy Bermeo (1997) finds that strike levels were high during transitions to democracy in Brazil, Chile, South Korea, Peru, and the Philippines. Glenn Adler and Eddie Weber (1995) argue that powerful social movements—and especially the labor movement—were instrumental to the demise of the apartheid regime in South Africa. Jon Kraus (2007) generalizes the argument across six states in Africa, finding that high levels of trade union militancy helped to create and maintain democracy. Recent quantitative studies reach similar conclusions. Mohammad Ali Kadivar, Adaner Usmani, and Benjamin Bradlow (2020) find that the more sustained the popular mobilization before a transition, the deeper the democracy that results. Stephan Haggard and Robert Kaufman (2016) find that democracies emerging from episodes of popular mobilization are deeper and more durable than those crafted from above.

The working class is not always important to the strength and success of democracy, and it allies with other actors when it moves the process forward (Collier 1999). But "docile," "patient," and "defeated" labor movements are not, as Adam Przeworski suggests (1986, 63), necessary for democratization to succeed. To the contrary, mass protests and labor activism can be decisive to the emergence, consolidation, and expansion of democracy. Whether war plays a similarly positive role is more doubtful.

War Is Rarely Good for Democracy

Scholars and activists should be skeptical of claims that war is good for democracy. Wartime states are often quick to limit civil liberties. The US war on terror increased presidential power and spawned a new generation of restrictions on rights (Tarrow 2015). Even the best-case scenarios for democracy's war-induced advance—mass mobilization warfare—are poor vehicles for democratic reform. Britain and Italy were easy cases for conventional arguments, yet World War I did little to advance political, civil, or social rights. In the Italian case, mobilization for war opened the way to Fascism's rise. British democracy survived the conflict, but the promise of further democratization went unfulfilled. Sometimes war does deliver social rights, especially when the scale and sophistication of war raises concerns about the size and quality of *human* resources. But many of the commonly cited examples of war-induced democratic advances, such as female suffrage, cannot withstand empirical scrutiny. The political opportunities that wartime creates are more constrained than often recognized. The growing distance from the total wars of the twentieth century makes it easy to both exaggerate the apparent benefits of large-scale wars and discount their costs.

Many states extended welfare benefits to society in the late nineteenth century as part of "national efficiency" campaigns to produce better educated and healthier populations to compete on the international stage (Titmuss 1963, 78–82). Fears about threats to Britain's supremacy as an industrial and imperial power prompted calls to emulate the German model of technological education. It became a patriotic necessity to expand higher education and to invest in the nation's brainpower (Searle 1971). Many governments also provided assistance for mothers and children to increase their population base and to ensure its health (Davin 1978). French nationalists were especially anxious about the German birth rate. Pronatalists distributed posters of five German solders bayoneting two French conscripts with the explanation that two French soldiers were born for every five German ones. France provided monetary and other material benefits to large families to address this "grave public concern." One deputy introduced an amendment to give men an additional vote for each additional child. That proposal was not endorsed, but the 1939 family code provided bonuses for the birth of every child and a tax on bachelors and couples without children to pay for it (Tomlinson 1985).

These forms of state assistance can make real and immediate differences in people's lives, but they can also undermine basic rights. Concerns about improving the quality of the "human stock" helped legitimize the British eugenics movement and furthered calls to adopt the "science" of race improvement (Searle 1976). Under a 1920 law designed to increase the birth rate, French women who had abortions and individuals who distributed information on contraception could be imprisoned. The Vichy regime guillotined one abortion provider (Stetson 1986). "National efficiency" policies are an odd "social egalitarianism" that is more akin to fattening a lamb for slaughter than a commitment to social rights. Indeed, one British woman received the queen's commendation in 1917 for her decade-long efforts to feed and exercise undersized working-class "lads" for the sole purpose of ensuring they met military standards (Gullace 2002, 59). Perhaps it is no accident that those states that assumed that they would fight with small volunteer forces, such as Canada and the United States, were reluctant to adopt child allowances.

Veterans and military personnel are often rewarded for their service. Pensions for Civil War veterans were the closest thing the United States had to comprehensive social welfare before the New Deal. The GI Bill opened up higher education to thousands, and the Veterans Affairs hospital system provides medical care to millions. The US military is the one entity in America with a comprehensive welfare system. While many civilian programs contracted from the 1970s to the early 1990s, the Pentagon built a social safety net that includes housing assistance, medical and dental care, education, child care, financial counseling, and legal services (Mittelstadt 2015). British servicemen also profited from their participation in World War I. Unemployment payments to veterans were more generous, and they lasted nearly twice as long as those for civilians (Mowat 1955, 45; Wilson 1986, 823). Electoral reform in 1918 gave all British men the right to vote, including two notable stipulations. Men on active service could start voting two years earlier—at nineteen—and conscientious objectors were disenfranchised for five years. The link between military service and political citizenship was clear.

But the extension of voting rights is also contingent: it depends as much on politics and identity as it does on service and sacrifice. During World War II, Congress twice attempted to ease access to voting for Americans living overseas. The public supported these efforts and the rationale was compelling—millions of Americans were abroad. Yet the first bill (1942) came up short. The complications involved meant that a fraction of sailors and soldiers had access to the ballot box. Less than 1 percent of all service members voted in elections later that year (Manning 2016, 336). Congress considered a second bill to address this shortfall, and "Washington was soon seething with controversy" (B. Martin 1945, 727). For many, it was simply a question of manipulating the process to buttress their side's electoral prospects. The 1944 presidential election was expected to be close, and polling showed that servicemembers overwhelmingly supported Franklin D. Roosevelt's reelection (Manning 2016, 368). But for many southern Democrats, this was about more than partisan politics. A "principle" was at stake. Not only would the proposed bill enfranchise thousands of African Americans who could not vote under state laws, but it would also set a dangerous precedent by allowing the federal government to intervene in the electoral process. In the end, the South won. The final bill (1944) left the initiative to states and preserved poll taxes. "We have to retain our constitutional rights to prescribe qualifications of electors," a senator from Louisiana declared. It was necessary, he explained, in order "to maintain white supremacy" (quoted in Manning 2016, 364). Even military service during a war of unprecedented dimensions was insufficient grounds for voting rights.

The extension of the suffrage to British women after World War I is often cited as evidence of war's democratizing effect (Marwick 1965). Former prime minister Herbert Asquith publicly claimed that the war persuaded him that women deserved the franchise: "Some years ago I ventured to use the expression, 'let women work out their own salvation,' Well, Sir, they have worked it out during this war" (quoted in Taylor 1965, 94). With more than a third of the male workforce in uniform (Wrigley 1987a, 23), women were pulled into factories and government work and, according to this argument, were rewarded for their efforts. Yet the women who *did* the war work did *not* get the vote. Women formed more than a third of the British industrial workforce by the war's end (Horne 1991, 401), but only women over thirty who were either property owners or married to property owners gained the suffrage in 1918. The vast majority of women who took hazardous jobs in munitions factories either were under thirty or did not meet the property qualifications. Another decade would pass before British working-class women could vote. Indeed, some historians argue that World War I *delayed* female suffrage (Holton 1986; Lloyd 1971, 99). Others contend that it would have occurred regardless of the war (Powell 2004, 85; Wilson 1986, 725). Whatever the case, focusing on enlightened male politicians granting "deserving" women the right to vote gives credit where credit is not due. Little policy change would have occurred if suffragists had not spent years fighting and organizing for equal rights.

The correlation between war and female suffrage is misleading. Despite their wartime service, British women who merited a payback got nothing. Suffragists who had patriotically joined the war effort had to accept truncated voting rights after the war. Two years before World War I, the suffrage movement had *rejected* the provisions for female suffrage contained in the 1918 act. "Women were made to swallow the very mixture that had been considered so unpalatable when offered to them in 1912" (Pugh 1974, 358). Adding insult to injury, nineteen-year-old boys who had served in the military could now vote, while older sisters who had volunteered for "men's work" around explosives and poisonous materials could not. A smaller proportion of Italian women entered the industrial workforce during World War I—about 23 percent—but their labor was vital to munitions production and the maintenance of agricultural yields (Tomassini 1991, 71). The Parliament had considered female suffrage before the war, and deputies returned to the question after 1918. But efforts to leverage women's war work to gain the suffrage also failed in Italy (Mancini 2012).

Some Canadian women gained the vote during the war. The Wartime Elections Act of 1917 enfranchised women with male relatives serving in the Canadian Expeditionary Force. But this correlation between war and female suffrage is again misleading: the timing is correct, but the process is not. This electoral reform was not a payback for wartime service. The governing party enfranchised women with family members fighting abroad to ensure support for its pro-conscription agenda (Lloyd 1971, 99–100). As with most extensions of rights, electoral calculations and political power, not gratitude for war work or newfound enlightenment about women's rights, explain this limited suffrage reform.

Rosie the Riveter conveys an appealing story, but it is mostly fiction. Beginning in the 1970s, feminist scholars revised the popular portrayal of the world wars as disrupting gender norms and transforming women's place in society (Rubio-Marín 2014; Summerfield 1997). More often than not, the desire to put women back into traditional roles drowned out hopes for female emancipation. Little has changed. Women were integral to the Libyan revolution that ousted Muammar Qaddafi in 2011. They smuggled bullets past checkpoints and helped NATO with target acquisition. Women assumed positions that had previously been inconceivable, and many were determined to participate in charting their country's future. "We will never again let anyone control us," one Libyan woman declared.[4] Yet despite the international community's rhetoric of "female empowerment" and Libyan activists' lobbying for female inclusion, women had no formal role in the UN-led peace process.[5]

Wars can provide opportunities for societal actors to bargain for rights. Activists can use wartime emergencies to frame demands for equality of treatment (Krebs 2006). But these wartime environments also constrain the pursuit of citizenship rights. In some cases, such as in Britain during World War I, the strength of labor's patriotism checks its willingness to wield labor scarcity to extract maximum advantage. After all, World War I was also its war and the British nation its nation. British labor sacrificed for the war without any explicit quid pro quo. In other cases, societal actors might not share British labor's political allegiance, or they might be willing, indeed eager, to exploit wartime leverage to extract concessions from the state. But in the high-octane environment of a total war, societal actors must walk a fine line between supporting the war and demanding rights.

The British campaign for female suffrage had escalated before World War I. Marches grew larger, more women were arrested, and some were thrown in jail and force-fed. Women heckled cabinet ministers, vandalized shops, and bombed a house under construction for Lloyd George. Yet most suffragists suspended their activism during the war. The main suffrage organizations plunged into the war effort, especially once it was clear that the war would not end soon. The largest group changed its name to the Women's Active Service Movement, and it used its well-run organization to direct relief work. "We know that a War Government cannot busy itself with legislation for franchise reform," its leader, Millicent Fawcett, obligingly declared (quoted in Pugh 1991, 3). The militant suffrage organization known for its civil disobedience soon followed suit. The Women's Social and Political Union pledged to put the war first. Leading figures in the organization spoke at recruiting rallies, and the union replaced its newspaper, the *Suffragette*, with a fiercely patriotic paper, the *Britannia*, that promoted military conscription and attacked dissenters, and especially pacifists, as pro-German (Angela Smith 2003).

Whether these organizations put their suffrage activity on hold for patriotic or tactical reasons, continuing the struggle for equal rights while soldiers were dying abroad would have been poorly received by the country at large. Many suffragists correctly feared that demanding equal rights during the war would hurt the suffrage cause. British parliamentarians who opposed electoral reform were eager "to deploy the argument that women as voters would hinder the Government from waging war." Fawcett used "sound political instinct" in refocusing her energies away from women's rights to relief work (Pugh 1974, 361). The need for patriotic unity took precedence over the attainment of basic rights.

Other rights claimants face similar barriers in wartime. Labor organizations risk losing their standing with the public if they appear unpatriotic. Radical union opposition to US entry in World War I led to charges of disloyalty and became a justification for government repression (Zolberg 1986, 407). The stigma of un-Americanism undermined calls for progressive change (Johnson 2000, 342–44). African Americans also faced repression and harassment when they pressed their claims while their country was at war. Although denied equal rights, they were still expected to display unflinching support. The federal government repressed the Black press during World War I if it hinted at dissent. The editor of the *San Antonio Inquirer* was imprisoned under the Espionage Act for his editorial about the unjust hanging of thirteen soldiers in the US Army.

The Roosevelt administration resisted FBI director J. Edgar Hoover's pressure to prosecute Black journalists with sedition during World War II. But this did not mean that the Black community was free to advocate for equal rights. Government officials just took a less direct approach in their efforts to censor wartime accounts of racial injustice. Federal agents visited Black editors to complain about press coverage. Some issued veiled threats about losing access to newsprint and mailing privileges or hinted at the possibility of criminal investigations. Even Roosevelt's wartime racial adviser—a Southern white liberal—condemned the Double V campaign as "extortion" (Finkle 1973, 696). Mainstream white editors and publications agreed. The *Atlantic Monthly* wrote a blistering attack on "extremist" Black newspapers for their wartime reports of racial injustice (Finkle 1975, 69). By mid-1942, the Black press had curbed its reporting despite minor progress in civil rights (Polenberg 1992, 306–7). Activists felt similarly constrained to limit their demands. They knew they could not appear to undermine the war effort (Steven White 2019, 126).

Paradoxically, it is those who are the most disenfranchised who are also the most likely to be caught in this bind: they have the most to gain from wartime bargains for their cooperation, but they are also the ones most susceptible to charges of disloyalty. They need to show that they are, for instance, good Americans, in order to gain the country's sympathy and to avoid government repression. But in doing so, they relinquish their leverage during the wartime emergency.

Although war can advance rights, there are many less destructive paths to democratic reform. This is an obvious but important point to reiterate. Female suffrage was introduced in Norway, Finland, New Zealand, and Australia *before* the first total war. Sweden introduced a comprehensive welfare state *without* participating in mass mobilization warfare. Strong labor unions *in peacetime* help to reduce inequality, benefiting both "labor aristocrats" and the poorest and most vulnerable workers (Chasse 2018). Indeed, there is a curious tone to recent literature linking war to democracy, and especially accounts stressing the role of mass mobilization. It is violence, and especially large-scale violence, that dramatically shrinks the "gap between the haves and the have nots," a historian at Stanford explains (Scheidel 2018, 6). "The manpower needs of warfare gave democracies a kind of built-in correction from the grassroots," two American scholars remark (Ferejohn and Rosenbluth 2017, 22).

Pessimism pervades these accounts. The disappearance of mass mobilization warfare makes progressive taxation "less credible" (Scheve and Stasavage 2016, 7). Today's reliance on machine-based warfare has dangerous implications for "the political power of the common man." Questions are raised about whether modern democracy can remain strong "under alien conditions of peace" (Ferejohn and Rosenbluth 2017, 12). Where will we be, they seem to imply, without "incessant warfare" to keep the march toward democracy moving forward? No one says "bring back total war," and there is often recognition of war's destructiveness. Yet the assumption that war is the ultimate democratizer is misguided, and not only because it slights the role of contentious politics in gaining rights and narrowing inequality in peacetime. This nostalgia for total war is likely an artifact of its origins in the United States, and of a political culture that labels a "good war" one that brought barbarity and horror to millions abroad. World War II was necessary to destroy Fascism, but the war was not "good," and no advance of rights at home merited its costs abroad.

The Political Role of Veterans

This book explores how the mobilization of Italian conscripts transformed their political beliefs, and it contrasts the treatment of Italian soldiers with policies in other combatant nations. But these cases merit greater investigation and broader comparisons. Veterans often participate in democracy as just another interest group, but sometimes they are key actors in democracy's future. It is important to unravel why military service sometimes inspires veterans to political action, and why some veterans support right-wing causes while others become left-wing or pacifists.

There is no meaning inherent in war. Many soldiers simply want to go home and resume their lives, with at most the conviction that they merit compensation for their service. In these cases, military service does not create a new political identity concerned with anything larger than organizing for benefits. Yet sometimes war confers an enveloping social identity. Soldiers return home yearning to recover the camaraderie they found in war and committed to an ideology of violence infused with extreme right-wing nationalism, as happened in many belligerents after World War I. And sometimes the experience of war instills in soldiers a commitment to a democratic and inclusive agenda. Jay Winter (2010) documents how the brutality of trench warfare led to a mass movement of French pacifist veterans who challenged traditional notions of raison d'état and gave rise to a commitment to human rights. By making war on war, these veterans helped transform and strengthen European democracies.

Some scholars suggest that victory and defeat are critical to explaining variation in the political activity of veterans. Consumed by a "violent rejection of an unexpected defeat," ex-officers in Germany, Austria, and Hungary returned from World War I to form right-wing paramilitary groups determined to avenge their imagined humiliation (Gerwarth 2008, 192). Defeat in war is important, but also indeterminate. Italy was among the victorious allies in 1918, yet war produced extremes on both sides of the political spectrum. Italian veterans split between left- and right-wing organizations, and the latter formed part of the ultraviolent right-wing movement that encompassed veteran groups in the defeated nations in Central Europe.

How veterans respond to war depends on how they experience the war (and not just whether their country wins or loses). The type of warfare may be crucial. The massive increase of civilian casualties during World War II blurred any bright line between the home front and the battlefield. Increasingly effective weapons targeted population centers. While 5 percent of those killed during World War I were civilians, half of the deaths in World War II were on the home front. Women, children, and soldiers suffered similar fates. Indeed, "innocents" often suffered more from war's deadly violence. This shared experience left little space for paramilitary groups to set themselves apart, to glamorize war, and to create a cult of masculine virility. Unlike their predecessors in 1918, these veterans could not claim a unique experience of war to bind themselves together or to claim they constituted a distinct and superior society. US reliance on a professional military in its open-ended wars may be encouraging a reversion to the World War I model. The small percentage of Americans experiencing modern warfare may explain the sense among servicemembers that they are a distinct group, alienated from society, and imbued with higher moral standards than the country they serve (Foster 2016, 36–37; Holsti 2001, 56–63).

The strategies states use to mobilize soldiers may also explain veterans' political attitudes and behavior. How the military treats its members shapes who they are and what they want. The Italian army imposed unrelentingly unjust policies that radicalized conscripts and alienated them from the state. Italian conscripts returned home determined to challenge the status quo. But their left-wing radicalization is just one side of the story. Italian veterans from the Great War did not form a cohesive group. The conscripts had a new set of ideas about what they wanted that contrasted sharply with the demands of a different (and infamous) group of Italian veterans—the middle-class volunteers who served as officers and noncommissioned officers, and especially those who fought in the *arditi* (shock troops). Joined by their experience and disillusioned with the liberal state, the *arditi* formed the backbone of Mussolini's Fascist squads that launched the anti-Socialist terrorist offensive in central and northern Italy. The majority of squad leaders and members were ex-officers (Snowden 1989, 158–60, 190–91; Valli 2000, 136). These men shared a hatred of socialism and Giolittian politicians, a veneration of violence and war, and a desire for national regeneration. Mussolini viewed these veterans as "the trenchocracy." He dismissed conscripts as "the stupid mass" (quoted in Wohl 1979, 173).

Italian conscripts and middle-class officers represented different demographics and they fought differently, especially the *arditi*. These hand-picked assault units had special training and equipment. They conducted raids that infiltrated enemy defenses with concentrated firepower to open the way for broad infantry attacks. They fought a war of maneuver that was often tactically successful. In other words, unlike conscripts, these men were not mired in the trenches. Although this difference may partially explain their different reactions to the war, all of Europe's soldiers experienced the horror of trench warfare (but not all responded as Italian conscripts did). There is an additional difference between these groups of Italian veterans that may explain their reactions to military service and their postwar political engagement. The middle-class officers and the *arditi* were an elite: they lived in nicer barracks, had higher pay, and ate better food. Most important, they also enjoyed more relaxed discipline (Pirocchi 2004). They did not experience the disciplinary terror inflicted on Italian conscripts. Identity influences experience just as assuredly as the experience of justice or injustice shapes identity.

Fear of Democracy and Its Consequences for War

Scholars posit a relationship between the anticipated consequences of war and its likelihood. Regimes that lose wars are punished for their policy failures and removed from power. Anticipation of this fate "dampen[s] any enthusiasm for risky foreign adventures" (Bueno de Mesquita, Siverson, and Woller 1992, 638). Here again the focus is on war outcomes (victory or defeat). Yet policy makers also fear how the *process* of mobilizing for large-scale wars may bring demands for domestic change that they consider unacceptable. This fear may temper calls for war and limit their length.

Conservatives have long feared war's (domestic) potential. Austrian chancellor Klemens von Metternich sought to avoid war so as to avoid domestic reform (Sheridan 1975, 47). German chancellor Bernhard von Bülow warned, "History shows us that every great war is followed by a period of liberalism, since a people demands compensation for the sacrifices and effort war has entailed" (quoted in D. Kaiser 1983, 456). A segregationist and prominent American lawyer worried that World War II "offered the opportunity for the rationalization of the position of the Negro as a citizen of the United States" (quoted in Steven White 2016, 40). An American's comment during the Revolutionary War succinctly captures this sentiment: "When the pot boils, the scum will arise" (quoted in Mann 1993, 152). This fear of the domestic consequences of large-scale wars is often unrelated to whether policy makers expect to win or lose the war. And it may affect the duration and likelihood of war.

The fear that long and costly wars will lead to democratic reform may push policy makers to the peace table. They may attempt to end a conflict before "damage" to domestic privilege is (apparently) done. Just three weeks after the Bolshevik-led government came to power, Lord Lansdowne—a senior British Conservative—went public with a proposal that he had privately urged cabinet colleagues to consider a year earlier. Lansdowne's celebrated "Peace Letter" in the *Daily Telegraph* called for a negotiated settlement with Germany. "We are not going to lose this war," he stressed, "but its prolongation will spell ruin for the civilized world." Lansdowne called for the revision of Allied war aims. Britain should not seek to destroy Germany or to undermine Germany's great-power status.[6] Lansdowne's "defeatism was utterly conservative," notes one historian. "He did not like what he saw of the social changes of wartime" (Turner 1988, 129). Popular calls for "a conscription of riches" and organized labor's growing power— not the prospect of a British defeat—worried this member of the land-owning elite. Lansdowne feared that prolonging the war would unleash democratizing forces. He hoped that a negotiated peace would halt that process (DeGroot 1996, 209). The British cabinet flatly rejected Lansdowne's proposal, but the idea did not die. Conservatives returned to this theme when another protracted war with Germany appeared on the horizon.

The slow pace of British and French rearmament, and their reluctance to confront the Nazi threat, can be traced back in part to fears of war-induced democracy. The rise of mass left-wing parties and the growth of organized labor frightened British and French conservatives. They were anxious about the westward spread of Bolshevism. They feared what another protracted war would mean for the established order. Just after the Armistice, Stanley Baldwin explained his apprehension: "We were in a new world . . . class conscious and revolutionary it was. If London [is] bombed three nights running, nothing [could] avert a revolution" (quoted in Halperin 1997, 144). As the German threat became clear, Conservative governments in Britain hesitated to kick-start rearmament in part because they feared collaboration with unions would allow labor to extract concessions (McKibbin 1990, 290). A cabinet minister advised against "direct contact with the trade unions . . . as consultation would encourage the unions to demand a high price as regards conditions and wages in return for cooperation" (quoted in Anievas 2010, 615). These politicians feared that nationalization and taxes on the rich would become inevitable. On the eve of World War II, a diplomat noted the calm of the patriarch of one of Britain's wealthiest aristocratic families: "I must say I do admire a man like that, who must realise that all his grandeur is gone forever, not showing the slightest sign of any gloom or apprehension" (quoted in McKibbin 1990, 290). War would be a crossroads, these traditionalists feared.

"Whether we win or lose," a prominent Tory politician cautioned in 1938, "it will be the end of everything we know" (quoted in Kennedy 1981, 298).

French conservatives were especially worried that a large-scale war against the Axis powers would empower the working class. Center and center-right politicians hoped to avoid war or, if that were not possible, to fight a short war on French terms. They worried that mobilization for total war would permanently restructure France's domestic political economy. It would require the type of economic planning that verged dangerously close to the Bolshevik model. War "would bring to our country measures of control, organization, in a word socialization, similar to those adopted in totalitarian countries," the editor of a business journal exclaimed (quoted in Imlay 2003, 270). Members of some of France's wealthiest families concurred that it was better to remain open to negotiations with the Fascist powers than to risk what another war might do to their status and privilege (Halperin 1997, 157). A few months before the French surrender to Hitler, the arch-conservative Pierre Laval (three-time prime minister, four-time foreign secretary, and later Vichy collaborator) declared to the Senate, "If the war lasts, the social consequences for capitalist regimes will be terrible" (quoted in Imlay 2003, 175).

Sometimes this quest for peace at all costs is counterproductive, as it was in appeasing Nazi Germany. But if fears of war-induced democratic reform are common, the anticipated (but unintended and frequently unrealized) consequences of war may decrease the likelihood and duration of war. War rarely serves democracy, but the fear of democracy can sometimes serve peace.

Notes

1. MOBILIZING LABOR FOR WAR AND ITS IMPLICATIONS FOR DEMOCRACY

1. Lasswell 1941 and Nef 1950 are classics. See also Cole 2005; Donohue 2008.

2. See also W. Thompson 1996; Gleditsch and Ward 2006.

3. Most consider World War I the first total war. The main belligerents devoted more than half of the national income to the war (Broadberry and Harrison 2005, 36).

4. Therborn 1977 and Rueschemeyer, Stephens, and Stephens 1992 are classics. See also Bermeo 1997; Collier 1999; Tilly 2003; Valenzuela 1989. For labor's role in transitions to democracy in Africa, see G. Adler and Webster 1995; Kraus 2007. In Southeast Asia, see Neureiter 2013. In the Middle East, see Arslanalp and Perlman 2017.

5. On the role of nonviolent protest, see Celestino et al. 2013; Kadivar and Ketchley 2018; Teorell 2010.

6. On labor's role in the durability of democracy, see Haggard and Kaufman 2016; Kadivar 2018.

7. The classics are Esping-Andersen 1985; Korpi 1983; Stephens 1979. On retrenchment, see Allan and Scruggs 2004; Anderson 2001; Huber, Rueschemeyer, and Stephens 1997; Zarate Tenorio 2014. See also n. 5 in chapter 8.

8. See Steven White 2019 for a critical review of this literature.

9. See also Brooke 1992; Hickson 2004. Kavanagh and Morris 1989 support the traditional view.

10. See "War Is Rarely Good for Democracy" in the conclusion for a discussion of war and female suffrage.

11. See Cronon (1969, 28) and Klinkner and Smith (1999, 11) for Black support for World War I. There were practical reasons to enlist and buy war bonds, but Jane Lang Scheiber and Harry Scheiber (1969, 454–55) stress that cooperation was not based on pragmatism or fear alone. Theodore Kornweibel (1981) disagrees.

12. See also Ellison 1992; Jennings and Markus 1976; Leal 1999. Blattman 2009 examines the effect of military service in insurgencies.

13. See also Carrell and Dittrich 1978; Greenberg and Cohen 1982; Walster, Walster, and Berscheid 1978. Most research on distributive justice focuses on equity (as opposed to equality or need). I use *equity* because theorists argue that it is the principle most likely to apply when the goal is to maximize productivity. See Mowday 1991, 121–23.

14. 346 Parl. Deb. H.C. (5th ser.) (April 27, 1939) col. 1343.

15. For reviews, see Bobocel and Gosse 2015; Colquitt et al. 2013; Greenberg and Lind 2000; Konovsky 2020; MacCoun 2005.

16. E. Allan Lind and Tom Tyler (1988) developed the noninstrumental (or "group value") model. See G. Leventhal 1980; and Thibaut and Walker 1975 for the instrumental view.

17. Scholars debate whether informal (also called interactional or informational) justice is a type of procedural justice or separate from it (Colquitte et al. 2001).

18. See Gregory 2008; Leff 1991; Levi 1997; Scheve and Stasavage 2016; Sparrow 2008; Winter and Robert 1997.

19. See also Folger and Konovsky 1989; Korsgaard, Schweiger, and Sapienza 1995.

20. Examples include Geary 1981, 19; Lipset 1985, 230; Katznelson 1986, 38; Marks 1989, 14–15; Poole 1986; Zolberg 1986, 408.

21. See also Mazerolle et al. 2014; Tyler 1997, 2017; Tyler and Lind 1992.

22. See also Cohen-Charash and Spector 2001; Folger and Konovsky 1989; Korsgaard, Schweiger, and Sapienza 1995.

23. See also Alexander and Ruderman 1987; Kernan and Hanges 2002; Lind and Tyler 1988; Mittal, Shubham, and Sengupta 2019; Van den Bos, Wilke, and Lind 1998.

24. For discussion, see "Procedural Justice Explains Compliance" and "Procedural Injustice Explains Revenge" in chapter 7.

2. DISCIPLINING ITALIAN LABOR

1. Royal Decree 993 created MI on May 24, 1915. Two additional decrees (June 27 and August 22, 1915) expanded its authority. MI became its own ministry in June 1917.

2. MI had a statistics department, but the data collected and it's location is unknown.

3. The notion that political insurrection caused Caporetto also appealed to the extreme Left. The army's recovery at the end of 1917 and its defense of Monte Grappa should have quashed this notion, but it persisted for years because it appealed to so many. The military historian Piero Pieri demolished this self-serving myth of a "soldiers' strike" in the 1950s. Operational problems, including incompetent officers, poor planning, and inadequate defensive preparations, explain the mass flight and surrenders. As in France, the appointment of a competent commander resolved the army's problems (Morselli 2001, ix–xi; M. Thompson 2008, 316, 325; Wilcox 2009).

4. There are no good figures on how many civilians passed through the military judicial system. Many courts did not send records to Rome, and the Venetia records were lost after Caporetto (Giovanna Procacci 2013, 162).

5. The index of wholesale prices in Italy climbed from 100 in 1914 to 425 in 1918; in Britain it rose from 100 to 227 (Toniolo 1990, 131). Accurate figures on the wartime Italian economy, such as the change in the gross national product, are not available (Galassi and Harrison 2005, appendix).

6. The northern regions were not all commercialized. Sharecroppers and small landowners worked in the foothills and mountains. *Braccianti* also worked in parts of Apulia.

7. Irene Guerrini and Marco Pluviano (2014, 186) identified 294 victims of summary executions. They believe there were many more. See also M. Thompson 2008, 274; Wilcox 2005, 81.

8. Exceptions include Bulgaria and possibly Russia.

9. For the harshness of British military law compared with that of Germany and France, see Johansen 2013, 58–60; Oram 2003, 18–20.

3. MANAGING BRITISH LABOR

1. Charles à Court Repington, "Need for Shells: British Attack Checked. Limited Supply the Cause," *Times* (London), May 14, 1915.

2. Additional amendments in 1916 and 1917 strengthened the act.

3. DORA was rushed through Parliament on August 8, 1914, and amended six times.

4. Henderson was forced out in August 1917, but another Labour member, George Barnes, replaced him.

5. Henderson chaired the Central Munitions Labour Supply Committee that produced the guidelines.

6. The government created the Whitley Committee in 1916 to investigate problems in industrial relations. It was composed of union representatives, employers, academics, and social reformers.

7. A spoiled wicket is when too much rain on the pitch softens the ground, making hitting the ball even harder (for the ball's trajectory can change when it digs into the pitch).

8. Quoted in "Mr. Lloyd George's Manchester Speech," *Colonist*, June 9, 1915, https://paperspast.natlib.govt.nz/newspapers/TC19150609.2.34.38; "Speech by Lloyd George," *Hawera and Normanby Star*, June 5, 1915, http://paperspast.natlib.govt.nz/cgi-bin/paperspast?a=d&d=HNS19150605.2.30.14.

9. Inflation outstripped wage increases for the vast majority of the working class by the start of 1917 (Gregory 2008, 194–96). Wholesale prices were 140 percent above prewar levels by 1918, and inflation was even higher for basic household items (Simmonds 2012, 172–73).

10. Some historians dispute this claim. See Bryder 1987; Gazely and Newell 2013; Winter 1988.

11. "How They Starve at the Ritz," *Herald*, November 24, 1917.

12. Editorial, "At the Front and at Home," *Economist*, November 28, 1917, 831.

13. On the use of troops to quell industrial unrest from 1910 to 1914, see Winter 1974, 18–21.

14. On the "servile state," see Hinton 1973. For contrary views, see Davidson 1974; Rubin 1984; Noel Whiteside 1992; and Wrigley 1987a.

15. See also A. Reid 1985, 50–51; Noel Whiteside 1992, 111–12.

16. See Commons 1922 for a list.

17. Benjamin Disraeli (1845) coined the expression "two nations" in his popular novel about upper-class indifference to the plight of the working class.

4. CHOOSING A MOBILIZATION STRATEGY: A COUNTERFACTUAL ANALYSIS

1. See "A Lost Opportunity for Nation Building" in chapter 5 for a discussion of whether Italy's participation in World War I could have built this imagined community.

2. For Paul Corner (2002b, 31) it was the "fundamental motive"; for Giuliano Procacci (1968, 322) it was the "deciding factor"; for Richard Webster (1960, 27, 42–44) it was "primary." See also Cardoza 1982, 211–13; Haywood 1999, 410, 433–34.

3. Some on the left, including Democrats and revolutionary Socialists (e.g., Benito Mussolini), also supported intervention as a way to destroy Giolittian liberalism (Cardoza 1982, 212–13; Lyttelton 2002, 7; Roberts 1979, 106).

4. Giolitti became premier for the fifth and final time in 1920.

5. See "No Explanation, Only Repression" and "A Mixed Record on Compensation" in chapter 2 for details.

5. ITALIAN LABOR'S REVOLUTIONARY SOCIALISM

1. See Giovanna Procacci 1989, 33, 36, 52–53; Seton-Watson 1967, 470; Tomassini 1990, 201–7.

2. A confusing variety of terms are used to refer to different factions of the PSI. In broad terms, the party was composed of "transigents" (moderate or reformist Socialists) and "intransigents" or "maximalists" (a heterogeneous group composed of revolutionaries and syndicalists; syndicalists believed that revolution would come through the direct action of labor unions, not parliamentary politics).

3. In the Po Valley in 1914, 87 percent of Federterra members were *braccianti*. The Federterra also represented agricultural workers in the southern regions of Apulia and Sicily. It otherwise had little support in southern and central Italy or among small farmers, renters, and sharecroppers in the north (De Grand 1989, 16).

4. In Italy, as in the rest of Europe, the Communist Party seceded from the Socialist Party. The division represented irreconcilable differences in most countries. Not in Italy: relatively minor issues led to the break.

5. See also Cardoza 1982, 246; Ledeen 1975, 109; Quine 2002, 107; Seton-Watson 1967, 521; Snowden 1986, 153.

6. The number of small peasant proprietors increased during the war, but they never constituted a mass movement comparable to the Socialist leagues. They aggressively resisted Federterra and turned to agrarian Fascism (Cardoza 1982, 321–23; Knox 2007, 226; C. Schmidt 1938, 27).

7. Unlike Emilia-Romagna in northern Italy (Po Valley), the Tuscan sharecropper in central Italy had virtually no ownership of the means of production. They had no interests to defend against encroachment from below (Snowden 1989, 72).

8. On labor's conviction that radical change was inevitable, see Cardoza 1982, 245; Lyttelton 2004, 3; Pernicone 1974, 208; Snowden 1989, 136.

9. On the fragmentation of Italian prewar labor, see Horowitz 1963, 50, 95; Pernicone 1974, 200–205; Seton-Watson 1967, 299–302.

10. MI officials required that cost-of-living demands be made on a factory-by-factory basis. This attempt to localize labor unrest cut the traditional ties between skilled workers across factories and encouraged labor solidarity within them (Tomassini 1990, 195–200).

11. On the Italian working class's weak nationalism, see Corner and Procacci 1997, 224; Koenig-Archibugi 2003, 85–91; Lyttelton 2004, 3–5; Saladino 1970, 24, 36, 234–35.

12. The Austrian requisition of foodstuffs made this reaction short-lived (M. Thompson 2008, 348).

13. John Tagliabue, "A New Legacy in Belgium for World War I Deserters," *New York Times*, November 25, 2008; Richard Norton-Taylor, "Executed World War I Soldiers to Be Given Pardons," *Guardian*, August 16, 2006.

14. The phrase is from the Italian poet Piero Jahier, who volunteered for the Italian army during World War I. Quoted in M. Thompson 2008, 387.

6. BRITISH LABOR'S MODERATE SOCIALISM

1. Historians reject George Dangerfield's claim (1935) that the Liberal Party was on its last legs in 1914. Duncan Tanner (1990) shows the Liberal Party's appeal to the working class and Labour's inability to distinguish itself from them.

2. Support for political action varied by sector. Craft unions, engineers, and electricians opposed it; some new sectors were more supportive (A. Reid 2000, 223).

3. The Conciliation Act of 1896 specified that state arbitration could only occur if both parties to the conflict requested it. The decisions were not legally binding (Davidson 1979, 175–78).

4. Ross McKibbin (1974) downplayed but later revised (1990) the war's role in Labour's "socialist turn." See Horne 1991, 258.

5. In response to demands from the railroad and mining unions, Labour endorsed state ownership of the railroads in 1908 and the mines in 1912 (Worley 2005, 12).

6. It later became controversial. In the late 1950s, Labour politician Hugh Gaitskell failed in his attempts to amend Clause IV. Tony Blair's "New Labour" succeeded in 1995, thus ending Labour's support for mass nationalization.

7. William Beveridge was a researcher for the report.

8. Early historiography on the shop stewards (e.g., Hinton 1973) overly relied on the papers of movement leaders. See McLean 1983 for a reassessment.

9. It was renamed the British Workers League (1916) and then the National Democratic and Labour Party (1918).

10. For details on British labor's reaction to the German offensive, see "Hooray for Caporetto!" in chapter 5.

11. On labor's involvement in government leading to tension between union leaders and their members, see Hardach 1977; Turner 1992, 106, 369; Wrigley 1982b, 82.

12. A khaki election is held shortly after a war in the expectation that the party in power will benefit from war enthusiasm. See "A Chamber of 'Hard-Faced Men'" in chapter 8 for details on the election results.

7. COMPLIANCE, REVENGE, AND THE RISE OF ITALIAN FASCISM

1. *Labour and the New Social Order* (1918) and the National Industrial Conference's joint report (March 1919) are two of Labour's most important statements on its plans for reconstruction. The Joint Committee on Labour Problems after the War (spring 1916) included union and Labour Party representatives; it developed many of these proposals.

2. "Classic Podium: A Humble Recognition of Heroes," *Independent* (London), November 6, 1998.

3. This section's title refers to the title of Trevor Wilson's (1986) chapter on British postwar reform.

4. "At the Front and at Home," *Economist*, November 24, 1917, 831; Bonar Law quoted in "Conscription of Wealth," *Economist*, December 29, 1917, 1024.

5. "Finding the Money," *Economist*, January 5, 1918, 3.

6. Ibid.

7. The quote references the title of Wilson's (1986) chapter on postwar education policy.

8. Dating from 1601 and last revised in 1834, the Poor Laws regarded poverty as a moral failing. The able bodied could gain relief only through employment in locally administered workhouses.

9. On retributive justice and revenge, see Carlsmith, Darley, and Robinson 2002; Darley and Pittman 2003; Tripp and Bies 2015; Vidmar 2002; Wenzel et al. 2008. This corresponds to the in-group favoritism effect (Brewer 2008).

10. This section's title is taken from Webster 1960, 65.

11. On the reliability of data on Italian and British wages and inflation, see Zamagni 1991, 144–46; and Cronin 1979, 197–201, respectively.

12. On the central importance of the countryside to Fascism's rise, see Cardoza 1982; Corner 2002a, 277; Linz 1976, 26–29; Snowden 1972.

13. On military and local police collaboration, see Corner 1975, 119–20; Lyttelton 2004, 39; Maier 1975, 177, 316–17; Salvemini 1928, 76, 107; Snowden 1989, 190, 198.

8. REVISITING COMPETING ACCOUNTS, AND THE FAILURE OF BRITISH REFORM

1. See "British Labor's Compliance" in chapter 7 for details on the unmet promises.

2. On British industrialists' postwar offensive against labor and the gulf between employers and labor, see Gospel 1987, 163; Lowe 1978b, 668–71; MacDonald 1976, 95; Wrigley 1987b, 2–4.

3. David Lloyd George election speech, November 24, 1918; "Classic Podium: A Humble Recognition of Heroes," *Independent* (London), November 6, 1998.

4. For details on British labor's reaction to the German offensive, see "Hooray for Caporetto!" in chapter 5.

5. Walter Korpi and Joakim Palme (2003) emphasize the role of partisanship and left-wing parties in retrenchment; other theorists stress the continued relevance of trade

unions (Fleckenstein and Lee 2019; Gordon 2015; Keune 2018; Rathgeb 2019). See end-note 7 in chapter 1 for additional citations.

6. Duncan Tanner (1983) argues that the increase in the number of working-class voters is less than Henry Matthew, Ross McKibbin, and John Kay (1976) estimate.

7. That would come in World War II. On the development of Labour's "social patrio-tism," see Field 1992.

8. Labour got 22 percent of the votes in 1918 and 33 percent in 1924 even though there had been no change in the franchise (Freeman 2018).

9. Andrew Bonar Law's Conservative government replaced Lloyd George's coalition in October 1922.

10. "Close the Ranks: Labour's Fight for Its Life," *Herald* (Glasgow), November 23, 1918. "Unionists" are Conservatives. The term has nothing to do with trade unions. Unionists sought to preserve the "union" with Ireland. The Conservative Party was offi-cially the Conservative and Unionist Party.

9. CONCLUSION: BRINGING THE POLITICS OF WAR INTO THE POLITICS OF PEACE

1. The nationalist Right saw the outcome as a "mutilated victory" because its territorial ambitions were not satisfied. Most Italians did not share this view.

2. Audie Cornish, "How a Proposal to Reduce Flood Risks in Ellicott City Nearly De-stroyed the Community," *All Things Considered*, NPR, October 9, 2019.

3. Skocpol et al. (2002) argue that victory encourages the growth of civil society but that defeat dampens it.

4. Anne Barnard, "Libya's War-Tested Women Hope to Keep New Power," *New York Times*, September 12, 2011.

5. Emily Burchfield, "How the Exclusion of Women Has Cost Libya," Atlantic Council, November 26, 2019, https://www.atlanticcouncil.org/blogs/menasource/how-the-exclusion -of-women-has-cost-libya/.

6. Lord Lansdowne, "Co-ordination of Allies' War Aims," *Daily Telegraph*, Novem-ber 29, 1917.

References

Abrams, Philip. 1963. "The Failure of Social Reform, 1918–1920." *Past and Present* 24:43–64.

Absalom, Roger. 1995. *Italy since 1800: A Nation in the Balance?* New York: Routledge.

Acemoglu, Daren, and James A. Robinson. 2005. *Economic Origins of Dictatorship and Democracy.* New York: Cambridge University Press.

Adams, Jad. 2014. *Women and the Vote: A World History.* Oxford: Oxford University Press.

Adams, R. J. Q. 1978. *Arms and the Wizard: Lloyd George and the Ministry of Munitions, 1915–1916.* London: Cassell.

Adams, Thomas Sewell. 1922. "Excess Profits Tax." In *The Encyclopedia Britannica.* New York: Encyclopedia Britannica.

Addison, Christopher. 1922. *The Betrayal of the Slums.* London: Herbert Jenkins.

Addison, Paul. 1975. *The Road to 1945: British Politics and the Second World War.* London: Cape.

Adler, Franklin Hugh. 1995. *Italian Industrialists from Liberalism to Fascism: The Political Development of the Industrial Bourgeoisie, 1906–1934.* Cambridge: Cambridge University Press.

Adler, Glenn, and Eddie Webster. 1995. "Challenging Transition Theory: The Labor Movement, Radical Reform, and Transitions to Democracy in South Africa." *Politics and Society* 23 (1): 75–106.

Agócs, Sándor. 1971. "Giolitti's Reform Program: An Exercise in Equilibrium Politics." *Political Science Quarterly* 86 (4): 637–53.

Alexander, Sheldon, and Marian Ruderman. 1987. "The Role of Procedural and Distributive Justice in Organizational Behavior." *Social Justice Research* 1 (2): 177–98.

Allan, James P., and Lyle Scruggs. 2004. "Political Partisanship and Welfare State Reform in Advanced Industrial Societies." *American Journal of Political Science* 48 (3): 496–512.

Ambrose, Maureen L., and Carole T. Kulik. 1999. "Old Friends, New Faces: Motivation Research in the 1990s." *Journal of Management* 25 (3): 231–92.

Anderson, Karen M. 2001. "The Politics of Retrenchment in a Social Democratic Welfare State: Reform of Swedish Pensions and Unemployment Insurance." *Comparative Political Studies* 34 (9): 1063–91.

Andreski, Stanislav. 1954. *Military Organization and Society.* Berkeley: University of California Press.

Anievas, Alexander. 2010. "The International Political Economy of Appeasement: The Social Sources of British Foreign Policy during the 1930s." *Review of International Studies* 37 (2): 601–29.

Aquino, Karl, Thomas M. Tripp, and Robert J. Bies. 2006. "Getting Even or Moving On? Power, Procedural Justice, and Types of Offense as Predictors of Revenge, Forgiveness, Reconciliation, and Avoidance in Organizations." *Journal of Applied Psychology* 91 (3): 653–68.

Arslanalp, Mert, and Wendy Perlman. 2017. "Mobilization in Military-Controlled Transitions: Lessons from Turkey, Brazil, and Egypt." *Comparative Sociology* 16 (3): 311–39.

Askwith, Lord [Sir George Ranken Askwith]. 1920. *Industrial Problems and Disputes.* London: John Murray.

August, Andrew. 2007. *The British Working Class, 1832–1940.* London: Pearson Longman.

Balderston, Theo. 1989. "War Finance and Inflation in Britain and Germany, 1914–1918." *Economic History Review* 42 (2): 222–44.

Bales, Kevin. 1999. "Popular Reactions to Sociological Research: The Case of Charles Booth." *Sociology* 33 (1): 153–68.

Barnes, George Nicoll. 1917. *Summary of the Reports of the Commission of Inquiry into Industrial Unrest.* London: H. M. Stationary Office.

Barrett, Lisa F., Batja Mesquita, Kevin N. Ochsner, and James J. Gross. 2007. "The Experience of Emotion." *Annual Review of Psychology* 58:373–403.

Bates, Robert H. 2001. *Prosperity and Violence: The Political Economy of Development.* New York: W. W. Norton.

Bauer, Michael, Christopher Blattman, Julie Chytilová, Joseph Henrich, Edward Miguel, and Tamar Mitts. 2016. "Can War Foster Cooperation?" *Journal of Economic Perspectives* 30 (3): 249–74.

Beneš, Jakub. 2016. "Labour, Labour Movements, Trade Unions, and Strikes (Austria-Hungary)." In *1914–1918 Online: International Encyclopedia of the First World War*, edited by Ute Daniel, Peter Gatrell, Oliver Janz, Heather Jones, Jennifer Keene, Alan Kramer, and Bill Nasson. Berlin: Freie Universität Berlin. https://encyclopedia .1914-1918-online.net/article/labour_labour_movements_trade_unions_and _strikes_austria-hungary.

Berger, Stefan. 1994. *The British Labour Party and the German Social Democrats, 1900–1931.* Oxford: Clarendon.

Berman, Sheri. 1997. "Civil Society and the Collapse of the Weimar Republic." *World Politics* 49 (3): 401–29.

———. 2006. *The Primacy of Politics: Social Democracy and the Making of Europe's Twentieth Century.* New York: Cambridge University Press.

Bermeo, Nancy. 1997. "Myths of Moderation: Confrontation and Conflict during Democratic Transitions." *Comparative Politics* 29 (3): 305–22.

———. 2003. "What the Democratization Literature Says—or Doesn't Say—about Postwar Democratization." *Global Governance* 9 (2): 159–77.

———. 2007. "War and Democratization: Lessons from the Portuguese Experience." *Democratization* 14 (3): 388–406.

Berta, Giuseppe. 1993. "The Interregnum: Turin, Fiat, and Industrial Conflict between War and Fascism." In *Challenges of Labour: Central and Western Europe, 1917–1920*, edited by Chris Wrigley, 105–24. London: Routledge.

Bertrand, Charles L. 1976. "War and Subversion in Italy: 1917–1918." *Historical Reflections* 3 (2): 105–22.

Bessel, Richard. 2000. "Mobilizing German Society for War." In *Great War, Total War: Combat and Mobilization on the Western Front, 1914–1918*, edited by Roger Chickering and Stig Forster, 437–52. Cambridge: Cambridge University Press.

Beugre, Constant D., and Robert A. Baron. 2001. "Perceptions of Systemic Justice: The Effects of Distributive, Procedural, and Interactional Justice." *Journal of Applied Social Psychology* 31 (2): 324–39.

Bianchi, Bruna. 2013. "Crimes des officiers italiens et condamnations infligées pendant la Premiére Guerre mondial." In *Justice militaires et guerres mondiales*, edited by Jean-Marc Berliére, Jonas Campion, and Luigi Lacché, 167–78. Belgium: Presses Universitaires de Louvain.

Bies, Robert J., and J. S. Moag. 1986. "Interactional Justice: Communications Criteria of Fairness." In *Research on Negotiation in Organizations*, edited by Roy Lewitcki, Max Bazerman, and Blair Sheppard, 43–55. Greenwich, CT: Jai.

Blader, Steven L., and Tom R. Tyler. 2015. "Relational Models of Procedural Justice." In *The Oxford Handbook of Justice in the Workplace*, edited by Russell S. Cropanzano and Maureen L. Ambrose, 351–70. New York: Oxford University Press.

Blattman, Christopher. 2009. "From Violence to Voting: War and Political Participation in Uganda." *American Political Science Review* 103 (2): 231–47.

Bobocel, D. Ramona. 2013. "Coping with Unfair Events Constructively or Destructively: The Effects of Overall Justice and Self–Other Orientation." *Journal of Applied Psychology* 98 (5): 720–31.

Bobocel, D. Ramona, and Leanne Gosse. 2015. "Procedural Justice: A Historical Review and Critical Analysis." In *The Oxford Handbook of Justice in the Workplace*, edited by Russell S. Cropanzano and Maureen L. Ambrose, 461–76. Oxford: Oxford University Press.

Boix, Charles. 2003. *Democracy and Redistribution*. New York: Cambridge University Press.

Bondi, Victor. 1995. *American Decades: 1940–1949*. Detroit: Gale Research.

Bosworth, R. J. B. 1979. *Italy, the Least of the Great Powers: Italian Foreign Policy before the First World War*. London: Cambridge University Press.

——. 2005. *Mussolini's Italy: Life under Dictatorship, 1915–1945*. New York: Penguin Books.

Bourne, J. M. 1989. *Britain and the Great War, 1914–1918*. London: Edward Arnold.

Bravo, Anna. 1989. "Italian Peasant Women and the First World War." In *War, Peace, and Social Change in Twentieth Century Europe*, edited by Clive Emsley, Arthur Marwick, and Wendy Simpson, 102–115. Philadelphia: Open University Press.

Brewer, Marilynn B. 2008. "Depersonalized Trust and Ingroup Cooperation." In *Rationality and Social Responsibility: Essays in Honor of Robyn Mason Dawes*, edited by Joachim I. Krueger, 215–32. New York: Psychology Press.

Broadberry, Stephen, and Mark Harrison. 2005. "The Economics of World War I: An Overview." In *The Economics of World War I*, edited by Stephen Broadberry and Mark Harrison, 3–40. Cambridge: Cambridge University Press.

Broadberry, Stephen, and Peter Howlett. 2005. "The United Kingdom during World War I: Business as Usual?" In *The Economics of World War I*, edited by Stephen Broadberry and Mark Harrison, 206–34. Cambridge: Cambridge University Press.

Brockner, Joel A. 2010. *A Contemporary Look at Organizational Justice: Multiplying Insult Times Injury*. New York: Routledge.

Brockner, Joel A., and Phyllis Siegel. 1996. "Understanding the Interaction between Procedural and Distributive Justice: The Role of Trust." In *Trust in Organizations: Frontiers of Theory and Research*, edited by Roderick M. Kramer and Tom R. Tyler, 390–413. Thousand Oaks, CA: Sage.

Brooke, Stephen. 1992. *Labour's War: The Labour Party during the Second World War*. Oxford: Clarendon.

Brown, Henry Phelps. 1983. *The Origins of Trade Union Power*. Oxford: Clarendon.

Bryder, Linda. 1987. "The First World War: Healthy or Hungry." *History Workshop Journal* 24: 141–57.

——. 2008. "New Zealand." In *Nations and Nationalism: A Global Historical Overview*, edited by Guntram Henrik Herb and David H. Kaplan, 862–73. Santa Barbara, CA: ABC-CLIO.

Bueno de Mesquita, Bruce, Randolph M. Siverson, and Gary Woller. 1992. "War and the Fate of Regimes: A Comparative Analysis." *American Political Science Review* 86 (3): 638–46.

Burk, Kathleen. 1982. Introduction to *War and the State: The Transformation of British Government, 1914–1919*, edited by Kathleen Burk, 1–6. London: George Allen and Unwin.

Bush, Julia. 1992. "Labor Politics in East London during and after the First World War." In *Strikes, Social Conflict and the First World War: An International Perspective*, edited by Leopold Haimson and Giulio Sapelli, 123–40. Milan: Fondazione Giangiacomo Feltrinelli.

Calder, Angus. 1995. "Britain's Good War." *History Today* 45 (5): 55–62.

Cardoza, Anthony L. 1982. *Agrarian Elites and Italian Fascism: The Province of Bologna, 1901–1926*. Princeton, NJ: Princeton University Press.

———. 1991. "Commercial Agriculture and the Crisis of Landed Power: Bologna, 1880–1930." In *Landownership and Power in Modern Europe*, edited by Ralph Gibson and Martin Blinkhorn, 181–98. New York: HarperCollins.

Carlsmith, Kevin M., John M. Darley, and Paul H. Robinson. 2002. "Why Do We Punish? Deterrence and Just Deserts as Motives for Punishment." *Journal of Personality and Social Psychology* 83 (2): 284–99.

Carrell, M. R., and John E. Dittrich. 1978. "Equity Theory: The Recent Literature and New Directions." *Academy of Management Review* 3 (2): 202–10.

Celestino, Mauricio Rivera, Kristian Skrede Gleditsch, Erica Chenoweth, and Kathleen Gallagher Cunningham. 2013. "Fresh Carnations or All Thorn, No Rose? Nonviolent Campaigns and Transitions in Autocracies." *Journal of Peace Research* 50 (3): 385–400.

Centeno, Miguel. 2002. *Blood and Debt: War and the Nation-State in Latin America*. University Park: Pennsylvania State University Press.

———. 2010. "Concluding Reflections: What Wars Do." In *In War's Wake: International Conflict and the Fate of Liberal Democracy*, edited by Elizabeth Kier and Ronald R. Krebs, 253–70. Cambridge: Cambridge University Press.

Chance, William. 1917. *Industrial Unrest: The Reports of the Commissioners (July 1917) Collated and Epitomised*. London: P. S. King and Son.

Charles, Rodger. 1973. *The Development of Industrial Relations in Britain, 1911–1939*. London: Hutchinson.

Chasse, J. Dennis. 2018. "How Necessary Are Unions? Insights from John R. Commons." *Journal of Economic Issues* 52 (2): 413–21.

Clark, Martin. 1977. *Antonio Gramsci and the Revolution That Failed*. New Haven, CT: Yale University Press.

———. 2014. *Modern Italy, 1871 to the Present*. 3rd ed. London: Routledge.

Cline, Peter. 1982. "Winding Down the War Economy: British Plans for Peacetime Recovery, 1916–19." In *War and the State: The Transformation of British Government, 1914–1919*, edited by Kathleen Burk, 157–81. London: George Allen and Unwin, 1982.

Clough, Shepard B. 1968. *A History of Modern Italy: Documents, Readings and Commentary*. New York: Columbia University Press.

Cohen-Charash, Yoshi, and Paul E. Spector. 2001. "The Role of Justice in Organizations: A Meta-analysis." *Organizational Behavior and Human Decision Processes* 86 (2): 278–321.

Cole, David. 2005. *Enemy Aliens: Double Standards and Constitutional Freedoms in the War on Terrorism*. New York: New Press.

Collier, Ruth Berins. 1999. *Paths toward Democracy: The Working Class and Elites in Western Europe and South America*. New York: Cambridge University Press.

Colquitt, Jason A., Donald E. Conlon, Michael J. Wesson, Christopher O. L. H Porter, and K. Yee Ng. 2001. "Justice at the Millennium: A Meta-analytic Review of 25 Years of Organizational Justice Research." *Journal of Applied Psychology* 86 (3): 425–45.

Colquitt, Jason A., Brent A. Scott, Jessica B. Rodell, David M. Long, Cindy P. Zapata, Donald E. Conlon, and Michael J. Wesson. 2013. "Justice at the Millennium, a Decade

Later: A Meta-analytic Test of Social Exchange and Affect-based Perspectives." *Journal of Applied Psychology* 98 (2): 199–236.

Commons, John Rogers. 1922. "Labour Supply and Regulation." In *The Encyclopedia Britannica*. New York: Encyclopedia Britannica.

Comstock, Alzada. 1920. "Proposals for the Taxation of Wealth in Great Britain." *Journal of Political Economy* 28 (5): 399–406.

Cook, Chris, and John Stevenson. 2014. *A History of British Elections since 1989*. London: Routledge.

Corfield, Tony. 1993. "War and Wages, 1914–18." *History Today* 43:21–28.

Corner, Paul. 1975. *Fascism in Ferrara, 1915–1925*. London: Oxford University Press.

———. 1981. Review of *The Syndicalist Tradition and Italian Fascism*, by David D. Roberts; *Young Mussolini and the Intellectual Origins of Fascism*, by A. James Gregor; and *Italian Fascism and Developmental Dictatorship*, by A. James Gregor. *European Studies Review* 11 (3): 409–12.

———. 1997. "Italy 1915–1945: Politics and Society." In *The Oxford Illustrated History of Italy*, edited by George Holmes, 264–90. Oxford: Oxford University Press.

———. 2002a. "The Road to Fascism: An Italian Sonderweg?" *Contemporary European History* 11 (2): 273–95.

———. 2002b. "State and Society, 1901–1922." In *Liberal and Fascist Italy, 1900–1945*, edited by Adrian Lyttelton, 17–43. Oxford: Oxford University Press.

Corner, Paul, and Giovanna Procacci. 1997. "The Italian Experience of 'Total' Mobilization." In *State, Society, and Mobilization in Europe during the First World War*, edited by John Horne, 223–40. Cambridge: Cambridge University Press.

Coser, Lewis. 1956. *The Functions of Social Conflict*. Glencoe, IL: Free Press.

Craig, Fred W. S., ed. 1970. *British General Election Manifestos, 1900–1974*. London: Macmillan.

Craig, Gordon A. 1964. *The Politics of the Prussian Army, 1640–1945*. New York: Oxford University Press.

Craver, Earlene. 1996. "The Third Generation: The Young Socialists in Italy, 1907–1915." *Canadian Journal of History* 31:199–226.

Creel, George. 1920. *Complete Report of the Chairman of the Committee on Public Information*. Washington, DC: Government Printing Office.

Cronin, James E. 1979. *Industrial Conflict in Modern Britain*. London: Croom Helm.

———. 1984. *Labour and Society in Britain, 1918–1979*. London: Batsford Academic and Educational.

———. 1986. "The British State and the Second World War." Working Paper No. 64, New School for Social Research, New York.

———. 1989. "The Crisis of State and Society in Britain, 1917–1922." In *Strikes, Wars, and Revolutions in an International Perspective: Strike Waves in the Late Nineteenth and Early Twentieth Centuries*, edited by Leopold H. Haimson and Charles Tilly, 457–72. Cambridge: Cambridge University Press.

———. 1991. *The Politics of State Expansion: War, State and Society in Twentieth Century Britain*. London: Routledge.

———. 1992. "Industry, Locality, and the State: Patterns of Mobilization in the Postwar Strike Wave in Britain." In *Strikes, Social Conflict, and the First World War: An International Perspective*, edited by Leopold Haimson and Giulio Sapelli, 93–106. Milan: Fondazione Giangiacomo Feltrinelli.

Cronin, James E., and Peter Weiler. 1991. "Working-Class Interests and the Politics of Social Democratic Reform in Britain, 1900–1940." *International Labor and Working-Class History* 40:47–66.

Cronon, Edward David. 1969. *Black Moses: The Story of Marcus Garvey and the Universal Negro Improvement Association*. Madison: University of Wisconsin Press.

Cropanzano, Russell, and Jerald Greenberg. 1997. "Progress in Organizational Justice: Tunneling through the Maze." In *International Review of Industrial and Organizational Psychology*, edited by Cary L. Cooper and Ivan T. Robertson, 317–72. New York: John Wiley and Sons.

Crosby, Travis L. 2014. *The Unknown Lloyd George: A Statesman in Conflict*. London: I. B. Tauris.

Cunningham, Hugh. 1981. "The Language of Patriotism, 1750–1914." *History Workshop* 12:8–33.

Currie, Robert. 1979. *Industrial Politics*. Oxford: Clarendon.

D'Alonzo, Luigi. 2001. "The Strange Death of Liberal Italy: A Study in the Politics of Modernization, 1919–1925." PhD diss., York University, Toronto, Ontario.

Damasio, Antonio R. 1994. *Descartes' Error: Emotion, Reason, and the Human Brain*. New York: Putnam.

Dangerfield, George. 1935. *The Strange Death of Liberal England*. New York: H. Smith and R. Haas.

Darley, John M., and Thane S. Pittman. 2003. "The Psychology of Compensatory and Retributive Justice." *Personality and Social Psychology Review* 7 (4): 324–36.

Daunton, Martin. J. 1996. "How to Pay for the War: State, Society, and Taxation in Britain." *English Historical Review* 111 (443): 882–919.

———. 2002. *Just Taxes: The Politics of Taxation in Britain, 1914–1979*. Cambridge: Cambridge University Press.

Davidson, Roger. 1974. "The Myth of the 'Servile State.'" *Bulletin of the Society for the Study of Labour History* 29:62–67.

———. 1979. "Social Conflict and Social Administration: The Conciliation Act in British Industrial Relations." In *The Search for Wealth and Stability: Essays in Economic and Social History*, edited by T. Christopher Smout, 175–98. London: Macmillan.

Davin, Anna. 1978. "Imperialism and Motherhood." *History Workshop* 5:9–65.

Davis, Allen F. 1967. "Welfare, Reform, and World War I." *American Quarterly* 19 (3): 516–33.

Deacon, Alan. 1982. Review of *Homes Fit for Heroes*, by Mark Swenarton. *Journal of Social Policy* 11 (1): 130–31.

Decalo, Samuel. 1992. "The Process, Prospects, and Constraints on Democratization in Africa." *African Affairs* 91:7–35.

De Cecco, Marcello. 2002. "The Economy from Liberalism to Fascism." In *Liberal and Fascist Italy, 1900–1945*, edited by Adrian Lyttelton, 62–82. New York: Oxford University Press.

De Grand, Alexander. 1989. *The Italian Left in the Twentieth Century: A History of the Socialist and Communist Parties*. Bloomington: Indiana University Press.

———. 2001a. "Giovanni Giolitti: A Pessimist as Modernizer." *Journal of Modern Italian Studies* 6 (1): 57–67.

———. 2001b. *The Hunchback's Tailor: Giovanni Giolitti and Liberal Italy from the Challenge of Mass Politics to the Rise of Fascism*. Westport, CT: Greenwood.

DeGroot, Gerald J. 1996. *Blighty: British Society in the Era of the Great War*. London: Longman.

Dewey, Peter E. 1984. "Military Recruiting and the British Labour Force during the First World War." *Historical Journal* 27 (1): 199–223.

Diamond, Larry. 1996. "Toward Democratic Consolidation." In *The Global Resurgence of Democracy*, 2nd ed., edited by Larry Diamond and Marc F. Plattner, 227–40. Baltimore: Johns Hopkins University Press.

Di Palma, Giuseppe. 1990. *To Craft Democracies: An Essay on Democratic Transitions.* Berkeley: University of California Press.

Disraeli, Benjamin. 1845. *Sybil: Or, The Two Nations.* London: Henry Colburn.

Donohue, Laura K. 2008. *The Cost of Counterterrorism: Power, Politics, and Liberty.* Cambridge: Cambridge University Press.

Douglas, Roy. 1972. "The National Democratic Party and the British Workers' League." *Historical Journal* 15 (3): 533–52.

Downing, Brian M. 1998. "Constitutionalism, Warfare, and Political Change in Early Modern Europe." *Theory and Society* 17 (1): 7–56.

Duggan, Christopher. 2008. *The Force of Destiny: A History of Italy since 1796.* Boston: Houghton Mifflin.

Dunbabin, John P. D. 1980. "British Elections in the Nineteenth and Twentieth Centuries, a Regional Approach." *English Historical Review* 95 (375): 241–67.

Dwork, Deborah. 1987. *War Is Good for Babies and Other Young Children: A History of the Infant and Child Welfare Movement in England, 1898–1918.* London: Tavistock.

Eichengreen, Barry. 1990. "The Capital Levy in Theory and Practice." In *Public Debt Management: Theory and History*, edited by Rudiger Dornbusch and Mario Draghi, 191–220. Cambridge: Cambridge University Press.

Elazar, Dahlia S. 2001. *The Making of Fascism: Class, State, and Counter-revolution, Italy, 1919–1922.* Westport, CT: Praeger.

Ellis, Mark. 1992. "'Closing Ranks' and 'Seeking Honors': W. E. B. Du Bois in World War I." *Journal of American History* 79 (1): 96–124.

Ellison, Christopher G. 1992. "Military Background, Racial Orientations, and Political Participation among Black Adult Males." *Social Science Quarterly* 73 (2): 360–78.

Emery, Robert E., Sheila G. Matthews, and Katherine M. Kitzmann. 1994. "Child Custody Mediation and Litigation: Parents' Satisfaction and Functioning One Year after Settlement." *Journal of Consulting Clinical Psychology* 62 (1): 124–29.

Engel, Jeffrey A. 2015. "The Scene, the Phrase, and the Debate." In *The Four Freedoms: Franklin D. Roosevelt and the Evolution of an American Idea*, edited by Jeffrey A. Engel, 15–38. NY: Oxford University Press.

Ermacora, Matteo. 2017. "Labour, Labour Movements, Trade Unions, and Strikes (Italy)." In *1914–1918 Online: International Encyclopedia of the First World War*, edited by Ute Daniel, Peter Gatrell, Oliver Janz, Heather Jones, Jennifer Keene, Alan Kramer, and Bill Nasson. Berlin: Freie Universität. https://encyclopedia.1914-1918-online.net /article/labour_labour_movements_trade_unions_and_strikes_italy.

Esping-Andersen, Gøsta. 1985. *Politics against Markets: The Social Democratic Road to Power.* Princeton, NJ: Princeton University Press.

Etzioni, Amitai. 1975. *A Comparative Analysis of Complex Organizations.* New York: Free Press.

Evans, Mark. 2003. *Constitution-Making and the Labour Party.* New York: Palgrave Macmillan.

Farneti, Paolo. 1978. "Social Conflict, Parliamentary Fragmentation, Institutional Shift, and the Rise of Fascism: Italy." In *The Breakdown of Democratic Regimes*, edited by Juan Linz and Alfred Stepan, 3–33. Baltimore: Johns Hopkins University Press.

Feinstein, Yuval. 2020. "Applying Sociological Theories of Emotions to the Study of Mass Politics: The Rally-Round-the-Flag Phenomenon in the United States as a Test Case." *Sociological Quarterly*, published online. https://doi.org/10.1080/00380253.2019 .1711255.

Feldman, Gerald D. 1966. *Army, Industry, and Labor in Germany, 1914–1918.* Princeton, NJ: Princeton University Press.

Ferejohn, John, and Frances McCall Rosenbluth. 2017. *Forged through Fire: War, Peace, and the Democratic Bargain.* New York: Norton.

Ferrera, Maurizio. 2018. "Wars, Political Extremism, and the Constraints to Welfare Reform." In *Warfare and Welfare: Military Conflict and Welfare State Development in Western Countries*, edited by Herbert Obinger, Klaus Petersen, and Peter Starke, 99–126. Oxford: Oxford University Press.

Field, Geoffrey. 1992. "Social Patriotism and the British Working Class: Appearance and Disappearance of a Tradition." *International Labor and Working-Class History* 42:20–39.

Finkle, Lee. 1973. "The Conservative Aims of Militant Rhetoric: Black Protest during World War II," *Journal of American History* 60: 692-713.

———. 1975. *Forum for Protest: The Black Press during World War II*. Rutherford, N.J.: Fairleigh Dickinson University Press.

Fischhoff, Baruch. 1982. "For Those Condemned to Study the Past: Heuristics and Biases in Hindsight." In *Judgment under Uncertainty*, edited by Daniel Kahneman, Paul Slovic, and Amos Tversky, 335–51. Cambridge: Cambridge University Press.

Fleckenstein, Timo, and Soohyun Christine Lee. 2019. "Organised Labour, Dualisation and Labour Market Reform: Korean Trade Union Strategies in Economic and Social Crisis." *Journal of Contemporary Asia* 49 (3): 452–72.

Folger, Robert, and Mary A. Konovsky. 1989. "The Effects of Procedural and Distributive Justice on Reactions to Pay Raise Decisions." *Academy of Management Journal* 32 (1): 115–30.

Foot, John M. 1996. "Socialist-Catholic Alliances and Gender: Work, War and the Family in Milan and Lombardy, 1914–21." *Social History* 21 (1): 37–53.

———. 1997. "'White Bolsheviks'? The Catholic Left and the Socialists in Italy, 1919–1920." *Historical Journal* 40 (2): 415–33.

———. 1999. "Analysis of a Defeat: Revolution and the Worker-Peasant Alliances in Italy, 1919–20." *Labour History Review* 64 (2): 159–78.

———. 2009. *Italy's Divided Memory*. New York: Palgrave Macmillan.

Foot, John M., and Samantha Owen. 2012. "Italy's 150th Anniversary: Commemorating the Past in a Divided Country." *Italian Politics* 27 (1): 262–78.

Forsyth, Douglas J. 1993. *The Crisis of Liberal Italy: Monetary and Financial Policy, 1914–1922*. Cambridge: Cambridge University Press.

Foster, Gregory. 2016. "Civil-Military Relations on Trial: Through the Eyes of Tomorrow's U.S. Military Leaders." *RUSI Journal* 161 (4): 34–41.

Franzosi, Roberto. 1999. "The Return of the Actor: International Networks among Social Actors during Periods of High Mobilization (Italy, 1919–1922)." *Mobilization: An International Journal* 4 (2): 131–49.

Freeman, Gavin. 2018. "The Liberal Party and the Impact of the 1918 Reform Act." *Parliamentary History* 37 (1): 47–63.

French, David. 1982. "The Rise and Fall of 'Business as Usual,' in *War and the State: The Transformation of British Government, 1914-1919*, edited by Kathleen Burk, 7–31. London: George Allen and Unwin.

———. 1995. *The Strategy of the Lloyd George Coalition*. Oxford: Clarendon.

Fuller, Jerry Bryan, and Kim Hester. 2001. "A Closer Look at the Relationship between Justice Perceptions and Union Participation." *Journal of Applied Psychology* 86 (6): 1096–105.

Galassi, Francesco, and Mark Harrison. 2005. "Italy at War, 1915–1918." In *The Economics of World War I*, edited by Stephen Broadberry and Mark Harrison, 276–309. Cambridge: Cambridge University Press.

Gatrell, Peter, and Mark Harrison. 1993. "The Russian and Soviet Economies in Two World Wars: A Comparative View." *Economic History Review* 46 (3): 425–52.

Gazely, Ian, and Andrew Newell. 2013. "The First World War and Working-Class Food Consumption in Britain." *European Review of Economic History* 17 (1): 71–94.

Geary, Dick. 1981. *European Labour Protest, 1848–1939.* London: Croom Helm.

Gellately, Robert. 2001. *Backing Hitler: Consent and Coercion in Nazi Germany.* New York: Oxford University Press.

Gerber, Larry G. 2005. *The Irony of State Intervention: American Industrial Relations Policy in Comparative Perspective, 1914–1939.* DeKalb: Northern Illinois University Press.

Gerwarth, Robert. 2008. "The Central European Counter-revolution: Paramilitary Violence in Germany, Austria, and Hungary after the Great War." *Past and Present* 200 (1): 175–209.

Gerwarth, Robert, and Erez Manela. 2014. "The Great War as a Global War: Imperial Conflict and the Reconfiguration of World Order, 1911–1923." *Diplomatic History* 38 (4): 796–800.

Gibelli, Antonio. 2010. "Italy." In *A Companion to World War I,* edited by John Horne, 464–78. Malden, MA: Wiley Blackwell.

Gilmour, David. 2011. *The Pursuit of Italy: A History of a Land, Its Regions and Their Peoples.* London: Allen Lane.

Gleditsch, Kristian Skrede, and Michael D. Ward. 2006. "Diffusion and the International Context of Democratization." *International Organization* 60 (4): 911–33.

Goldman, Barry. 2003. "The Application of Referent Cognitions Theory to Legal-Claiming by Terminated Workers: The Role of Organizational Justice and Anger." *Journal of Management* 29 (5): 705–28.

Goldstone, Jack A. 1991. *Revolution and Rebellion in the Early Modern World.* Berkeley: University of California Press.

Gooch, John. 1986. "Clausewitz Disregarded: Italian Military Thought and Doctrine, 1815–1943." *Journal of Strategic Studies* 9 (2–3): 303–24.

———. 2010. "Italy during the First World War." In *Military Effectiveness,* vol. 1, *The First World War,* edited by Allan R. Millett and Williamson Murray, 157–89. Cambridge: Cambridge University Press.

———. 2014. *The Italian Army and the First World War.* Cambridge: Cambridge University Press.

Gordon, Joshua C. 2015. "Protecting the Unemployed: Varieties of Unionism and the Evolution of Unemployment Benefits and Active Labor Market Policy in the Rich Democracies." *Socio-economic Review* 13 (1): 79–99.

Gorgolini, Luca. 2015. "Prisoners of War (Italy)." In *1914–1918 Online: International Encyclopedia of the First World War,* edited by Ute Daniel, Peter Gatrell, Oliver Janz, Heather Jones, Jennifer Keene, Alan Kramer, and Bill Nasson. Berlin: Freie Universität. https://encyclopedia.1914-1918-online.net/article/prisoners_of_war_italy.

Gospel, Howard F. 1987. "Employers and Managers; Organisation and Strategy, 1914–29." In *A History of British Industrial Relations,* vol. 2, *1914–1939,* edited by Chris Wrigley, 159–84. London: Harvester.

Graziano, Manlio. 2010. *The Failure of Italian Nationhood: The Geopolitics of a Troubled Identity.* New York: Palgrave Macmillan.

Greenberg, Jerald. 1990. "Employee Theft as a Reaction to Underpayment Inequity: The Hidden Costs of Pay Cuts." *Journal of Applied Psychology* 75 (5): 561–68.

Greenberg, Jerald, and Ronald L. Cohen, eds. 1982. *Equity and Justice in Social Behavior.* San Diego: Academic Press.

Greenberg, Jerald, and Allen E. Lind. 2000. "The Pursuit of Organizational Justice: From Conceptualization to Implication to Application." In *Industrial and Organizational Psychology: Linking Theory with Practice,* edited by Cary L. Cooper and Edwin A. Locke, 72–108. Oxford: Blackwell.

Gregor, Neil. 2006. "Politics, Culture, Political Culture: Recent Work on the Third Reich and Its Aftermath." *Journal of Modern History* 78 (3): 643–83.

Gregory, Adrian. 2008. *The Last Great War: British Society and the First World War*. Cambridge: Cambridge University Press.

Grieves, Keith. 1989. *Sir Eric Geddes: Business and Government in War and Peace*. Manchester: Manchester University Press.

Grimes, Marcia. 2006. "Organizing Consent: The Role of Procedural Fairness in Political Trust and Compliance." *European Journal of Political Research* 45 (2): 285–315.

Guerrini, Irene, and Marco Pluviano. 2014. "Extrajudicial Executions in the Italian Army during World War I." In *Justice militaires et guerres mondiales*, edited by Jean-Marc Berliere, Jonas Camion, and Luigi Lacche, 179–92. Belgium: Presses Universitaires de Louvain.

Gullace, Nicoletta. 2002. *The Blood of Our Sons: Men, Women, and the Renegotiation of British Citizenship during the Great War*. New York: Palgrave Macmillan.

Gunitsky, Seva. 2017. *Aftershocks: Great Powers and Domestic Reforms in the Twentieth Century*. Princeton, NJ: Princeton University Press.

Gurfein, M. I., and Morris Janowitz. 1946. "Trends in Wehrmacht Morale." *Public Opinion Quarterly* 10 (1): 78–84.

Haggard, Stephan, and Robert R. Kaufman. 2016. *Dictators and Democrats: Masses, Elites, and Regime Change*. Princeton, NJ: Princeton University Press.

Halperin, Sandra. 1997. "The Politics of Appeasement: The Rise of the Left and European International Relations during the Interwar Period." In *Contested Social Orders and International Politics*, edited by David Skidmore, 128–65. Nashville, TN: Vanderbilt University Press.

Hancock, Eleanor. 1991. *National Socialist Leadership and Total War, 1941–45*. New York: St. Martin's.

Hardach, Gerd. 1977. *The First World War, 1914–1918*. London: Allen Lane.

Harries, Meirion, and Susie Harries. 1997. *The Last Days of Innocence: America at War, 1917–1918*. New York: Vintage Books.

Harris, Jose. 2000. "Labour's Political and Social Thought." In *Labour's First Century*, edited by Duncan Tanner, Pat Thane, and Nick Tiratsoo, 8–45. Cambridge: Cambridge University Press.

Harrison, Royden. 1971. "The War Emergency Workers' National Committee, 1914–1920." In *Essays in Labour History, 1886–1923*, edited by Asa Briggs, John Saville, and Benjamin Britten, 211–59. Hamden, CT: Archon Books.

Haywood, Geoffrey A. 1999. *Failure of a Dream: Sidney Sonnino and the Rise and Fall of Liberal Italy, 1847–1922*. Florence: Fondazione Luigi Einaudi.

Herbst, Jeffrey. 1990. "War and the State in Africa." *International Security* 14 (4): 117–39.

Hicks, Alexander. 1999. *Social Democracy and Welfare Capitalism: A Century of Income Security Politics*. Ithaca, NY: Cornell University Press.

Hicks, Daniel L. 2013. "War and the Political *Zeitgeist*: Evidence from the History of Female Suffrage." *European Journal of Political Economy* 31 (C): 60–81.

Hickson, Kevin. 2004. "The Postwar Consensus Revisited." *Political Quarterly* 75 (2): 142–54.

Higley, John, and Michael G. Burton. 1989. "The Elite Variable in Democratic Transitions and Breakdowns." *American Sociological Review* 54 (1): 17–32.

Hilton-Young, W. 1949. *The Italian Left: A Short History of Political Socialism in Italy*. London: Longmans.

Hinton, James. 1973. *The First Shop Stewards' Movement*. London: Allen and Unwin.

———. 1995. "Voluntarism versus Jacobinism: Labor, Nation, and Citizenship in Britain, 1850–1950." *International Labor and Working-Class History* 48:68–90.

Hoague, Francis, Russell M. Brown, and Philip Marcus. 1940. "Wartime Conscription and Control of Labor." *Harvard Law Review* 54 (1): 50–105.

Hochschild, Adam. 2011. *To End All Wars: A Story of Loyalty and Rebellion, 1914–1918.* Boston: Houghton Mifflin Harcourt.

Hoffenberg, Peter H. 2001. "Landscape, Memory, and the Australian War Experience, 1915–18." *Journal of Contemporary History* 36 (1): 111–31.

Holsti, Ole R. 2001. "Of Chasms and Convergences: Attitudes and Beliefs of Civilians and Military Elites." In *Soldiers and Civilians: The Civil-Military Gap and American National Security*, edited by Peter D. Feaver and Richard H. Kohn, 15–99. Cambridge, MA: MIT Press.

Holton, Sandra Stanley. 1986. *Feminism and Democracy: Women's Suffrage and Reform Politics in Britain, 1900–1918.* New York: Cambridge University Press.

Hopkin, Deian. 1970. "Domestic Censorship in the First World War." *Journal of Contemporary History* 5 (4): 151–69.

Horne, John. 1991. *Labour at War: France and Britain, 1914–1918.* Oxford: Clarendon.

———. 1997. "Remobilizing for 'Total War': France and Britain, 1917–1918." In *State, Society, and Mobilization in Europe during the First World War*, edited by John Horne, 195–211. Cambridge: Cambridge University Press.

———. 2010. "Public Opinion and Politics." In *A Companion to World War I*, edited by John Horne, 279–94. Malden, MA: Wiley Blackwell.

———. 2014. "Socialism, Peace, and Revolution, 1917–1918." In *The Oxford Illustrated History of the First World War*, new ed., edited by Hew Strachan, 226–37. Oxford: Oxford University Press.

Horowitz, Daniel L. 1963. *The Italian Labor Movement.* Cambridge, MA: Harvard University Press.

Huber, Evelyne, Dietrich Rueschemeyer, and John D. Stephens. 1997. "The Paradoxes of Contemporary Democracy: Formal, Participatory, and Social Dimensions." *Comparative Politics* 29 (3): 323–42.

Huntington, Samuel P. 1991a. "Democracy's Third Wave." *Journal of Democracy* 2 (2): 12–34.

———. 1991b. *The Third Wave: Democratization in the Late Twentieth Century.* Norman: University of Oklahoma Press.

Huo, Yuen J., Heather J. Smith, Tom R. Tyler, and E. Allan Lind. 1996. "Superordinate Identification, Subgroup Identification, and Justice Concerns." *Psychological Science* 7 (1): 40–45.

Hyman, Richard. 1987. "Rank-and-File Movements and Workplace Organisation, 1914–39." In *A History of British Industrial Relations*, vol. 2, *1914–1939*, edited by Chris Wrigley, 129–58. London: Harvester.

Imlay, Talbot C. 2003. *Facing the Second World War: Strategy, Politics, and Economics in Britain and France, 1938–1940.* New York: Oxford University Press.

Ingesson, Tony, Mårten Lindvall, Johannes Lindvall, and Jan Teorell. 2018. "The Martial Origins of Democracy: A Global Study of Military Conscription and Suffrage Extensions since the Napoleonic Wars." *Democratization* 25 (4): 633–51.

Janowitz, Morris. 1983. *The Reconstruction of Patriotism: Education for Civic Consciousness.* Chicago: University of Chicago Press.

Jefferys, Kevin. 1987. "British Politics and Social Policy during the Second World War." *Historical Journal* 30 (1): 123–44.

Jenkins, Roy. 2001. *Churchill: A Biography.* London: Macmillan.

Jennings, M. Kent, and Gregory B. Markus. 1976. "Political Participation and Vietnam War Veterans: A Longitudinal Study." In *The Social Psychology of Military Service*, edited by Nancy L. Goldman and David R. Segal, 175–200. Beverly Hills: Sage.

Johansen, Anja. 2013. "License Not to Kill: British Opposition to Military Justice during the First World War." In *Justice militaires et guerres mondiales*, edited by Jean-Marc

Berlière, Jonas Campion, and Luigi Lacchè, 57–72. Belgium: Presses Universitaires de Louvain.

Johnson, Victoria. 2000. "The Cultural Foundation of Resources, the Resource Foundation of Political Cultures: An Explanation for the Outcomes of Two General Strikes." *Politics and Society* 28 (3): 331–65.

Jones, Simon. 1985. "Antonio Salandra and the Politics of Italian Intervention in the First World War." *European History Quarterly* 15 (2): 157–72.

Kadivar, Mohammad Ali. 2018. "Mass Mobilization and the Durability of New Democracies." *American Sociological Review* 83 (2): 390–417.

Kadivar, Mohammad Ali, and Neil Ketchley. 2018. "Sticks, Stones, and Molotov Cocktails: Unarmed Collective Violence and Democratization." *Socius: Sociological Research for a Dynamic World* 4:1–16.

Kadivar, Mohammad Ali, Adaner Usmani, and Benjamin H. Bradlow. 2020. "The Long March: Deep Democracy in Cross-National Perspective." *Social Forces* 98 (3): 1311–38.

Kage, Rieko. 2010. "The Effects of War on Civil Society: Cross-National Evidence from World War II." In *In War's Wake: International Conflict and the Fate of Liberal Democracy*, edited by Elizabeth Kier and Ronald R. Krebs, 253–70. Cambridge: Cambridge University Press.

Kaiser, David E. 1983. "Germany and the Origins of the First World War." *Journal of Modern History* 55 (3): 442–74.

Kaiser, Kimberly A., and Kristy Holtfreter. 2015. "An Integrated Theory of Specialized Court Programs: Using Procedural Justice and Therapeutic Jurisprudence to Promote Offender Compliance and Rehabilitation." *Criminal Justice Behavior* 43 (1): 45–62.

Kasza, Gregory J. 2002. "War and Welfare Policy in Japan." *Journal of Asian Studies* 61 (2): 417–35.

Katznelson, Ira. 1986. "Working-Class Formation: Constructing Cases and Comparisons." In *Working-Class Formation: Nineteenth-Century Patterns in Western Europe and the United States*, edited by Ira Katznelson and Aristide R. Zolberg, 3–44. Princeton, NJ: Princeton University Press.

Kavanagh, Dennis, and Peter Morris. 1989. *Consensus Politics from Atlee to Major*. Oxford: Basil Blackwell.

Kealey, Gregory S. 1992. "State Repression of Labour and the Left in Canada, 1914–20: The Impact of the First World War." *Canadian Historical Review* 73 (3): 281–314.

Kellogg, Paul Underwood, and Arthur Gleason. 1919. *British Labour and the War: Reconstructors for a New World*. New York: Boni and Liveright.

Kelly, Matthew Kraig. 2012. "An Ambivalent Nation: Australian Nationalism and Historical Memory." *UCLA Historical Journal* 23 (1): 1–11.

Kennedy, Paul. 1981. *The Realities behind Diplomacy: Background Influences on British External Policy, 1865–1980*. London: Allen and Unwin.

Keohane, Nigel. 2010. *The Party of Patriotism: The Conservative Party and the First World War*. New York: Ashgate.

Keohane, Robert O. 1984. *After Hegemony: Cooperation and Discord in the World Political Economy*. Princeton, NJ: Princeton University Press.

Kernan, Mary C., and Paul J. Hanges. 2002. "Survivor Reactions to Reorganization: Antecedents and Consequences of Procedural, Interpersonal, and Informational Justice." *Journal of Applied Psychology* 87 (5): 916–28.

Keune, Maarten. 2018. "Opportunity or Threat? How Trade Union Power and Preferences Shape Occupational Pensions." *Social Policy and Administration* 52 (2): 463–76.

Kier, Elizabeth. 1997. *Imagining War: French and British Military Doctrine between the Wars*. Princeton, NJ: Princeton University Press.

Kinnear, Michael. 1973. *The Fall of Lloyd George: The Political Crisis of 1922.* London: Palgrave Macmillan.

——. 1981. *The British Voter: An Atlas and Survey since 1885.* London: Batsford.

Kirk, Neville. 1998. *Change, Continuity, and Class: Labour in British Society, 1850–1920.* Manchester: Manchester University Press.

Kivimaki, Ville. 2012. "Between Defeat and Victory: Finnish Memory Culture of the Second World War." *Scandinavian Journal of History* 37 (4): 482–504.

Klausen, Jytte. 2001. *War and Welfare: Europe and the United States, 1945 to the Present.* Basingstoke, UK: Palgrave Macmillan.

Klinkner, Philip A., and Rogers M. Smith. 1999. *The Unsteady March: The Rise and Decline of Racial Equality in America.* Chicago: University of Chicago Press.

Knox, MacGregor. 2007. *To the Threshold of Power, 1922/33: Origins and Dynamics of the Fascist and National Socialist Dictatorships.* New York: Cambridge University Press.

Koenig-Archibugi, Mathias. 2003. "National and European Citizenship: The Italian Case in Historical Perspective." *Citizenship Studies* 7 (1): 85–109.

Konovsky, Mary A. 2020. "Understanding Procedural Justice and Its Impact on Business Organizations." *Journal of Management* 26 (3): 489–511.

Kornweibel, Theodore. 1981. "Apathy and Dissent: Black America's Negative Response to World War I." *South Atlantic Quarterly* (80): 322-38.

——. 1998. *Seeing Red: Federal Campaigns against Black Militancy, 1919–1925.* Bloomington: Indiana University Press.

Korpi, Walter. 1983. *The Democratic Class Struggle.* Boston: Routledge and Kegan Paul.

——. 1989. "Power, Politics, and State Autonomy in the Development of Social Citizenship." *American Sociological Review* 54 (3): 309–28.

Korpi, Walter, and Joakim Palme. 2003. "New Politics and Class Politics in the Context of Austerity and Globalization: Welfare State Regress in 18 Countries, 1975–95." *American Political Science Review* 97 (3): 425–46.

Korsgaard, Audrey M., and Loriann Roberson. 1995. "Procedural Justice in Performance Evaluation: The Role of Instrumental and Non-instrumental Voice in Performance Appraisal Discussions." *Journal of Management* 21 (4): 657–69.

Korsgaard, Audrey M., David M. Schweiger, and Henry J. Sapienza. 1995. "Building Commitment, Attachment, and Trust in Strategic Decision-Making Teams: The Role of Procedural Justice." *Academy of Management Journal* 38 (1): 60–84.

Kramer, Alan. 2014. "Recent Historiography of the First World War." *Journal of Modern European History* 12 (1): 5–27.

Kramer, Roderick M., Marilynn B. Brewer, and Benjamin A. Hanna. 1996. "Collective Trust and Collective Action: The Decision to Trust as a Social Decision." In *Trust in Organizations: Frontiers of Theory and Research,* edited by Roderick M. Kramer and Tom R. Tyler, 357–89. Thousand Oaks, CA: Sage.

Kraus, Jon. 2007. "Conclusion: Trade Unions and Democratization in Africa." In *Trade Unions and the Coming of Democracy in Africa,* edited by Jon Kraus, 255-86. New York: Palgrave Macmillan.

Krebs, Ronald R. 2006. *Fighting for Rights: Military Service and the Politics of Citizenship.* Ithaca, NY: Cornell University Press.

Kryder, Daniel. 2000. *Divided Arsenal: Race and the American State during World War II.* New York: Cambridge University Press.

Lake, David. 1992. "Powerful Pacifists: Democratic States and War." *American Political Science Review* 86 (1): 24–37.

Lane, Robert E. 1962. *Political Ideology: Why the American Common Man Believes What He Does.* New York: Free Press of Glencoe.

Lasswell, Harold D. 1941. "The Garrison State." *American Journal of Sociology* 46 (4): 455–68.

Lawrence, Jon. 1993. "State and Society in the Shadow of War." *Historical Journal* 36 (4): 993–1001.

———. 2011. "Labour and the Politics of Class, 1900–1940." In *Structures and Transformations in Modern British History*, edited by David Feldman and Jon Lawrence, 237–60. Cambridge: Cambridge University Press.

Leal, David. 1999. "It's Not Just a Job: Military Service and Latino Political Participation." *Political Behavior* 21 (2): 153–74.

Ledeen, Michael A. 1975. "Italy: War as a Style of Life." In *The War Generation: Veterans of the First World War*, edited by Stephen R. Ward, 104–34. Port Washington, NY: Kennikat.

Leff, Mark H. 1991. "The Politics of Sacrifice on the American Home Front in World War II." *Journal of American History* 77 (4): 1296–1318.

Le magazine de la Grande Guerre. 2005. "Les soldats fusillés en Italie." 29:14–21.

Lentz-Smith, Adrienne. 2009. *Freedom Struggles: African Americans and World War I.* Cambridge, MA: Harvard University Press.

Leventhal, F. M. 1989. *Arthur Henderson.* Manchester: Manchester University Press.

Leventhal, Gerald S. 1980. "What Should Be Done with Equity Theory? New Approaches to the Study of Fairness in Social Relationship." In *Social Exchange: Advances in Theory and Research*, edited by Kenneth J. Gergen, Martin S. Greenberg, and Richard H. Willis, 27–55. New York: Plenum.

Levi, Margaret. 1997. *Consent, Dissent, and Patriotism.* Cambridge: Cambridge University Press.

Levitsky, Steve, and Scott Mainwaring. 2006. "Organized Labor and Democracy in Latin America." *Comparative Politics* 39 (1): 21–42.

Levy, Carl. 2002. "The Centre and the Suburbs: Social Protest and Modernization in Milan and Turin, 1898–1917." *Modern Italy* 7 (2): 171–88.

Lind, E. Allan, Carol T. Kulik, Maureen Ambrose, and Marie V. de Vera Park. 1993. "Individual and Corporate Dispute Resolution: Using Procedural Fairness as a Decision Heuristic." *Administrative Science Quarterly* 38 (2): 224–51.

Lind, E. Allan, and Tom R. Tyler. 1988. *The Social Psychology of Procedural Justice.* New York: Plenum.

Linz, Juan J. 1976. "Some Notes toward a Comparative Study of Fascism in Sociological Historical Perspective." In *Fascism: A Reader's Guide: Analyses, Interpretations, Bibliography*, edited by Walter Laqueur, 3–124. London: Wildwood House.

Linz, Juan J., and Alfred Stepan. 1996. *Problems of Democratic Transition and Consolidation.* Baltimore: Johns Hopkins University Press.

Lipset, Seymour Martin. 1985. *Consensus and Conflict: Essays in Political Sociology.* New Brunswick, NJ: Transaction Books.

Lloyd, Trevor. 1971. *Suffragettes International: The World-Wide Campaign for Women's Rights.* London: American Heritage.

Lloyd George, David. 1933. *War Memoirs of David Lloyd George.* Vol. 1. London: I. Nicholson and Watson.

Lowe, Rodney. 1978a. "The Erosion of State Intervention in Britain, 1917–24." *Economic History Review* 31 (2): 270–86.

———. 1978b. "The Failure of Consensus in Britain: The National Industrial Conference, 1919–21." *Historical Journal* 21 (3): 649–75.

———. 1982. "The Ministry of Labour, 1916–19: A Still, Small Voice?" In *War and the State: The Transformation of British Government, 1914–1919*, edited by Kathleen Burk, 108–34. London: George Allen and Unwin.

Ludtke, Alf. 1994. "The 'Honor of Labor': Industrial Workers and the Power of Symbols under National Socialism." In *Nazism and German Society, 1933–1945*, edited by David F. Crew, 67–109. London: Routledge.

Lyttelton, Adrian. 1982. "Fascism and Violence in Post-war Italy: Political Strategy and Social Conflict." In *Social Protest, Violence, and Terror in Nineteenth- and Twentieth-Century Europe*, edited by Wolfgang J. Mommsen and Gerhard Hirschfeld, 257–74. London: Berg.

———. 2002. Introduction to *Liberal and Fascist Italy, 1900–1945*, edited by Adrian Lyttelton, 1–16. Oxford: Oxford University Press.

———. 2004. *The Seizure of Power: Fascism in Italy*. London: Routledge.

MacCoun, Robert. 2005. "Voice, Control, and Belonging: The Double-Edged Sword of Procedural Fairness." *Annual Review of Law and Social Science* 1:171–201.

MacDonald, Donald F. 1976. *The State and the Trade Unions*. London: Macmillan.

MacIntyre, Stuart. 1975. Review of *The Evolution of the Labour Party*, by Ross McKibbin. *Bulletin of the Society for the Study of Labour History* 31:101–11.

Maclure, Stuart. 2005. *Education Documents: 1816 to the Present Day*. London: Taylor and Francis.

Magalhaes, Pedro C., and Luis Aguiar-Conraria. 2019. "Procedural Fairness, the Economy, and Support for Political Authorities." *Political Psychology* 40 (1): 165–81.

Maier, Charles S. 1975. *Recasting Bourgeois Europe: Stabilization in France, Germany and Italy in the Decade after World War I*. Princeton, NJ: Princeton University Press.

Malefakis, Edward. 1993. "A Comparative Analysis of Workers' Movements in Spain and Italy." In *Politics, Society, and Democracy: The Case of Spain*, edited by Richard Gunther, 57–69. Boulder, CO: Westview.

Mancini, Susanna. 2012. "From the Struggle for Suffrage to the Construction of a Fragile Gender Citizenship: Italy 1861–2009." In *The Struggle for Female Suffrage in Europe: Voting to Become Citizens*, edited by Blanca Rodríguez-Ruiz and Ruth Rubio-Marín, 373–88. Boston: Brill.

Mann, Michael. 1988. *States, War, and Capitalism: Studies in Political Sociology*. Cambridge, UK: Blackwell.

———. 1993. *The Sources of Social Power*. Vol. 2, *The Rise of Classes and Nation-States, 1760–1914*. Cambridge: Cambridge University Press.

Manning, Molly Guptill. 2016. "Fighting to Lose the Vote: How the Soldier Voting Acts of 1942 and 1944 Disenfranchised America's Armed Forces." *New York University Journal of Legislation and Public Policy* 19:336–73.

Marks, Gary. 1989. *Unions in Politics: Britain, Germany, and the United States in the Nineteenth and Early Twentieth Centuries*. Princeton, NJ: Princeton University Press.

Marshall, T. H. 1950. *Citizenship and Social Class, and Other Essays*. Cambridge: Cambridge University Press.

Martin, Boyd A. 1945. "The Service Vote in the Elections of 1944." *American Political Science Review* 39 (4): 720–32.

Markwica, Robin. 2018. *Emotional Choices: How the Logic of Affect Shapes Coercive Diplomacy*. Oxford: Oxford University Press.

Marwick, Arthur. 1965. *The Deluge: British Society and the First World War*. London: Bodley Head.

———. 1974. *War and Social Change in the Twentieth Century: A Comparative Study of Britain, France, Germany, Russia, and the United States*. London: Macmillan.

Matthew, Henry C. G., Ross I. McKibbin, and John A. Kay. 1976. "The Franchise Factor in the Rise of the Labour Party." *English Historical Review* 91 (361): 723–52.

Maylander, Alfred. 1922. "Labor Unrest in Italy." *Monthly Labor Review* 12:1253–75.

Mayo, Elton. 1933. *The Human Problems of an Industrial Civilization.* New York: Macmillan.

Mazerolle, Lorraine Green, Elise Sargeant, Adrian Cherney, Sarah Bennett, Kristina Murphy, Emma Antrobus, and Peter Martin. 2014. *Procedural Justice and Legitimacy in Policing.* New York: Springer.

McCrillis, Neal R. 1998. *The British Conservative Party in the Age of Universal Suffrage.* Columbus: Ohio State University Press.

McKibbin, Ross. 1974. *The Evolution of the Labour Party, 1910–1924.* Oxford: Oxford University Press.

——. 1990. *The Ideologies of Class: Social Relations in Britain, 1880–1950.* Oxford: Clarendon.

——. 2010. *Parties and People: England, 1914–1951.* Oxford: Oxford University Press.

McLean, Iain. 1983. *The Legend of Red Clydeside.* Edinburgh: John Donald.

McNally, Mark. 2017. "Socialism and Democratic Strategy in Italy's *Biennio Rosso*: Gramsci contra Treves." *Journal of Modern Italian Studies* 22 (3): 314–37.

Mead, Robert. 2006. "The Italians' Great War: A Translation of *La Grande Guerra degli Italiani*." PhD diss., Drew University.

Meeker, Royal. 1917. *Industrial Unrest in Great Britain: Reprints of: 1. Reports of the Commission of Inquiry into Industrial Unrest; and 2. Interim Report of the Reconstruction Committee, on Joint Standing Industrial Councils.* Washington, DC: Government Printing Office.

Mercer, Jonathan. 2005. "Rationality and International Politics." *International Organization* 59 (1): 77–106.

——. 2010. "Emotional Beliefs." *International Organization* 64 (1): 1–31

Mershon, Sherie, and Steven Schlossman. 1998. *Foxholes and Color Lines: Desegregating the U.S. Armed Forces.* Baltimore: Johns Hopkins University Press.

Messick, David M., Suzanne Bloom, Janet P. Boldizar, and Charles D. Samuelson. 1985. "Why We Are Fairer than Others." *Journal of Experimental Social Psychology* 21 (5): 480–500.

Messinger, Gary S. 1992. *British Propaganda and the State in the First World War.* Manchester: Manchester University Press.

Mettler, Suzanne. 2005. *Soldiers to Citizens: The G.I. Bill and the Making of the Greatest Generation.* New York: Oxford University Press.

Mikkelsen, Vincent P. 2009. "Fighting for Sergeant Caldwell: The NAACP Campaign against 'Legal' Lynching after World War I." *Journal of African American History* 94 (4): 464–86.

Miller, James Edward. 1990. *From Elite to Mass Politics: Italian Socialism in the Giolittian Era, 1900–1914.* Kent, OH: Kent State University Press.

Milward, Alan S. (1977) 1987. *War, Economy, and Society, 1939–1945.* Harmondsworth, UK: Penguin Books.

Misner, Paul. 2015. *Catholic Labor Movements in Europe: Social Thought and Action, 1914–1965.* Washington, DC: Catholic University of America Press.

Mitchison, Naomi. 1985. *Among You Taking Notes: The Wartime Diary of Naomi Mitchison, 1939–1945.* Oxford: Oxford University Press.

Mittal, Shashank, Atri Shubham, and Altri Sengupta. 2019. "Multidimensionality in Organizational Justice-Trust Relationship for Newcomer Employees: A Moderated-Mediation Model." *Current Psychology* 38 (3): 737–48.

Mittelstadt, Jennifer. 2015. *The Rise of the Military Welfare State.* Cambridge, MA: Harvard University Press.

Monger, David. 2012. *Patriotism and Propaganda in First World War Britain: The National War Aims Committee and Civilian Morale.* Liverpool: Liverpool University Press.

Morgan, Kenneth O. 2011. *Ages of Reform: Dawns and Downfalls of the British Left.* New York: Palgrave Macmillan.

Morselli, Mario A. 2001. *Caporetto 1917: Victory or Defeat*. London: Frank Cass.

Mowat, Charles Loch. 1955. *Britain between the Wars*. Chicago: University of Chicago Press.

Mowday, Richard T. 1991. "Equity Theory Predictions of Behavior in Organizations." In *Motivation and Work Behavior*, 5th ed., edited by Richard M. Steers and Lyman W. Porter, 110–130. New York: McGraw-Hill.

Musso, Stefano. 1990. "Political Tension and Labor Union Struggle: Working Class Conflicts in Turin during and after the First World War." In *Strikes, Social Conflict, and the First World War: An International Perspective*, edited by Leopold Haimson and Giulio Sapelli, 213–46. Milan: Fondazione Giangiacomo Feltrinelli.

Nef, John U. 1950. *War and Human Progress: An Essay on the Rise of Industrial Civilization*. Cambridge, MA: Harvard University Press.

Neufeld, Maurice F. 1961. *Italy: School for Awakening Countries*. Ithaca, NY: Cayuga.

Neureiter, Michael. 2013. "Organized Labor and Democratization in Southeast Asia." *Asian Survey* 53 (6): 1063–86.

Newton, Douglas. 2002. "The Lansdowne 'Peace Letter' of 1917 and the Prospect of Peace by Negotiation with Germany." *Australian Journal of Politics and History* 48 (1): 16–39.

Newton, Kenneth. 2001. "Trust, Social Capital, Civil Society, and Democracy." *International Political Science Review* 22 (2): 201–14.

Norris, Pippa. 1999. *Critical Citizens: Global Support for Democratic Governance*. Oxford: Oxford University Press.

North, Douglass, and Barry Weingast. 1989. "Constitutions and Commitment: The Evolution of Institutions Governing Public Choice in Seventeenth-Century England." *Journal of Economic History* 49 (4): 813–32.

Obinger, Herbert, Klaus Petersen, and Peter Starke. 2018. Introduction to *Warfare and Welfare: Military Conflict and Welfare State Development in Western Countries*, edited by Herbert Obinger, Klause Petersen, and Peter Starke, 1–35. Oxford: Oxford University Press.

O'Brien, Paul. 2006. "Summary Executions in Italy during the First World War: Findings and Implications." *Modern Italy* 11 (3): 353–59.

O'Donnell, Guillermo, and Philippe C. Schmitter. 1986. *Transitions from Authoritarian Rule: Tentative Conclusions about Uncertain Democracies*. Baltimore: Johns Hopkins University Press.

Oram, Gerard. 2003. *Military Executions during World War I*. Basingstoke, UK: Palgrave Macmillan.

Panayi, Panikos. 1989. "Anti-German Riots in London during the First World War." *German History* 7 (2): 184–203.

Parker, Christopher. 2009. *Fighting for Democracy: Black Veterans and the Struggle against White Supremacy in the Postwar South*. Princeton, NJ: Princeton University Press.

Peacock, Alan T., and Jack Wiseman. 1961. *The Growth of Public Expenditure in the United Kingdom*. Princeton, NJ: Princeton University Press.

Peck, George Terhune. 1942. "Giovanni Giolitti and the Fall of Italian Democracy, 1919–1922." PhD diss., University of Chicago.

Pelling, Henry. 1963. *A History of British Trade Unionism*. London: Macmillan.

———. 1968. *Popular Politics and Society in Late Victorian Britain*. London: Macmillan.

Pernicone, Nunzio. 1974. "The Italian Labor Movement." In *Modern Italy: A Topical History Since 1861*, edited by Edward R. Tannenbaum and Emiliana P. Noether, 197–231. New York: New York University Press.

Phillips, Gordon. 1989. "The British Labour Movement before 1914." In *Labour and Socialist Movements in Europe before 1914*, edited by Dick Geary, 11–47. Oxford: Berg.

Pigou, Arthur C. 1941. *The Political Economy of War*. New York: Macmillan.

Pimlott, Ben. 1985. *Hugh Dalton*. London: Macmillan.

Pirocchi, Angelo. 2004. *Italian Arditi: Elite Assault Troops*. Oxford: Osprey.

Pironti, Pierluigi. 2016. "Nitti, Francesco Saverio." In *1914–1918 Online: International Encyclopedia of the First World War*, edited by Ute Daniel, Peter Gatrell, Oliver Janz, Heather Jones, Jennifer Keene, Alan Kramer, and Bill Nasson. Berlin: Freie Universität. https://encyclopedia.1914-1918-online.net/article/nitti_francesco_saverio.

Pluviano, Marco, and Irene Guerrini. 2000. "Italy: Extreme Crisis, Resistance and Recovery." In *The Great World War, 1914–45*, vol. 2, *The Peoples' Experience*, edited by Peter Liddle, John Bourne, and Ian Whitehead, 106–20. London: HarperCollins.

Polenberg, Richard. 1992. "The Good War?: A Reappraisal of How World War II Affected American Society." *Virginia Magazine of History and Biography* 100 (3): 295–322.

Pollard, John. 1998. *The Fascist Experience in Italy*. London: Routledge.

Pollard, Sidney. 1983. *The Development of the British Economy, 1914–1980*. London: Edward Arnold.

Poole, Michael. 1986. *Industrial Relations: Origins and Patterns of National Diversity*. London: Routledge and Kegan Paul.

Pope, Rex. 1991. *War and Society in Britain, 1899–1948*. London: Longman.

Porter, Bruce D. 1994. *War and the Rise of the State: The Military Foundations of Modern Politics*. New York: Free Press.

Powell, David. 2004. *British Politics, 1910–35: The Crisis of the Party System*. London: Routledge.

Price, Richard. 1972. *An Imperial War and the British Working Class*. Toronto: University of Toronto Press.

Procacci, Giovanna. 1989. "Popular Protest and Labour Conflict in Italy, 1915–18." *Social History* 14 (1): 31–58.

——. 1992. "State Coercion and Worker Solidarity in Italy: The Moral and Political Content of Social Unrest." In *Strikes, Social Conflict, and the First World War: An International Perspective*, edited by Leopold Haimson and Giulio Sapelli, 145–78. Milan: Fondazione Giangiacomo Feltrinelli.

——. 1995. "A 'Latecomer' in War: The Case of Italy." In *Authority, Identity, and the Social History of the Great War*, edited by Frans Coetzee and Marilyn Shevin-Coetzee, 3–28. Providence, RI: Berghahn Books.

——. 2013. "La Justice militaire en Italie pendant la Première Guerre mondial: Le front intérieur." In *Justice militaires et guerres mondiales*, edited by Jean-Marc Berlière, Jonas Campion, and Luigi Lacchè, 157–65. Belgium: Presses Universitaires de Louvain.

Procacci, Giuliano. 1968. *History of the Italian People*. New York: Harper and Row.

——. 1979. *The Italian Working Class from the Risorgimento to Fascism*. Lectures at the Center for European Studies. Cambridge, MA: Center for European Studies, Harvard University.

Przeworski, Adam. 1986. "Problems in the Study of the Transition to Democracy." In *Transitions from Authoritarian Rule: Comparative Perspectives*, edited by Guillermo O'Donnell, Philippe C. Schmitter, and Laurence Whitehead, 47–63. Baltimore: Johns Hopkins University Press.

Przeworski, Adam, and John Sprague. 1986. *Paper Stones: A History of Electoral Socialism*. Chicago: University of Chicago Press.

Pugh, Martin. 1974. "Politicians and the Woman's Vote 1914–1918." *History* 59 (197): 358–74.

——. 1991. *Women and the Women's Movement in Britain, 1914–1959*. Basingstoke, UK: Macmillan.

——. 2002. *The Making of Modern British Politics, 1867–1945*. Oxford: Blackwell.

——. 2010. *Speak for Britain! A New History of the Labour Party*. London: Bodley Head.

Putnam, Robert D. 1993. *Making Democracy Work: Civic Traditions in Modern Italy*. Princeton, NJ: Princeton University Press.

——. 2000. *Bowling Alone: The Collapse and Revival of American Community*. New York: Simon and Schuster.

Quine, Maria Sophia. 2002. *Italy's Social Revolution: Charity and Welfare from Liberalism to Fascism*. New York: Palgrave.

Rathgeb, Philip. 2019. "No Flexicurity without Trade Unions: The Danish Experience." *Comparative European Politics* 17 (1): 1–21.

Ravetz, Alison. 2001. *Council Housing and Culture: The History of a Social Experiment*. London: Routledge.

Reid, Alastair J. 1985a. "Dilution, Trade Unionism, and the State in Britain during the First World War." In *Shop Floor Bargaining and the State*, edited by Steven Tolliday and Jonathan Zeitlin, 26–74. Cambridge: Cambridge University Press.

——. 1985b. "The Division of Labour and Politics in Britain." In *The Development of Trade Unionism in Great Britain and Germany, 1880-1914*, edited by Wolfgang J. Mommsen and Hans-Gerhard Husung, 150–65. London: George Allen and Unwin.

——. 1988a. "The Impact of the First World War on British Workers." In *The Upheaval of War: Family, Work, and Welfare in Europe, 1914–1918*, edited by Richard Wall and Jay Winter, 221–34. Cambridge: Cambridge University Press.

——. 1988b. "World War I and the Working Class in Britain." In Arthur Warwick, ed., *Total War and Social Change*, edited by Arthur Warwick, 16–24. London: Macmillan.

——. 2000. "Labour and the Trade Unions." In *Labour's First Century*, edited by Duncan Tanner, Pat Thane, and Nick Tiratsoo, 221–47. Cambridge: Cambridge University Press.

——. 2010. *The Tide of Democracy: Shipyard Workers and Social Relations in Britain, 1870–1950*. Manchester: Manchester University Press.

Reid, Stewart J. H. 1955. *The Origins of the British Labour Party*. Minneapolis: University of Minnesota Press.

Reiter, Dan, and Allan C. Stam. 2002. *Democracies at War*. Princeton, NJ: Princeton University Press.

Renzi, William A. 1988. *In the Shadow of the Sword: Italy's Neutrality and Entrance into the Great War, 1914–1915*. New York: Peter Lang.

Riddell, Neil. 1999. "Arthur Henderson." In *Leading Labour: From Keir Hardie to Tony Blair*, edited by Kevin Jefferys, 41–60. New York: I. B. Tauris.

Riley, Dylan. 2005. "Civic Associations and Authoritarian Regimes in Interwar Europe: Italy and Spain in Comparative Perspective." *American Sociological Review* 70 (2): 288–310.

——. 2010. *The Civic Foundations of Fascism in Europe: Italy, Spain and Romania, 1870–1945*. Baltimore: Johns Hopkins University Press.

Robbins, Tina L., Timothy P. Summers, Janis L. Miller, and William H. Hendrix. 2000. "Using the Group-Value Model to Explain the Role of Noninstrumental Justice in Distinguishing the Effects of Distributive and Procedural Justice." *Journal of Occupational and Organizational Psychology* 73 (4): 511–18.

Roberts, David D. 1979. *The Syndicalist Tradition and Italian Fascism*. Chapel Hill: University of North Carolina Press.

Rochat, Giorgio. 2010. "The Italian Front, 1915–18." In *A Companion to World War I*, edited by John Horne, 82–96. Malden, MA: Wiley Blackwell.

Rockoff, Hugh. 1998. "The Peace Dividend in Historical Perspective." *American Economic Review* 88 (2): 46–60.

——. 2005. "Until It's Over, Over There: The U.S. Economy in World War I." In *The Economics of World War I*, edited by Stephen Broadberry and Mark Harrison, 310–43. Cambridge: Cambridge University Press.

Rubin, Gerry R. 1977. "The Origins of Industrial Tribunals: Munitions Tribunals during the First World War." *Industrial Law Journal* 6:149–64.

——. 1979. "Wartime Industrial Relations Legislation and Legal Institutions and Procedures: The British Munitions of War Acts, 1915–1917." In *The Imposition of Law*, edited by Sandra B. Burman and Barbara E. Harrell-Bond, 257–72. New York: Academic Press.

——. 1984. "Law, War and Economy: The Munitions Acts, 1915–17 and Corporatism in Context." *Journal of Law and Society* 11 (3): 317–33.

——. 1987a. "Explanations for Law Reform: The Case of Wartime Labour Legislation in Britain, 1915–1916." *International Review of Social History* 32 (3): 250–70.

——. 1987b. *War, Law, and Labour: The Munitions Acts, State Regulation, and the Unions, 1915–1921.* Oxford: Clarendon.

——. 2013. "The Last Word on the Capital Court Martial Controversy in Britain? Toward a History of British Military Law in World War I." In *Justice militaires et guerres mondiales*, edited by Jean-Marc Berliére, Jonas Campion, and Luigi Lacché, 39–56. Belgium: Presses Universitaires de Louvain.

Rubinstein, William D. 2003. *Twentieth-Century Britain: A Political History.* New York: Palgrave MacMillan.

Rubio-Marín, Ruth. 2014. "The Achievement of Female Suffrage in Europe: On Women's Citizenship." *International Journal of Constitutional Law* 12 (1): 4–34.

Rueschemeyer, Dietrich, Evelyne Huber Stephens, and John D. Stephens. 1992. *Capitalist Development and Democracy.* Chicago: University of Chicago Press.

Runciman, Walter G. 1993. "Has British Capitalism Changed since the First World War?" *British Journal of Sociology* 44 (1): 53–67.

Rustow, Dankwart A. 1970. "Transitions to Democracy: Toward a Dynamic Model." *Comparative Politics* 2 (3): 337–63.

Sabbatucci, Giovanni. 1996. "The PSI and the Postwar Crisis." In *Italian Socialism: Between Politics and History*, edited by Spencer M. Di Scala, 45–53. Amherst: University of Massachusetts Press.

Saladino, Salvatore. 1970. *Italy from Unification to 1919: Growth and Decay of a Liberal Regime.* New York: Thomas Y. Crowell.

Saldin, Robert P. 2010. *War, the American State, and Politics since 1898.* New York: Cambridge University Press

Salvemini, Gaetano. 1928. *The Fascist Dictatorship in Italy.* Vol. 1, *Origins and Practices.* London: Jonathan Cape.

——. 1973. *The Origins of Fascism in Italy.* New York: Harper and Row.

Sarti, Roland. 2004. *Italy: A Reference Guide from the Renaissance to the Present.* New York: Facts on File.

Scheiber, Jane Lang, and Harry N. Scheiber. 1969. "The Wilson Administration and the Wartime Mobilization of Black Americans, 1917–18." *Labor History* 10 (3): 433–58.

Scheidel, Walter. 2018. *The Great Leveler: Violence and the History of Inequality from the Stone Age to the Twenty-First Century.* Princeton, NJ: Princeton University Press.

Scheve, Kenneth F., and David Stasavage. 2016. *Taxing the Rich: A History of Fiscal Fairness in the United States and Europe.* Princeton, NJ: Princeton University Press.

Schmidt, Carl T. 1938. *The Plough and the Sword: Labor, Land, and Property in Fascist Italy.* New York: Columbia University Press.

Schmidt, Regin. 2000. *Red Scare: FBI and the Origins of Anticommunism in the United States, 1919–1943.* Copenhagen: Museum Tusculanum Press.

Schuker, Stephen A. 1981. Comments on "The Two Postwar Eras and the Conditions for Stability in Twentieth Century Western Europe," by Charles S. Maier. *American Historical Review* 86 (2): 353–62.

Scott, James C. 1976. *The Moral Economy of the Peasant Rebellion and Subsistence in South-east Asia*. New Haven, CT: Yale University Press.

Searle, Geoffrey Russell. 1971. *The Quest for National Efficiency: A Study in British Politics and Political Thought, 1899–1914*. Berkeley: University of California Press.

——. 1976. *Eugenics and Politics in Britain, 1900–1914*. Leiden: Noordhoff International.

——. 2004. *A New England? Peace and War, 1886–1918*. Oxford: Clarendon.

Seldon, Anthony, and David Walsh. 2013. *Public Schools and the Great War*. Barnsley, UK: Pen and Sword.

Seton-Watson, Christopher. 1967. *Italy from Liberalism to Fascism, 1870–1925*. London: Methuen.

Sewell, William H., Jr. 1996. "Historical Events as Transformations of Structures: Inventing Revolution at the Bastille." *Theory and Society* 25 (6): 841–81.

Shapiro, Debra L., Linda Klebe Trevino, and Bart Victor. 1995. "Correlates of Employee Theft: A Multi-dimensional Justice Perspective." *International Journal of Conflict Management* 6 (4): 404–14.

Shapiro, Stanley. 1971. "The Great War and Reform: Liberals and Labor, 1917–19." *Labor History* 12 (3): 323–44.

Shepherd, John, and Keith Laybourn. 2006. *Britain's First Labour Government*. New York: Palgrave Macmillan.

Sheridan, William Allen. 1975. "The Appeal of Fascism and the Problem of National Disintegration." In *Reappraisals of Fascism*, edited by Henry A. Turner Jr., 44–68. New York: New Viewpoints.

Sherington, Geoffrey E. 1976. "The 1918 Education Act: Origins, Aims, and Development." *British Journal of Educational Studies* 24 (1): 66–85.

Sibley, David. 2005. *The British Working Class and Enthusiasm for War*. London: Frank Cass.

Simmel, Georg. 1955. *Conflict: The Web of Group Affiliations*. New York: Free Press.

Simmonds, Alan G. V. 2012. *Britain and World War One*. New York: Routledge.

Sirianni, Carmen J. 1980. "Workers' Control in the Era of World War I: A Comparative Analysis of the European Experience." *Theory and Society* 9 (1): 29–88.

Skarlicki, Daniel P., and Robert Folger. 1997. "Retaliation in the Workplace: The Roles of Distributive, Procedural, and Interactional Justice." *Journal of Applied Psychology* 82 (3): 434–43.

Skocpol, Theda. 1979. *States and Social Revolutions: A Comparative Analysis of France, Russia, and China*. New York: Cambridge University Press.

——. 1992. *Protecting Soldiers and Mothers: The Political Origins of Social Policy in the United States*. Cambridge, MA: Harvard University Press.

Skocpol, Theda, Ziad Munson, Andrew Karch, and Bayliss Camp. 2002. "Patriotic Partnerships: Why Great Wars Nourished American Civic Voluntarism." In *Shaped by War and Trade: International Influences on American Political Development*, edited by Ira Katznelson and Martin Shefter, 134–80. Princeton, NJ: Princeton University Press.

Smith, Angela K. 2003. "The Pankhursts and the War: Suffrage Magazines and First World War Propaganda." *Women's History Review* 12 (1): 103–18.

Smith, Anthony D. 1981. "War and Ethnicity: The Role of Warfare in the Formation, Self-Images and Cohesion of Ethnic Communities." *Ethnic and Racial Studies* 4 (4): 375–95.

Smith, Denis Mack. 1969. *Italy: A Modern History*. Ann Arbor: University of Michigan Press.

——. 1989. *Italy and Its Monarchy*. New Haven, CT: Yale University Press.

Smith, Leonard V. 1991. "The Disciplinary Dilemma of French Military Justice, September 1914–April 1917: The Case of the 5e Division d'Infanterie." *Journal of Military History* 55 (1): 47–68.

——. 2010. "France." In *A Companion to World War I*, edited by John Horne, 418–31. Malden, MA: Wiley Blackwell.

Snowden, Frank M. 1972. "On the Social Origins of Agrarian Fascism in Italy." *European Journal of Sociology* 13 (2): 268–95.

——. 1986. *Violence and Great Estates in the South of Italy: Apulia, 1900–1922.* Cambridge: Cambridge University Press.

——. 1989. *The Fascist Revolution in Tuscany, 1919–1922.* Cambridge: Cambridge University Press.

Snyder, Jack L., and Edward Mansfield. 2010. "Does War Influence Democratization?" In *War's Wake: International Conflict and the Fate of Liberal Democracy*, edited by Elizabeth Kier and Ronald R. Krebs, 23–49. New York: Cambridge University Press.

Sorenson, Georg. 1993. *Democracy and Democratization Processes and Prospects in a Changing World.* Boulder, CO: Westview.

Sparrow, James T. 2008. "Buying Our Boys Back: The Mass Foundations of Fiscal Citizenship in World War II." *Journal of Policy History* 20 (2): 263–86.

Spero, Sterling D., and Abram L. Harris. 1931. *The Black Worker: The Negro and the Labor Movement.* New York: Columbia University Press.

Squeri, Lawrence. 1983. "The Italian Local Elections of 1920 and the Outbreak of Fascism." *Historian* 45 (3): 324–36.

Stein, Arthur A., and Bruce M. Russett. 1980. "Evaluating War: Outcomes and Consequences." In *Handbook of Political Conflict: Theory and Research*, edited by Ted Robert Gurr, 399–422. New York: Free Press.

Stephens, John D. 1979. *The Transition from Capitalism to Socialism.* London: Macmillan.

Stetson, Dorothy M. 1986. "Abortion Law Reform in France." *Journal of Comparative Family Studies* 17 (3): 277–90.

Stevenson, John. 1990. "More Light on World War One." *Historical Journal* 33 (1): 195–210.

Summerfield, Penny. 1997. "Gender and War in the Twentieth Century." *International History Review* 19 (1): 1–15.

Swidler, Ann. 1986. "Culture in Action: Symbols and Strategies." *American Sociological Review* 51 (2): 273–86.

Tanner, Duncan. 1983. "The Parliamentary Electoral System, the 'Fourth' Reform Act and the Rise of Labour in England and Wales." *Historical Research* 56 (134): 205–19.

——. 1990. *Political Change and the Labour Party, 1900–1918.* New York: Cambridge University Press.

——. 1997. "The Development of British Socialism, 1900–1918." *Parliamentary History* 16 (1): 48–66.

——. 2003. "The Politics of the Labour Movement, 1900–1939." In *A Companion to Early Twentieth-Century Britain*, edited by Chris Wrigley, 38–55. Oxford: Blackwell.

Tarrow, Sidney G. 2015. *War, States, and Contention: A Comparative Historical Study.* Ithaca, NY: Cornell University Press.

Tasca, Angelo. 1938. *The Rise of Italian Fascism, 1918–1922.* London: Methuen.

Tawney, R. H. 1943. "The Abolition of Economic Controls, 1918–1921." *Economic History Review* 13 (1/2): 1–30.

Taylor, A. J. P. 1965. *English History, 1914–1945.* Oxford: Clarendon.

Teorell, Jan. 2010. *Determinants of Democratization: Explaining Regime Change in the World, 1972–2006.* New York: Cambridge University Press.

Tepora, Tuomas. 2007. "Redirecting Violence: The Finnish Flag as a Sacrificial Symbol, 1917–1945." *Studies in Ethnicity and Nationalism* 7 (3): 153–70.

Tetlock, Philip E., and Aaron Belkin. 1996. "Counterfactual Thought Experiments in World Politics: Logical, Methodological, and Psychological Perspectives." In *Counterfac-*

tual Thought Experiments in World Politics: Logical, Methodological, and Psychological Perspectives, edited by Philip E. Tetlock and Aaron Belkin, 1–38. Princeton, NJ: Princeton University Press.

Thayer, John A. 1964. *Italy and the Great War: Politics and Culture.* Madison: University of Wisconsin Press.

Therborn, Göran. 1977. 'The Rule of Capital and the Rise of Democracy." *New Left Review* 103:3–41.

Thibaut, John, and Laurens Walker. 1975. *Procedural Justice: A Psychological Analysis.* Hillsdale, NJ: Lawrence Erlbaum.

Thompson, E. P. 1971. "The Moral Economy of the English Crowd in the Eighteenth Century." *Past and Present* 50 (1): 76–136.

Thompson, J. A. 1971. "Labour and the Modern British Monarchy." *South Atlantic Quarterly* 70:341–49.

Thompson, J. Lee. 2007. *Forgotten Patriot: A Life of Alfred, Viscount Milner of St. James's and Cape Town.* Madison, NJ: Fairleigh Dickinson University Press.

Thompson, Mark. 2008. *The White War: Life and Death on the Italian Front, 1915–1919.* London: Faber and Faber.

Thompson, William R. 1996. "Democracy and Peace: Putting the Cart before the Horse?" *International Organization* 50 (1): 141–74.

Thorpe, Andrew. 1997. *A History of the British Labour Party.* New York: St. Martin's.

Tilly, Charles. 1975. "Western State Making and Theories of Political Transformation," In *The Formation of National States in Western Europe*, edited by Charles Tilly, 601-38. Princeton, NJ: Princeton University Press.

——. 1992a. *Coercion, Capital, and European States, AD 990–1992.* Cambridge, MA: Blackwell.

——. 1992b. "Where Do Rights Come From?" In *Contributions to the Comparative Study of Development*, edited by Lars Mjoset, 9–37. Oslo: Institute for Social Research.

——. 1993. *European Revolutions, 1492–1992.* Cambridge, MA: Blackwell.

——. 1995. "To Explain Political Processes." *American Journal of Sociology* 100 (6): 1594–610.

——. 2003. *Contention and Democracy in Europe, 1650–2000.* Cambridge: Cambridge University Press.

——. 2006. *Regimes and Repertoires.* Chicago: University of Chicago Press.

Titmuss, Richard M. 1950. *Problems of Social Policy.* London: H. M. Stationery Office.

——. 1963. *Essays on the Welfare State.* London: George Allen and Unwin.

Tocqueville, Alexis de. (1835) 1945. *Democracy in America.* New York: Alfred A. Knopf.

Tomassini, Luigi. 1990. "Industrial Mobilization and State Intervention in Italy in the First World War: Effects on Labor Unrest." In *Strikes, Social Conflict, and the First World War. An International Perspective*, edited by Leopold Haimson and Giulio Sapelli, 179–212. Milan: Fondazione Giangiacomo Feltrinelli.

——. 1991. "Industrial Mobilization and the Labour Market in Italy during the First World War." *Social History* 16 (1): 59–87.

——. 1996. "The Home Front in Italy." In *Facing Armageddon: The First World War Experience*, edited by Hugh Cecil and Peter Liddle, 577–95. London: Leo Cooper.

Tomlinson, Richard. 1985. "The 'Disappearance' of France, 1896–1940: French Politics and the Birth Rate." *Historical Journal* 28 (2): 405–15.

Toniolo, Gianni. 1990. *An Economic History of Liberal Italy, 1850–1918.* New York: Routledge.

Towers, Graham. 1995. *Building Democracy: Community Architecture in the Inner Cities.* London: University College London Press.

Toye, Richard. 2010. "Winston Churchill's 'Crazy Broadcast': Party, Nation, and the 1945 Gestapo Speech." *Journal of British Studies* 49 (3): 655–90.

Trebilcock, Clive. 1981. *The Industrialisation of the Continental Powers, 1780–1914*. London: Routledge.

Tripp, Thomas M., and Robert J. Bies. 2015. "Doing Justice: The Role of Motives for Revenge in the Workplace." In *The Oxford Handbook of Justice in the Workplace*, edited by Russell S. Cropanzano and Maureen L. Ambrose, 461–76. Oxford: Oxford University Press.

Turner, John. 1988. "British Politics and the Great War." In *Britain and the First World War*, edited by John Turner, 117–39. London: Unwin Hyman.

———. 1992. *British Politics and the Great War: Coalition and Conflict*. New Haven, CT: Yale University Press.

Tyler, Tom R. 1984. "The Role of Perceived Injustice in Defendants' Evaluations of Their Courtroom Experience." *Law and Society Review* 18 (1): 51–74.

———. 1990. *Why People Obey the Law*. New Haven, CT: Yale University Press.

———. 1997. "The Psychology of Legitimacy: A Relational Perspective on Voluntary Deference to Authorities." *Personality and Social Psychology Review* 1:322–45.

———. 2017. "Procedural Justice and Policing: A Rush to Judgment?" *Annual Review of Law and Social Science* 13 (1): 29–53.

Tyler, Tom R., and Steven L. Blader. 2013. *Cooperation in Groups: Procedural Justice, Social Identity, and Behavioral Engagement*. London: Taylor and Francis.

Tyler, Tom R., Robert J. Boeckmann, Heather J. Smith, and Yuen J. Huo. 1997. *Social Justice in a Diverse Society*. Boulder, CO: Westview.

Tyler, Tom R., Jonathan D. Casper, and Bonnie Fisher. 1989. "Maintaining Allegiance toward Political Authorities: The Role of Prior Attitudes and the Use of Fair Procedures." *American Journal of Political Science* 33 (3): 629–52.

Tyler, Tom R., and Peter Degoey. 1995. "Collective Restraint in Social Dilemmas: Procedural Justice and Social Identification Effects on Support for Authorities." *Journal of Personality and Social Psychology* 69 (3): 482–97.

Tyler, Tom R., and Yuen J. Huo. 2002. *Trust in the Law: Encouraging Public Cooperation with the Police and Courts*. New York: Russell Sage Foundation.

Tyler, Tom R., and E. Allan Lind. 1992. "A Relational Model of Authority in Groups." In *Advances in Experimental Social Psychology*, edited by M. Zanna, 115–91. Boston: McGraw-Hill.

Tyler, Tom R., and Gregory Mitchell. 1994. "Legitimacy and the Empowerment of Discretionary Legal Authority: The United States Supreme Court and Abortion Rights." *Duke Law Journal* 43 (4): 703–815.

Tyler, Tom R., Kenneth A. Rasinski, and Nancy Spodick. 1985. "Influence of Voice on Satisfaction with Leaders: Exploring the Meaning of Process Control." *Journal of Personality and Social Psychology* 48 (1): 72–81.

Tyler, Tom R., and Heather J. Smith. 1998. "Social Justice and Social Movements." In *Handbook of Social Psychology*, 4th ed., edited by Daniel Gilbert, Susan T. Fiske, and Gardner Lindzey, 595–632. New York: McGraw-Hill.

Vagts, Alfred. 1959. *A History of Militarism*. New York: Meridian Books.

Valenzuela, Samuel J. 1989. "Labor Movements in Transitions to Democracy: A Framework for Analysis." *Comparative Politics* 21 (4): 445–72.

Valli, Roberta Suzzi. 2000. "The Myth of Squadrismo in the Fascist Regime." *Journal of Contemporary History* 35 (2): 131–50.

Van den Bos, Kees, Henk A. M. Wilke, and E. Allan Lind. 1998. "When Do We Need Procedural Fairness? The Role of Trust in Authority." *Journal of Personality and Social Psychology* 75 (6): 449–558.

Ventrone, Angelo. 2011. "Fascism and the Legacy of the Great War." In *The Legacies of Two World Wars: European Societies in the Twentieth Century*, edited by Lothar Kettenacker and Torsten Riotte, 90–119. New York: Berghahn.

Vidmar, Neil. 2002. "Retributive Justice: Its Social Context." In *The Justice Motive in Everyday Life*, edited by Michael Ross and Dale T. Miller, 291–313. New York: Cambridge University Press.

Viswesvaran, Chockalingam, and Deniz Ones. 2002. "Examining the Construct of Organizational Justice: A Meta-analytic Evaluation of Relations with Work Attitudes and Behaviors." *Journal of Business Ethics* 38 (3): 193–203.

Waites, Bernard A. 1976. "The Effect of the First World War on Class and Status in England, 1910–20." *Journal of Contemporary History* 11 (1): 27–48.

———. 1987. *A Class Society at War: England.* New York: Berg.

Walster, Elain G., William Walster, and Ellen Berscheid. 1978. *Equity: Theory and Research.* Boston: Allyn and Bacon.

Watkins, Gordon S. 1920. *Labor Problems and Labor Administration in the United States during the World War.* Urbana: University of Illinois.

Webb, Sidney. 1918. *Labour and the New Social Order: A Report on Reconstruction.* London: Labour Party.

Webb, Sidney, and Beatrice Webb, eds. 1909. *Minority Report of the Poor Law Commission.* London: Longmans, Green.

Weber, Eugene. 1976. *Peasants into Frenchmen: The Modernization of Rural France, 1870–1914.* Stanford, CA: Stanford University Press.

Weber, Max. (1923) 1983. *General Economic History,* New Brunswick, NJ: Transaction.

Webster, Richard A. 1960. *The Cross and the Fasces: Christian Democracy and Fascism in Italy.* Stanford, CA: Stanford University Press.

Welch, Steven R. 2014. "Military Justice." In *1914–1918 Online: International Encyclopedia of the First World War,* edited by Ute Daniel, Peter Gatrell, Oliver Janz, Heather Jones, Jennifer Keene, Alan Kramer, and Bill Nasson. Berlin: Freie Universität. https://encyclopedia.1914-1918-online.net/article/military_justice.

Wenzel, Michael, Tyler G. Okimoto, Norman T. Feather, and Michael J. Platow. 2008. "Retributive and Restorative Justice." *Law and Human Behavior* 32 (5): 375–89.

White, Stephen. 1974. "Soviets in Britain: The Leeds Convention of 1917." *International Review of Social History* 19 (2): 165–83.

White, Steven. 2016. "Civil Rights, World War II, and U.S. Public Opinion." *Studies in American Political Development* 30 (1): 38–61.

———. 2019. *World War II and American Racial Politics: Public Opinion, the Presidency, and Civil Rights Advocacy.* Cambridge: Cambridge University Press.

Whiteside, Noel. 1987. "Social Welfare and Industrial Relations." In *A History of British Industrial Relations,* vol. 2, *1914–1939,* edited by Chris Wrigley, 211–42. London: Harvester.

———. 1992. "Concession, Coercion or Cooperation? State Policy and Industrial Unrest in Britain, 1916–1920." In *Strikes, Social Conflict, and the First World War. An International Perspective,* edited by Leopold Haimson and Giulio Sapelli, 107–22. Milan: Fondazione Giangiacomo Feltrinelli.

Whiteside, Noelle. 1980. "Welfare Legislation and the Unions during the First World War." *Historical Journal* 23 (4): 857–74.

Whittam, John. 1975. "War and Italian Society, 1914–16." In *War and Society: A Yearbook of Military History,* edited by Brian Bond and Ian Roy, 144–61. London: Croom Helm.

Wickenden, Dorothy. 1990. "Lincoln and Douglass: Dismantling the Peculiar Institution." *Wilson Quarterly* 14 (4): 102–12.

Wilcox, Vanda. 2005. "Discipline in the Italian Army." In *War and Belligerence: Perspectives in First World War Studies,* edited by Pierre Purseigle, 73–100. Boston: Brill.

———. 2009. "Generalship and Mass Surrender during the Italian Defeat at Caporetto." In *1917: Beyond the Western Front,* edited by Ian Frederick William Beckett, 25–46. Leiden: Brill.

——. 2011. "Encountering Italy: Military Service and National Identity during the First World War." *Bulletin of Italian Politics* 3 (2): 283–302.

——. 2012. "Weeping Tears of Blood: Exploring Italian Soldiers' Emotions in the First World War." *Modern Italy* 17 (2): 171–84.

——. 2014. "La bataille de Caporetto: Un tournant pour le moral des troupes italiennes?" In *Accepter, endurer, refuser*, edited by Nicolas Beaupré, Heather Jones, and Anne Rasmussen, 229–50. Paris: Les Belles Lettres.

——. 2016. *Morale and the Italian Army during the First World War*. Cambridge: Cambridge University Press.

Wilensky, Harold L. 1975. *The Welfare State and Equality: Structural and Ideological Roots of Public Expenditures*. Berkeley: University of California.

Williams, Gwyn A. 1975. *Proletarian Order: Antonio Gramsci, Factory Councils, and the Origins of Italian Communism, 1911–1921*. London: Pluto.

Wilson, Trevor. 1964. "The Coupon and the British General Election of 1918." *Journal of Modern History* 36 (1): 28–42.

——. 1966. *The Downfall of the Liberal Party, 1914–1935*. London: Collins.

——. 1986. *The Myriad Faces of War: Britain and the Great War, 1914–1918*. Cambridge, UK: Polity.

Winter, Jay M. 1974. *Socialism and the Challenge of War: Ideas and Politics in Britain*. London: Routledge and Kegan Paul.

——. 1985a. *The Great War and the British People*. London: Macmillan.

——. 1985b. "Some Paradoxes of the First World War." In *The Upheaval of War: Family, Work, and Welfare in Europe*, edited by Richard Wall and Jay Winter, 9–42. Cambridge: Cambridge University Press.

——. 1985c. "Trade Unions and the Labour Party in Britain." In *The Development of Trade Unionism in Great Britain and Germany, 1880–1914*, edited by Wolfgang J. Mommsen and Hans-Gerhard Husung, 359–71. London: George Allen and Unwin.

——. 1988. "Public Health and the Political Economy of War: A Reply to Linda Bryder." *History Workshop Journal* 26:163–73.

——. 2010. "Veterans, Human Rights, and the Transformation of European Democracy." In *In War's Wake: International Conflict and the Fate of Liberal Democracy*, edited by Elizabeth Kier and Ronald R. Krebs, 121–38. Cambridge: Cambridge University Press.

Winter, Jay M., and Jean-Louis Robert, eds. 1997. *Capital Cities at War: London, Paris, Berlin, 1914–1919*. Cambridge: Cambridge University Press.

Wohl, Robert. 1979. *The Generation of 1914*. Cambridge, MA: Harvard University Press.

Womack, Brantly. 1987. "The Party and the People: Revolutionary and Postrevolutionary Politics in China and Vietnam." *World Politics* 39 (4): 479–507.

Wood, Elisabeth Jean. 2003. *Insurgent Collective Action and Civil War in El Salvador*. New York: Cambridge University Press.

Worley, Matthew. 2005. *Labour Inside the Gate: A History of the British Labour Party between the Wars*. London: I. B. Tauris.

Wright, Quincy. 1942. *A Study of War*. Chicago: University of Chicago Press.

Wrigley, Chris. 1976. *David Lloyd George and the British Labour Movement: Peace and War*. Hassocks, UK: Harvester.

——. 1982a. "The Ministry of Munitions: An Innovatory Department." In *War and the State: The Transformation of British Government, 1914–1919*, edited by Kathleen Burk, 32–56. London: George Allen and Unwin.

——. 1982b. "Trade Unions and Politics in the First World War." In *Trade Unions in British Politics*, edited by Ben Pimlott and Chris Cook, 79–97. London: Longman.

———. 1987a. "The First World War and State Intervention in Industrial Relations." In *A History of British Industrial Relations*, vol. 2, *1914–1939*, edited by Chris Wrigley, 23–70. London: Harvester.

———. 1987b. Introduction to *A History of British Industrial Relations*, vol. 2, *1914–1939*, edited by Chris Wrigley, 1–22. London: Harvester.

———. 1987c. "The Trade Unions between the Wars." In *A History of British Industrial Relations*, vol. 2, *1914–1939*, edited by Chris Wrigley, 71–128. London: Harvester.

———. 1992. *Lloyd George*. Oxford: Blackwell.

———. 2003. "The Impact of the First World War." In *A Companion to Early Twentieth-Century Britain*, edited by Chris Wrigley, 502–16. Oxford: Blackwell.

———. 2018. "The Labour Party and the Impact of the 1918 Reform Act." *Parliamentary History* 37 (1): 64–80.

Wynn, Neil A. 1977. "War and Social Change: The Black American in Two World Wars." In *War and Society*, vol. 2, *A Yearbook of Military History*, edited by Brian Bon and Ian Roy, 40–64. London: Routledge.

———. 1986. *From Progressivism to Prosperity; World War I and American Society*. New York: Holmes and Meier.

———. 2010. *The African American Experience during World War II*. Lanham, MD: Rowman and Littlefield.

Zamagni, Vera. 1991. "Industrial Wages and Workers' Protest in Italy during the 'Biennio Rosso,' 1919–1920." *Journal of European Economic History* 20 (1): 137–53.

———. 1993. *The Economic History of Italy, 1860–1990*. Oxford: Clarendon.

Zarate Tenorio, Barbara. 2014. "Social Spending Responses to Organized Labor and Mass Protests in Latin America, 1970–2007." *Comparative Political Studies* 47 (14): 1945–72.

Zolberg, Aristide R. 1986. "How Many Exceptionalisms?" In *Working-Class Formation: Nineteenth-Century Patterns in Western Europe and the United States*, edited by Ira Katznelson and Aristide R. Zolberg, 397–456. Princeton, NJ: Princeton University Press.

Index

Acemoglu, Daren, 191
Addison, Christopher, 141, 143, 164, 176
Addison, Paul, 6, 11
Addison Act (1919, UK), 143
Adler, Glenn, 191
affect, importance of, 29, 184–85. *See also* emotional bonds
agricultural cooperatives, 149–50, 156
agricultural labor. *See braccianti;* Federterra (Italy); Italian economy; *mezzadri*
alienation from the state, 22–24, 104–115, 140, 153–54, 186–87. *See also* labor mobilization; procedural (in)justice
allegiance to the state, 22–24, 92, 112, 118, 130–36, 147, 185. *See also* nationalism and war; patriotism; procedural (in)justice
Amalgamated Society of Engineers, ASE (UK), 59–60, 108, 134, 137
American Federation of Labor, 13
Andreski, Stanislav, 12, 14
antiwaste campaign, 163–64, 176
arditi, 199–200. *See also* Italian army
Asquith, Herbert, 54, 57–59, 121, 194
Associated Society of Locomotive Engineers and Firemen (UK), 137
Austria-Hungary, 14, 21, 51, 198
auxiliary firms in Italy, 31, 33–34, 106, 154–55. *See also* Italian labor mobilization

Baldwin, Stanley, 176, 201
Bates, Robert, 12
The Battle of the Somme (film), 64
battle deaths, 41, 87, 100, 113, 169, 199; officer *vs.* enlisted, 51, 70–71
Bauer, Michael, 189
Belkin, Aaron, 84
Berman, Sheri, 189, 191
Bermeo, Nancy, 9–10, 191
Beveridge Report, 8–9
Bevin, Ernest, 21, 61, 125
Bismarck, Otto von, 177
Boer War (1899), 10, 11, 130, 131
Boix, Charles, 191
Bolshevism. *See* Russian Revolution
Booth, Charles, 167–68

Boselli, Paolo, 32, 36
braccianti, 41, 49, 94, 98–99, 204n6 (ch. 2), 205n3 (ch. 5). *See also* Federterra (Italy); Italian labor mobilization
Bradlow, Benjamin, 191
British army: data on, 169; distributive (in) justice in, 49; military justice in, 45–46, 56; war memorials for, 111. *See also* battle deaths
British economy: development of, 74; inflation in, 63, 68–69, 132, 133–34, 171, 205n9. *See also* corporate wartime profits; taxation
British India, 13–14
British labor mobilization, 26–27; distributive injustice in, 69–72; effect on allegiance, 108–9, 128, 130–36, 172, 182–83; effect on compliance, 141–47; effect on labor solidarity, 136–38; effect on preferences, 125–130; effect on trust, 118–23; formal procedural justice in, 57–62, 71–72, 122, 128–31, 206n3; informal procedural justice in, 62–67; material rewards in, 67–68; merging of state and society by, 117–18; organization of, 53–57; postwar reform failures and, 141–47, 172–77, 201–2; propaganda used in, 62–64. *See also* labor mobilization
British political reform: collective bargaining for, 54–55, 59–62, 118–19, 121, 136–38, 169–72; labor activism for, 55–56, 60, 126–28, 133, 145–47, 171–72; moderate socialism, 118, 122–30; payback arguments and, 14, 169–72, 195–96; postwar democracy, 5–6, 8, 162–72, 181, 182–83, 185–86, 190, 195–96; postwar failure of, 141–47, 172–77, 201–2; prewar Labourism, 118–22; social solidarity arguments and, 8–9, 162–65, 195–96; state capacity arguments and, 10, 165–69. *See also* democracy; welfare state; *names of specific political parties*
Bülow, Bernhard von, 200
Burton, Michael, 182

Cadorna, Luigi: mobilization propaganda and, 36–37, 46–47, 87; support for unjust army procedures, 41–46, 85, 96–97. *See also* Italian Army